Luchino Visconti and the Alchemy of Adaptation

THE SUNY SERIES

HORIZONS OF CINEMA

MURRAY POMERANCE | EDITOR

Luchino Visconti and the Alchemy of Adaptation

Brendan Hennessey

Published by State University of New York Press, Albany

Printed in the United States of America

For information, contact State University of New York Press, Albany, NY
www.sunypress.edu

Library of Congress Cataloging-in-Publication Data

Name: Hennessey, Brendan, 1977– author.
Title: Luchino Visconti and the alchemy of adaptation / Brendan Hennessey.
Description: Albany : State University of New York, [2021] | Series: SUNY series, horizons of cinema | Includes bibliographical references and index.
Identifiers: LCCN 2021016731 (print) | LCCN 2021016732 (ebook) | ISBN 9781438484976 (hardcover : alk. paper) | ISBN 9781438484990 (ebook)
Subjects: LCSH: Visconti, Luchino, 1906–1976—Criticism and interpretation. | Film adaptations—History and criticism.
Classification: LCC PN1998.3.V57 H46 2021 (print) | LCC PN1998.3.V57 (ebook) | DDC 791.4302/33092—dc23
LC record available at https://lccn.loc.gov/2021016731
LC ebook record available at https://lccn.loc.gov/2021016732

10 9 8 7 6 5 4 3 2 1

For Susan

One is far more an author making a film, even if it is a film derived from literature.

—Luchino Visconti

Contents

Illustrations

Acknowledgments

This volume would not have been possible without encouragement and support from a number of colleagues, friends, and institutions. I have received substantial assistance from various libraries and archives in the United States and Italy. Among others, thanks to Caryl Ward at Bartle Library at Binghamton University, Giovanna Bosman at the Fondazione Istituto Gramsci, the staff at the Biblioteca Nazionale Centrale di Roma, and the people at Harvard University's Widener Library. I owe a debt of gratitude to the wonderful staff in the Main Reading Room at the Library of Congress, where much of this book was written. Special thanks to Lucia Re for her early guidance through the many thorny questions Visconti introduces. The intellectual engagement at Binghamton University has been particularly important and I recognize Mario Moroni, Rachel Samiani, Alexandra Lee, Maria Cook, Ana Ros, and my dear friend Dana Stewart for all of their help and inspiration. An earlier version of chapter 6 originally appeared in *The Italianist*. The manuscript benefited from comments by Christopher Wagstaff and Charles L. Leavitt IV, Pamela Erins's thoughtful editing, and assistance with images from Sean Donnelly. Thanks to Murray Pomerance, Laura Poole, and the entire team at SUNY Press for transforming my manuscript into a book. The entire project profited immensely from my conversations with Zyg and Maggie Baranski, James Kriesel, and Laurence Hooper. I also extend my gratitude to Barry Steelman at Cinema 93 for sharing his immense knowledge and eclectic film collection.

None of this would be possible without the support of my parents and the entire Hennessey clan. Finally, I thank my wife, son, and daughter for tolerating my absences and enduring countless screenings of beautiful Italian films.

Preface

Alongside such figures as John Huston, Stanley Kubrick, and Jean-Luc Godard, Luchino Visconti's legacy will be forever rooted in the cinematic transformation of literature. "Of the great Italian filmmakers," Lino Micciché once noted, "none had as special, intense, or enduring a relationship with literature" (Micciché 2002, 85). This omnipresence of adaptation reflects Italian cinema, a national film tradition that is perhaps "the most bound to the structures, models and history of universal literature of all time" (Brunetta 2008, 28). Still, more than forty years since his death and despite a voluminous bibliography dedicated to his life and work, few studies examine more than a select number of adaptations. The absence of a unifying monograph is revealing. It is embedded in the contradictions of the artist himself and in the thorny question of adaptation that his films disclosed. Twelve of the Visconti's eighteen fiction films were based on books. Nine made explicit reference to the novels or short stories they were based on: *Ossessione*, 1942 (*The Postman Always Rings Twice*, James M. Cain); *La terra trema*, 1948 (*The House by the Medlar Tree*, Giovanni Verga); *Senso*, 1954 (Camillo Boito); *Le notti bianchi*, 1957 (Fyodor Dostoevsky); *Il lavoro*, 1962 (*On the Edge of the Bed*, Guy de Maupassant); *Il Gattopardo*, 1963 (Giuseppe Tomasi di Lampedusa); *Lo straniero*, 1967 (*The Stranger*, Albert Camus); *Morte a Venezia*, 1971 (*Death in Venice*, Thomas Mann); and *L'innocente* 1975 (Gabriele D'Annunzio). Three others represent hybrid variations that amalgamate more than a single author's work: *Rocco e i suoi Fratelli*, 1960 (Giovanni Testori, Dostoevsky, Mann, Arthur Miller); *Vaghe stelle dell'Orsa*, 1965 (Aeschylus, Sophocles, Euripides, D'Annunzio); and *La caduta degli dei* (*Götterdämmerung*), 1969 (Shakespeare, Dostoevsky, Richard Hughes).

In recent years, some of Visconti's films have been adapted to theater, demonstrating how the director's legacy continues to evolve through different forms of adaptation. On April 25, 2017, *Obsession*, a one-act play by Belgian director Ivo van Hove, opened at the Barbican Centre in London. *Obsession* is based on Visconti's first film, also titled *Obsession* (*Ossessione*), itself an adaptation of James M. Cain's hard-boiled novel *The Postman Always Rings Twice*. Starring Jude Law and Halina Reijn, the play featured an unembellished script by Jan Peter Gerrits and a minimalistic stage design by Jan Versweyveld. "Hidden in this naturalistic drama," van Hove remarked, "there's a Greek tragedy. It's inescapable somehow. Fate" (Trueman 2019). *Obsession* is one of numerous forays into theatrical adaptations of films undertaken by van Hove and the Toneelgroep Amsterdam, which has recently adapted movies by Ingmar Bergman, Michelangelo Antonioni, Pier Paolo Pasolini, and Ang Lee to stages around the world. Together, they also adapted the Visconti films *Rocco and His Brothers*, *Ludwig* (1973), and, more recently, *The Damned* (Willinger 2018).

Comparing play to film, critics of van Hove's adaptation identified a number of shortcomings that, in many respects, echo critiques levied against Visconti's original book-to-film adaptations. For Michael Billington of *The Guardian*, van Hove's play "becomes a psychological study in erotic obsession but with none of Visconti's atmospheric details," adding that "it is well executed, but lacks the power of the Visconti movie that shows passion arising out of sordidness and poverty" (Billington 2017). In another *Guardian* review titled "Jude Law Is Stranded in Treacle-Slow Adaptation," Susannah Clapp claimed that "No amount of writhing and roaring can enliven Ivo van Hove's self-absorbed take on Visconti" (Clapp 2017). Arguing that the play was all style, no content, Henry Hitching of *The Stage* opined that "the script is trite and mired in cliché. Instead of an intoxicating experience, we're left with something coolly stylish and portentous" (Morgan 2017). *Obsession*, it would seem, did not quite live up to the work it was adapting. Accurate or not, these critiques reveal how little perceptions of adaptation have evolved since the twentieth century. These critics rehearse one of the most hackneyed notions of adaptation: that the copy is inferior to the original. This concept continues to plague adaptations across media and has traditionally been targeted at films adapted from literary texts. Attending to what is lost rather than what is gained in the adaptive process has been common in studies of literary adaptation, where inevitably "the book is better than the film," and comparisons frequently exhibit a sense of loss and displacement.

What critics of the theatrical *Obsession* ignore is how linkages with and departures from the original film generate the same unmistakable vitality that Visconti channeled when he adapted Cain's novel in 1942. Novel, film, and theatrical performance all emphasize sight, the erotic catalyst of looking, and the lethal potential of unchecked physical desire in ways that are kindred and divergent. In van Hove's play, Hanna's face lights up when Gino enters from the rear of the stage, leering wantonly in her direction. In Visconti's film, the camera operates a delicate display of point of view when Giovanna (Clara Calamai) is startled by the sight of Gino (Massimo Girotti), who was previously shown gazing intently at her bare, provocatively dangling legs. In Cain's novel, Frank describes his immediate reaction to beholding Cora: "Then I saw her. She had been out back, in the kitchen, but she came in to gather up my dishes. Except for the shape, she really wasn't any raving beauty, but she had a sulky look to her, and her lips stuck out in a way that made me want to mash them in for her" (Cain 1992, 4). In a differing depiction of their first sexual encounter, van Hove uses the effect of pouring oil from a car's transmission suspended above the characters, soiling the lovemaking couple in flagrante delicto—a stagey symbolism of erotic delight and extramarital transgression. Visconti does not display their coupling at all in his film, instead choosing to employ a self-conscious ellipsis that highlights the erasure of the physical act. Although Cain refuses to narrate the lovemaking, he does mark out the deviance of the literary murderess—a hallmark of hard-boiled fiction—when he alludes to the masochism of Cora's unbridled sexual impulses.

These types of textual permutations proliferating across media are at the heart of Visconti's cinema. *Luchino Visconti and The Alchemy of Adaptation* traces the evolution of cinema's relationship with literature by analyzing the individual adaptations that dominated Visconti's oeuvre. Attention to his literary-based works is nothing new, and from early on, Visconti was admired as a transnational figure who filmed books from Europe and elsewhere. The most comprehensive studies of Visconti's oeuvre (Giori 2012, 2018; Rondolino 2003; Bacon 1998) include detailed discussions of literary antecedents and their influences on both screenwriting and production phases. These are just some of the critics and scholars who have analyzed his adaptations with great enthusiasm, examining how they reinforced, resisted, and were contoured by the various -isms of postwar Italy: neorealism, Marxism, auteurism, and aestheticism. The present work takes our understanding of Viscontian adaptation in new directions, reasserting the crucial position of books on film in postwar Italy by accounting for approaches from the history of ideas on adaptation (fidelity, textual analysis, Marxist-inspired adaptation) while introducing more recent developments from film and adaptation studies. I argue that Visconti adapted literature not only to reflect on the nature of cinema in a high modernist sense but also to parry cinematic quandaries that arose from categories of filmmaking circulating widely in Italy during the pre- and postwar periods. Although some cinematic types (documentary, melodrama, the historical film) are well established in studies of Visconti's adaptations, I emphasize some less appreciated ones as well: the diva, boxing, and auteur films; queer and heritage cinema, the legal drama, the gothic, the Italian *giallo*; and film adaptation as a discrete form of filmmaking. By viewing adaptations as based on literary and cinematic pillars, without one bearing more weight than the other, I hope to shed light on the pleasure of a Visconti adaptation, where spectators are invited to vacillate between literary and cinematic works in a "conceptual flipping back and forth between the work we know and the work we are experiencing" (Hutcheon 2006, 139). Freed from the strictures of an exclusively comparative analysis of films and books or the limits of a single theoretical paradigm to describe such a large number of adaptations, this book revels in adaptation's essential duality as it developed across the career of a single artist.

The book begins with an introduction and then is separated into three sections comprising nine chapters. The introduction outlines essential frameworks for this study, placing Visconti in a discourse on book-to-film transformations that appeared from the time of cinema's birth in the late nineteenth century to the mid-1970s. Adaptation, I argue, has frequently been subordinated to notions of realism and political cinema that dominate studies of Visconti's cinema. The foundations of his films, however, were more often textual than real. "The entirety of his oeuvre," writes Youssef Ishaghpour, "is not born from a direct encounter between cinema and the world; in a broad sense, it is founded on "texts" (Ishaghpour 1997, 186). Through a reading of Visconti's 1941 essay, "Tradition and Invention," with specific attention paid to adaptation's unique position in Italian culture and media, the introduction suggests alternative means for studying his adaptations. The issues of acting and stardom, mise-en-scène, editing, literary and cinematic genres, gender, and dramatic intermediality introduced here are further explored in the chapters that follow.

The remainder of the book presents Visconti's adaptations in a somewhat chronological fashion. Part I (chapters 1–3) examines his early films made during fascism and neorealism. Despite many adaptations occurring from 1939 until 1954, neorealist thinkers mostly muted the presence of literary antecedents, instead preferring to lavish their attention on cinema's relationship with reality. This section reinforces adaptation's influence in Italy's "new" cinema of neorealism, arguing that film theorists have generally emphasized landscape as a privileged space for defining neorealism at the expense of cinematic interiors based on literature. That interpretations of neorealist cinema placed literary sources in a secondary position and cinematic categories such as melodrama in a tertiary position, reveals some of the limitations of thoughts on the neorealist phenomenon that endure today. Chapter 1 explores the inside spaces of the Valastro family home in *The Earth Trembles*, a version of Giovanni Verga's *The House by the Medlar Tree* (1881), where a documentary intent is satisfied through a literary rendition. Chapter 2 transitions to the interior locations of the fascist-era *Obsession*, noting how these areas network the ominous atmosphere of Cain's *The Postman Always Rings Twice*, French poetic realism, and literary and cinematic noir in Europe and Hollywood. Chapter 3 examines the use of voiceover in *Senso* and *White Nights* to demonstrate how interior, literary narration was embodied by female stars of the screen. This chapter bridges the age of neorealism that dominated the 1940s and 1950s and the 1960s, when Italian cinema solidified its position at the forefront of international film production.

Part II (chapters 4–6) reviews how Visconti's adaptations achieved a blockbuster scale, known in Italian film histories as the age of the *superspettacolo d'autore* or auteur super-spectacles, in which auteur filmmakers (among others, Federico Fellini, Visconti, then Pasolini and Bernardo Bertolucci) addressed their cinema to massive domestic and international audiences. Reflecting the Italian film industry's increased international clout, Visconti mediated literary sources through generic forms that were common in global film cultures of the era, outfitting literary inspiration in cinematic costume. Chapter 4 takes up the boxers from *Rocco and His Brothers* to suggest how literary pugilists from Giovanni Testori's *The Bridge of Ghisolfa* (1958) became cinematic fighters who were widely popular in both Italian and Hollywood film of the 1950s. Chapter 5 examines how Visconti secured adaptation's position on the largest scale of Italian super-productions with *The Job* and *The Leopard*, presenting the question of a "good" adaptation through themes of marriage and betrayal found in the Guy de Maupassant and Giuseppe Tomasi di Lampedusa texts on which they were based. Chapter 6 suggests how Visconti queers Shakespeare's *Macbeth* in the extravagant Nazi historical film *The Damned*, borrowing from while also helping establish a tradition of sexually deviant Nazis on screen.

The final part of the book, part III (chapters 7–9), considers the late-period Visconti adaptations. These films were frequently interpreted as emblematic of cinematic "decadence," characterized by a detachment from social and political realities into an enclosed bubble of literary and autobiographical subjectivity. This section examines how forms of cinema (the *giallo* and gothic, the legal drama, the film adaptation) expand concepts of fidelity, subjectivity, and signature style that complicate the decadent label. Chapter 7 analyzes two adaptations based on works by Italian fin-de-siècle author Gabriele D'Annunzio, whose notion of masculinity is overturned in the gothic *giallo Sandra* and the period drama *The Intruder.* Chapter 8 examines *The Stranger*, illustrating how Visconti's least-beloved film, an adaptation of Albert Camus's existentialist novel, bolstered orthodox expectations about the impossibility of adapting classics of literary modernism. Chapter 9 concludes by unfurling the narrative layers of *Death in Venice*, Visconti's rereading of Thomas Mann's novella. This final chapter illuminates adaptation's enigmatic position in both popular and critical interpretations of Visconti's cinema, celebrating the power of book-to-film transformations that defined his career in the decades that followed.

Introduction

Literary Sources, Cinematic Frameworks

Figure I.1. Luchino Visconti's hand turning the pages of the novel being adapted in his final film, *L'innocente* (Luchino Visconti, 1976).

Visconti's 1941 essay "Tradition and Invention" represents his manifesto on the art of adaptation. Therein, he voiced his desire to render the "rhythm" of Giovanni Verga's 1881 novel, *The House by the Medlar Tree*:

> Then I was encouraged by the thought that even a common reader, in a first trivial contact with Verga's novel, finds its power and suggestiveness to rely completely on its *intimate*

> *and musical rhythm*; and that the key to a cinematic version of *The House by the Medlar Tree* might lie exclusively here—i.e., in the attempt to re-experience and assemble the magic of that rhythm, of that vague yearning for the unknown, of that knowledge that people are not well off, or could be better off, which makes up the poetic substance of a play of destinies, which cross without ever touching one another. (*LV*, 19–20; emphasis in original)

In foregrounding as musical and poetic a term as *rhythm* to describe the transformation from book to film, Visconti introduces a synthetic quality commonly associated with his filmmaking. Perhaps more than the films of any other Italian director of his generation, Visconti's works are consistently defined through a series of noncinematic modifiers (operatic, literary, painterly, etc.) that locate them at the juncture of the literary, visual, and dramatic arts. As we will see, this heterogenous characterization of his filmmaking creates a rather intriguing set of issues for the notion of literary adaptation in the twentieth and twenty-first centuries. For the time being, in this intermedial landscape, literature occupies a crucial position. "He uses film," Mario Serandrei once commented, "like a writer uses ink" (Serandrei 1979, 329). In this essay, Visconti's use of the term *rhythm* to describe his intent to adapt Verga's novel to film, harmonizing cinema with one of its sister arts, harkens back to many silent-period examinations of cinema in Italy. In 1908, Ricciotto Canudo announced the birth of cinema in similarly cadenced terms, noting film's capacity to merge the pulses of the other arts: "And this expression of art will be the conciliation between the Rhythm of Space (the Plastic Arts) and the Rhythm of Time (Music and Poetry). . . . The new art form should instead be precisely a Painting and a Sculpture unfolding in time; like Music and Poetry, which have life, they rhythmically mark the air during the time of their execution" (Canudo 2017, 68).

In the subsequent "Manifesto to the Seven Arts," Canudo observed that "The forms and rhythms which are called Life gush forth from the turning crank of a projector," establishing cinema as "The Seventh Art [that] reconciles all the others. Moving Painting, Plastic Art developing according to the norms of rhythmic art" (Canudo 1975, 254). Canudo offers some early paeans to "intermediality"—a critical term for the connections between media—in which cinema was shaped by intermixing multiple artforms in a single platform. Sebastiano Arturo Luciani soon concurred with Canudo's praise for artistic blending, claiming in 1916 that "this visual rhythm must be the rudimentary norm of the entire poetics of the new art" (Luciani 2017, 330). Canudo and Luciani's position was most enthusiastically espoused by the Italian futurists, who employed a similarly musical terminology in championing cinema's revolutionary potential. Futurists eagerly declared how "the *Futurist cinematographer* today creates the POLIEXPRESSIVE SYMPHONY," which they believed extended across artistic forms, "from chromatic and plastic music to the music of objects" (Marinetti 1976, 12). To these early thinkers, art forms across the spectrum constituted the various notes and intervals synchronized to create a consonant cinematic harmony. In 1914, writer Gabriele D'Annunzio announced cinema as a *gesamtkunstwerk* (all-embracing art form), claiming how "this newest of arts sends flames through the eyes" (Brunetta 1999, 23).

Much in line with the composite cinema promoted by these figures from the silent period (and later by Italian thinkers like Carlo Ludovico Ragghianti, Antonio Costa, and Leonardo De Franceschi), Visconti's postwar films have been hailed for balancing multiple forms of media, especially opera, theater, literature, and painting, in an integrated cinematic program. This polyartistic characterization stemmed first and foremost from the director's activities outside of cinema. Born to a musical family (he trained as a cellist in his youth), Visconti harbored literary ambitions early on, writing two unfinished novels, *Angelo* and *I tre* (*The Three*); a short story "Il cappello di paglia" ("The Straw Hat"); two acts of a play; and later, a one-act theatrical production, *Il gioco della verità* (*The Game of Truth*) that he composed with Livio dell'Anna (D'Amico de Carvalho and Favino 2003b, 30). Outside of cinema, he led a veritable revolution on Italian stages from the 1940s through the 1970s, directing classic and modern theater from Italy, the United States, Europe, and Russia (Puppa 2007, 43–54). This theater work extended to the opera, where a cycle of works starring Maria Callas between 1954 and 1957 (*The Vestal Virgin*, *The Sleepwalker*, *La Traviata*, *Anna Bolena*, *Iphigenia in Tauris*) inaugurated the director's equally profound activity in Italy's lyric venues. Although not a painter, Visconti has been associated with various Italian pictorial traditions. Darbellay (2011) and Blom (2017a) analyze how the director made overt and allusive references to painting through a notable use of mise-en-scène, especially framing devices such as mirrors and doorways but also through costumes, photographs, and other material elements. These are part of what Ilaria Serra calls "imagistic substitutions" that are typical connections between film and the figurative arts in Italy (Serra 2011). The international character of his activities cannot be understated, and Visconti's efforts reflect a truly transnational approach to Italian artmaking. It is notable that his work in cinema began in France as an assistant to Jean Renoir in the 1930s, and over the course of his prolific career, he borrowed liberally from sources and traditions around the world. When asked which art form he preferred—film, opera, or theater—Visconti suggested that all dramatic forms at his disposal might fit equally beneath the same umbrella of spectacle: "I don't know, honestly," he claimed in "La mia carriera teatrale" ("My Career in Theater") published in *L'Europeo* in 1966, "Cinema, theater, opera: I would say it is all the same work. Despite the enormous diversity of the means they use. The issue of bringing a spectacle to life is always equal" (*LV*, 62). This interartistic blending was not always viewed enthusiastically by critics, and although his films were periodically maligned for being too operatic or overly theatrical, his opera and theater works were likewise disparaged for their striking cinematicity (Rondolino 2003, 353).

Visconti's reliance on literary adaptation also factored into this vocabulary of totalizing artistic practice. For Mikhail Bakhtin, the novel was distinct from other literary genres in its ability to create a dialogic exchange of speech types, cultural forms, vernacular and literary languages. As Robert Stam observes, the cinema takes this appropriation of other forms and genres "to its paroxysm," expanding the novel's heteroglossia by becoming "a receptacle open to all kinds of literary and pictorial symbolism, to all types of collective representation, to all ideologies, to all aesthetics, and to the infinite play of influences within cinema, within the other arts, and within culture generally" (Stam 2000, 61). Although novels were the primary texts used to root Visconti's films, secondary ones appeared as well. Through allusion, referencing, and recall, a Visconti film might signal any number of literary, political, and historical works and authors. In this framework, Viscontian adaptation might be viewed as a broad threshold opening out to an almost countless set of textual linkages, motioning toward Stam's poststructural reading of adaptation's polyphonic capacities, where the "ongoing whirl of intertextual reference and transformation, of texts generating other texts an endless process of recycling, transformation and transmutation, with no clear point of origin" (Stam 2000, 66). Visconti perceived his tendency toward intertextuality not as a goal but as a natural by-product of the artistic act:

> If I wrote a book, exactly as is the case when I make a film, I would be writing on the basis of all the input I have received from my reading and from my artistic predilections. And there is little doubt that what I would then say would already have

> been said by someone else. I would be at liberty not to indicate my sources. They would exist nonetheless. A man who had never read a book, never looked at a painting, never heard any music? His gaze, his sense of hearing absolutely virgin? And who would be using a camera to look at the world and translate it into images? Yes, that person could certainly practice "pure cinema." But . . . (translated by Testa 2012, 23)

While not exactly dismissing the multiartistic input to his cinematic interface, here and elsewhere Visconti naturalized the "ongoing whirl of intertextual reference and transformation" as a normal feature of his—and perhaps any—artistic creation. What he emphasized as fundamental to his production as a filmmaker, however, were the literary antecedents he adapted to screen. It should be noted that his use of the term *rhythm* in "Tradition and Invention" does not refer to a seemingly infinite intertextuality outlined by Stam, or the sort of interartistic cinematic field buttressed by the silent-era thinkers. Rather, the essay underscores the process of bringing one book—Verga's *House by the Medlar Tree*—to screen. From the beginning, Visconti defended the originality of such literary adaptation, noting that relative to directing opera and theater, "one is far more an author making a film, even if it is a film derived from literature" (*LV*, 62). From the Greek *rythmos*, "measured flow or movement" but also "arrangement, order; form, shape," the term *rhythm* superbly evokes the complex process of literary adaptation: a semiotic reordering in which words from literature gather new cadence in the spatial-temporal medium of cinema. Rather than being haunted by some "dead hand of literature," Visconti mined literary texts and authors at will, breaking new ground through the conscious and unabashed manipulation of literary originals (Leitch 2008a, 65). He did so by mixing appropriation with invention: "When I choose a specific literary work, it is so that I can give it a new dimension," he stated, "or rather, a dimension which it already possesses implicitly, but which only 'another' gaze is able to give it—precisely the gaze called for by the creator, a gaze that is creative in and of itself" (translated by Testa 2012, 23). By accentuating his position as creator, in touch with "a specific literary work," Visconti suggests that the book on which he based his films has a unique status in his oeuvre, different than those other arts with which his cinema tends to echo.

Recent critical approaches have not necessarily highlighted adaptation's individuality. As Sarah Cardwell has suggested, the emphasis on adaptation as a form of intertextuality, popular since the 1990s (Stam 2000; Stam and Raengo 2004, 2005), and an interest in adaptation as a type of intermediality and transmediality, prominent since the early 2000s (Ellestrøm 2013), risk losing sight of what makes adaptation distinct from these broader categories (Cardwell 2018, 9). Intertextuality and intermediality, she argues, are "necessary but not sufficient condition[s] for adaptation," with adaptation a "special case of both intertextuality and intermediality," in which the "primary concern is to adapt" (Cardwell 2018, 12). As I demonstrate in the following pages, Visconti put his intent to adapt on full display, engineering a skeletal substrate composed of a distinctively literary substance to structure his works. Considering how complex literary frameworks interact in *Rocco and His Brothers*, Mauro Giori outlined what he calls Visconti's "bovarism"—the way the reality of Flaubert's title character Madame Bovary is shaped by the various fictional texts read in her past—as an essential component of his poetics of cinema evident throughout Visconti's filmography: "The quest for drama passes through an interpretation of reality and its themes beneath the light of many accumulated readings. If everything recalls to the Flaubertian heroine (in the sentimental reality that she tries to construct around herself) some of her past readings, likewise in *Rocco* almost every sequence has a literary root, every character numerous ones, every motive recalls entire genres and traditions [*filoni*], every theme is immersed in a fictional imaginary" (Giori 2011a, 101–2). Perhaps unsurprisingly, this literary origination characterized all of his adaptations, where literature was the starting point for his cinematic projects. As we will see, adaptation was not always accorded as prominent a position in the interpretations of his films as one might expect. Despite the fluctuating stress Visconti placed on the literary sources subtending his films in his public comments, his intent was always to adapt, always to "attempt to re-experience and assemble the magic of that rhythm, of that vague yearning for the unknown" (*LV*, 19). The concern to adapt was present throughout his career, literature and cinema becoming the Janus face of his idiosyncratic creative gaze.

Authors, Auteurs, Adaptation

In the same period in which D'Annunzio, the futurists, and others lauded the new art of cinema, there were literary authors who viewed this upstart form with some apprehension. In a letter to Dina di Sordevolo, dated February 20, 1912, Giovanni Verga grumbled about a film version of his *Cavalleria Rusticana*, stating that "*Cavalleria* or no *Cavalleria*, these days the cinematographer has utterly invaded the field in need of *subjects* or themes to disfigure the public and blind the people" (Verga 1984a, 30). Verga, in a letter from April 25, 1912, pleaded with Sordevolo not to identify him with the sale of his intellectual property or reveal that he had anything to do with what he called "this culinary manipulation of my things"(Verga 1984b, 33). Other literary figures viewed the neonate cinema with a similar degree of misgiving. Some perceived the film-book pairing as a marriage in conflict, with cinema making a crass modern spouse for noble literature. Adaptation was the strange vow that united this odd couple, and aspersions against it came early and often. In a much-cited essay titled "The Cinema" from 1926, Virginia Woolf interprets cinema as a parasite, feasting on the body of a literary host. In contrast to the harmonious confluence of arts described by Canudo, Woolf found cinema's appropriation of literature to be superficial and unsophisticated, like complex musical instruments in the hands of brutes: "It is as if the savage tribe . . . had found, scattering the seashore, fiddles, flutes, saxophones, trumpets, grand pianos by Erard and Bechstein, and had begun with incredible energy, but without knowing a note of music, to hammer and thump upon them all at the same time" (Woolf 1926, 383). The juxtaposition of the savage cinematic "eye" (senses) with the sophisticated literary "brain" (reason) betrays all of the anticorporeality, iconophobia, and logophilia that plagued studies of adaptation that followed (Stam 2000, 58). To Woolf, adaptation was not to create, or to use the *Oxford English Dictionary* definition "an altered or amended version of a text, musical composition, etc., (now *esp.*) one adapted for filming," but to damage, ruin, mutilate (*OED* 2021). Even cinema's most celebratory of literary works represented the discomfort inflicted by the fast-moving new medium. In Luigi Pirandello's 1916 novel *Shoot! The Notebooks of Serafino Gubbio, Cinematograph Operator*, itself proof of the newfound fascination with all things cinematic, the protagonist grouses in irritation: "Already my eyes and my ears too, from force of habit, are beginning to see and hear everything in the guise of this rapid, quivering, ticking mechanical reproduction" (Pirandello 2005a, 8). Gone is the rapturous encomium for cinema's melodies, replaced by the reservations of those remarking on an audiovisual assault by cinema's maddening, disruptive cacophony.

For some critics, cinema, to become a legitimate cultural form, had to carve its own path, not retread what was already established by literature. This is the essentialism of the medium-specificity thesis, in which each art form, by virtue of its individual medium, is thought to occupy an exclusive domain. From the 1776 essay "Laocoon," in which Gotthold Ephraim Lessing argued for the separation of art forms (poetry progresses in time; painting endures in space), to Clement Greenberg's 1940 "Towards a New Laocoon," where he asserted that modernist paintings maintain their virtue "by acting solely in terms of their separate and irreducible selves," arguments for the purity of media have an extended and august tradition (Greenberg 1961, 139). When Visconti wrote "Tradition and Invention" in 1941, he was addressing those who viewed literary-based films in Italy as a form of miscegenation, as much culturally retrograde as they were ideologically suspect. At the time, some Italian filmmakers and film theorists regarded adaptations as being synonymous with the "calligraphist" filmmaking of fascism, with the term *calligraphism* etymologically tied to "pretty writing," indicating a group of films during late fascism that advanced cinematic form through their explicit use of its sister arts. Large-scale adaptations by directors Mario Soldati, Luigi Chiarini, Fernando Maria Poggioli, Renato Castellani, Alberto Lattuada, and Luigi Zampa foregrounded nineteenth-century literary sources from France, Russia, and Italy to develop a cinematic formalism. The calligraphic filmmakers were inspired by French poetic realism of the 1930s, the "poetic" evocative of a cinema that was somehow literary (Martini 1992). The omnipresence of literary films in this period points to literature's cultural importance under fascism, where it was still the "privileged terrain" of Italian cultural production from which filmmakers could borrow (Brunetta 2009). In the postwar period, Zavattini, Chiarini, and others panned calligraphism's emphatic literariness, bourgeois and historical settings, and melodramatic structures as the quintessence of the fascist art of illusion. Highly mediated and condemned as empty formalism, calligraphism thus appeared to conspire with fascist cultural policy of "bread and circus." In the postwar period, Italian filmmakers created neorealism, a moment in Italy's film history when directors were tasked with encapsulating the devastating present of the nation torn apart by war and exposing the real-life struggles of the Italian commoner, calligraphism became a convenient prewar foil for postwar claims to cinematic authenticity. Critic Guido Aristarco, in a review of *Obsession* published in *Il Corriere Padano* in 1943, noted how Visconti's first film offered a potential new direction for Italian cinema against the calligraphists: "Castellani, Soldati, Lattuada, Poggioli e Chiarini have fallen into grave danger: into empty formalism: or better, in an arid and frigid decorativism, devoid of spiritual research, lyrical momentum, human values" (Brunetta 2017, 209). As we will see in chapter 2, attention to *Obsession*'s depictions of the Italian landscape and documentation of life in Italy's hinterlands eclipsed the film's identity as an adaptation and muted associations with literature.

Adaptation's unenviable status in the years following fascism extended outside the sphere of film criticism and into the courtroom. It is easily forgotten that Visconti's first adaptation, *Obsession*, made during the same period "Tradition and Invention" was written, also marked his first lawsuit for copyright infringement. The plaintiff was the French production company Gladiator, who owned the rights to James M. Cain's novel *The Postman Always Rings Twice* and produced its 1939 adaptation, *Le dernier tournant* (*The Last Turning*), by director Pierre Chenal (Foose 1976, 6) (see fig. I.2).

Figure I.2. Poster for the French film *Le dernier tournant* (Pierre Chenal, 1939).

The court case dragged on for over a decade and was an inaugural chapter in a developing portrayal of Visconti as a "liberal" adaptor of literary sources in film and theater whose lack of respect for literary antecedents was the source of praise and scorn. Many years later, after attending Visconti's 1973 performance of *Old Times* in Rome, dramaturge Harold Pinter was so offended by the frank exhibition of nudity and lesbianism that he whistled his displeasure. Pinter immediately revoked Visconti's rights to continue to direct it, noting: "I can't be said to feel too happy about such idiocies" (Drake 1985, VI: 1, 6). Such censure aligns with a historical hostility to adaptation by the likes of Viktor Shklovsky in Russia in the 1920s or Jean Mitry in France in the 1960s, for whom adaptation was simply impossible (Testa 2008, 76–78).

Despite adaptation's troublesome position for notions of originality and questions of authorship, much of Visconti's aura of creative authority was built on his cinematic readings of books. In a time when many Italian literary and intellectual figures engaged in what Gian Piero Brunetta has called a "fatal attraction" with the cinema, Visconti became famous for his counterhegemonic interpretations of literature on screen. A Marxist aristocrat known as the "Red Count," Visconti was the darling of Italy's Communist Party. Consequently, his films were read as undermining dominant political ideologies at the time, offering transgressive, politically charged works that exemplified the militancy of communist-affiliated filmmaking in Italy. Such political engagement was inseparable from Italian neorealism. Difficult to define, neorealism is some mixture of an ideological program, a historical movement, an aesthetic sensibility, and an ethical approach to artmaking (Marcus 1986, 22). Lino Micciché famously coined neorealism's "ethics of the aesthetic," pointing to shared notions of reliability, accuracy, and honesty similar to the documentarian standard, where filmmakers are tasked with telling real-life stories straightforwardly. Visconti concurred, once replying to the question of "What was neorealism?" with: "It was a moral position that we took up with regards to power, with regards to the social situation in Italy, of the postwar disorder, to clarify certain issues, or at least denounce them" (Rondi 2006, 284). Neorealism's prestige and association with antifascism protected Visconti's later films from the French New Wave hostility to adaptation, which François Truffaut regarded as the quintessence of France's tired *cinéma de papa* or "Daddy's cinema." Sheltered by his Marxist leanings and the antagonistic challenges to both fascist (prewar) and Christian Democratic (postwar) concepts of "Italian clean living" forwarded in his films, Visconti was permitted to explore adaptation as part of his wide-ranging artistic vision. He was one of the first Italian auteurs interviewed by *Cahiers* when they began publishing dialogues with admired filmmakers such as Welles, Hitchcock, Hawks, and Rossellini between 1954 and 1957. Critics Andrew Sarris, Peter Wollen, and others followed the notion of the auteur set forth by Truffaut and the *Cahiers*, and Visconti was soon elevated to "classic" auteur status in Italy by Pio Baldelli (1965) and Geoffrey Nowell-Smith in England (1967), the latter of whom argued for Visconti's place at the center of a "structuralist-auteur" school (an association referenced approvingly in Wollen's influential *Signs and Meaning in the Cinema*, first published in 1969). For Nowell-Smith, adaptation was just another means for expressing a "structural hard core of basic and often recondite motifs" that characterized a system of codes and patterns making up the auteur's trademark aura (Nowell-Smith 1967, 10). This brand of auteurism was successfully contested by semiotic and poststructuralist theories, and by the early 1970s, the concept that film (at least of a certain scale) was a collective rather than individual endeavor became mainstream. Today, no one would deny that Visconti benefited from screenwriters Suso Cecchi d'Amico or Enrico Medioli, cinematographers G. R. Aldo or Giuseppe Rotunno, Mario Garbuglia's set designs, Piero Tosi's costuming, and Mario Serandrei's editing, for example. The role of "star" producers like Franco Cristaldi, Goffredo Lombardo, and Dino de Laurentiis—once called the *politiques des producteurs*—also subverts ideas on the director as a film's lynchpin in favor of a notion of creative collaboration (Micciché 1975, 41–57; Small 2016, 109).

The legacy of auteur structuralism endures today, especially with regard to Visconti's adaptations. Interpretations of these films continue to focus on a sui generis artist, influenced by select authors whose ideas were seen to structure his textual borrowings. Above all others, critics have identified two individuals—Antonio Gramsci and Marcel Proust—as Visconti's most important reference points. Their significance was reasserted by scholars across the decades, helping determine ideas on Visconti's methods of adaptation. Carlo Testa, for example, once bifurcated all Italian literary adaptations into two camps, placing Visconti as co-figurehead of one: "Verily there seem to be two separate and largely non-communicating film-and-literature traditions: the one that developed within the Gramscian-Viscontian context, and the one that didn't" (Testa 2002a, 8). Ideologically, the ruminations on Italian politics, art, and history published in Gramsci's *Prison Notebooks* were seen to affect many of Visconti's films, especially those in the early phases. Although the Gramscian intertext behind historical films *Senso* and *The Leopard* is indeed noteworthy, I argue that Gramsci's connection to films like *The Earth Trembles* and *Rocco and His Brothers* overshadowed questions of adaptation in negative ways. Aesthetically, Visconti declared time and again his allegiance to Proust, a writer he adored (Mann, Chekhov, Dostoevsky, and Shakespeare also deserve mention). He shared various biographical elements with Proust, such as an aristocratic background, an adulation for his mother, and his identification as homosexual. Yet his long-planned adaptation of Proust's magnum opus, *In Search of Lost Time*, was ultimately abandoned, and he never projected a Proust work on film. Although Visconti did borrow characters and even sequences (as in *The Leopard*) from Proust's writing, I argue that Proust was just one of many literary figures whose textual production Visconti liberally resourced. "Proustian" themes of memory, nostalgia, and aestheticism, I contend, represent as much of a shared artistic mien between writer and filmmaker as they do a direct influence.

While acknowledging the influence of Gramsci and Proust, *Luchino Visconti and The Alchemy of Adaptation* trains its focus on some specific literary sources directly involved in the screenwriting process, exploring how individual texts helped shape the films they became. More important, this book examines the cinematic end product that results from the art of adaptation. Viewing adaptations as films in and of themselves unearths both the literary and cinematic substrates (a combination that will be called "cine-literary") that buttressed these films. To date, Visconti has rightly been tied to forms of melodrama, what Christine Gledhill deciphers as a composite form of its own or a "modality" but, as I will demonstrate, there are other genres and modalities at play as well (Bayman 2014; Gledhill 2000). Either explicitly or implicitly, his films toured modern Italian and international film conventions and forms, high-to-low: noir (*Obsession*) and documentary (*Giorni di Gloria*, *Appunti su un fatto di cronaca*, *The Earth Trembles*, *Alla ricerca di Tadzio*); historical costume dramas set in Italy (*Senso*, *The Intruder*) and Germany (*The Damned*, *Ludwig*); chamber films (*White Nights*, *The Job*, *Conversation Piece*), the boxing film (*Rocco and His Brothers*) and diva films (*Bellissima*, *Anna Magnani*, *The Witch Burned Alive*); the gothic, together with the Italian mystery or *giallo* (*Sandra*); the Italian heritage film (*The Leopard*) and legal drama (*The Stranger*); and even adaptation itself (*Death in Venice*). Many of these categories have largely been ignored in scholarly works on Visconti, which focus more on politics (Gramsci) and high art (Proust) that would place him above and beyond such a generic purview.

This book assumes a more contemporary notion of the auteur filmmaker that was introduced in the Italian context by Mary P. Wood, who argues that "Italian *auteur* cinema is not so much a distinct entity in itself, as the intellectual and/or better funded end of national genre production," referencing how auteur concerns operated within the same realm as genre ones (Wood 2005, 111). The connection between auteur and genre illustrates the simultaneous rise of auteurs and genre cinema in postwar Italian film, usually seen as isolated traditions. In many respects, Wood echoes the classic study on auteur-genre interaction by Robin Wood, who in 1977 argued for a more "synthetic" view of Alfred Hitchcock's *Shadow of a Doubt* (1943) and Frank Capra's *It's a Wonderful Life* (1946), one that stretches past the individual auteur to consider how these directors handled the ideological and generic conventions circulating in Hollywood (Wood 1977). Including film types only expands what is already a wide-ranging understanding of Visconti's identity as an auteur, whose "stardom," Marcia Landy notes, "has been nourished by critics who identify his works with his aristocratic background, his involvement with La Scala Opera, his left-leaning politics, and the erudition and precision of his cinematic style" (Landy 2008, 191). Visconti's attention to lower cultural forms has been well documented, if not usually accentuated, but as David Bordwell argued long ago, the art film is also itself a genre (Bordwell 1979). "Genre," as Andrew Tudor (1974, 139) suggests, "is what we collectively believe it to be," indicating a set of conventions that are recognizable to an audience or critics and adhere to or resist a set of expectations. I argue that in his consistent signaling of literary sources and resonances, in the marketing of his cinema as iterative of literary classics, and in the reception of his films by audiences primed to interpret a literary work at the movies, Visconti forwarded a set of conventions and structures that move centrifugally from literature to generic forms familiar to film spectators at the time.

Cryptographs and Code-Breakers: Tradition and Invention

Along with Visconti's essays from the early 1940s, "Anthropomorphic Cinema" and "Cadavers," "Tradition and Invention" is commonly understood in the antifascist context of the Italian film journal *Cinema*, where contributors argued for cinematic renewal that would only come about in the antifascist resistance poetics of neorealism. Unlike "Anthropomorphic

Cinema," an essay allegedly ghostwritten by Gianni Puccini, Visconti probably wrote "Tradition and Invention" himself. Mino Argentieri once remarked: "Visconti never picked up a pen . . . there are articles published and signed by Visconti that weren't written by Visconti. For declarations of his poetics and things of that sort he always found someone: as a good artist, he entrusted them to people who had their hands in things with which he was scarcely familiar. Visconti, Puccini and Peppe De Santis worked collegially together on the famous article 'Anthropomorphic Cinema,' then one of them was tasked with a draft, like you do with a screenplay" (Argentieri 2013, 362; translation mine). As a kind of travelogue of his trip to Sicily, "Tradition and Invention" fits in with the various written accounts in Visconti's diary and letters of trips to France, the Greek islands, and the United States during the mid- to late 1930s (Rondolino 2003, 60–70). He begins "Tradition and Invention" by addressing the debate over adaptation that was circulating during those years before filming *Obsession*:

> A recent dispute over the relationship between literature and film has found me spontaneously in the camp of those who place their faith in the richness and validity of a "literary" inspired cinema. I must confess that in the intention to begin a cinematographic activity, one of the primary difficulties that seem to impede my desire and my ambition to understand the film only as a poetic work, is the consideration of banality, forgive my use of the term, of misery that is so often at the basis of ordinary scriptwriting. (*LV*, 19)

His preference for a literary cinema echoes that of Giuseppe De Santis and Mario Alicata, who also in 1941 published two essays on the literature of Giovanni Verga as an important model for the more authentic cinema to come. (Their interventions are discussed in depth in chapter 2.) For all three, filmmakers needed not invent anything from scratch to move past conventions of fascist cinema. Visconti continues:

> It will seem perhaps obvious, but I've asked myself more than once, why it is that while a solid literary tradition exists, in one-hundred different forms of novels and stories realized in the sincere and pure "truth" of human life, cinema, in its meaning outside this life would seem to be the documentarian, content to accustom audiences to a taste for the small

> intrigue, the melodramatic rhetoric in which a mechanical coherence protects the spectator from the risk of inspiration and invention. (*LV*, 19)

The prose tradition, the director argues, featured an archive of authentic life expressed in a way that is already "poetic" or artistic. Noting the need to advance Italian cinema beyond the banal conventions that lull rather than challenge spectators, Visconti rehearses a common criticism during this era, that is, that fascist cinema was designed as a form of distraction, wrapping spectators in a prophylactic bubble that kept them out of contact with the truth. This point would be expressed more explicitly in the image of the decomposing bodies from the essay "Cadavers," a sardonic portrayal of the world of cinema as populated by the walking dead, stumbling about "in the belief that they are alive" (*LV*, 21–22). Throughout "Tradition and Invention," Visconti underscores the vitality of the literary artifact, an instrument for realism that fulfilled film's capacity to respect life and "tell the stories of living men," as famously stated in "Anthropomorphic Cinema."

"Tradition and Invention" is also prescriptive in nature: "In such a situation it is natural for those who sincerely believe in the filmmaker, to turn their eyes with nostalgia to the great narrative constructions of the classics of the European novel and to consider them today as a source of an even truer inspiration. It is good to have the courage to say truer, even if some might accuse our affirmation of impotency or at least scarce "cinematographic" purity" (*LV*, 19). That literary-based films are somehow weakened by their essential duality—film and literature together, both or neither—references adaptation's odd position in the history of medium-specific ideas and a preference that each art form adhere to its unique dimensions. Yet in considering the possibility that a literary-inspired cinema might actually be "truer" to human life than a documentary cinema, Visconti promotes a cinema that is not purely indexical. Turning toward an Aristotelian notion of mimesis, the director argues that cinema is not required to copy nature or an "imitation of men doing something," but can refashion or reconfigure the "essence of reality" in narrative form (Bacon 1998, 30–31). Although today this differentiation between documentary (naturalism) and narrative film (realism) might seem self-evident, in the 1940s when "Tradition and Invention" was written, filmmakers were still examining various models of cinema in their attempt to craft a new, nonfascist cinema in Italy. As demonstrated in part 1, what resulted in neorealism would not conclude a search for "a certain cinema, in a certain direction," to use the words of neorealism's greatest theorist, Cesare Zavattini. Instead, it was a platform for the continued discussion of cinema, reality, and truth that continued in the decades to come.

In "Tradition and Invention," Visconti suggests that author and auteur imbibe an artistic imaginary based on the same real geographic spaces. This is evidenced by the next section of the essay, where he declares his own presence as the primary "focalizer" (dominant origin of perspective) of the physical place of Sicily and is simultaneously a reader and interpreter of Verga's literary works. Significantly, this interpreter is an emotional one—an observer who not only reads but "falls in love" with another author. This affective quality is decisive:

> With a head full of these thoughts, walking around one day in the streets of Catania and crossing the plane of Caltagirone on a windy morning, I fell in love with Giovanni Verga. To me, a Lombard reader, accustomed by traditional custom to the clear rigor of Manzonian fantasy, the primitive and gigantic world of the fishermen of Aci Trezza and the shepherds of Marineo always appeared elevated in an imaginative and violent epic: to my Lombard eyes, contented by my land's sky "così bello quand'è bello," Verga's Sicily appeared truly as the island of Ulysses, an island of adventures and lively passions, located immobile and proud against the Ionian breakers. (*LV*, 19)

This image of Sicily is unquestionably that of an actual geographic place (the streets of Catania; the Caltagirone highland). But it is also from Verga's Sicily and the fishermen of Acitrezza who populated *The House by the Medlar Tree*, then his film *The Earth Trembles* (fig. I.3).

Most important, Sicily is that which is perceived by the artist, just one link in an ancient chain of interlocutors who have viewed, visualized, and represented the island. Visconti's vision and imagination are interconnected with that of Homer and his *Odyssey*, where Sicily was the mythical home of the Laestrygonians and the Cyclops. Together, these multiple interpreters link their representations of Sicily in the literary tradition in an "infinite regress of intertextual borrowings," with Visconti furthermore identifying himself with author Alessandro Manzoni's northern "Lombard reader," whose rational "clear rigor" he contrasts the "primitive" and "lively passions" of the island as constructed by Verga (Marcus 1993, 26). This confession of love is followed by a series of other emotional sensations

Figure I.3. Poster for *The Earth Trembles* (Luchino Visconti, 1948).

stirred by the specific thought of *The House by the Medlar Tree* ("Thus, I thought of a film on *The House by the Medlar Tree*"), which elicits "the enthusiasm to be able to give a visual and plastic reality to those heroic figures who symbolize all of the allusive and secret power without its abstract or rigid detachment" (*LV*, 19). On this overdetermination of sound, Visconti reestablishes his creative perspective on the book and Sicily:

> I would like to immediately note that if one day I have the good luck and the power to produce the film I have dreamed up on *The House by the Medlar Tree*, the most valid justification for my effort will certainly be the illusion that touched my

> soul in a distant hour, convincing me that for all spectators just as for myself, the mere sounds of those names—padron 'Ntoni Malavoglia, Bastianazzo, la Longa, Sant'Agata, "La provvidenza"—and of those places—Aci Trezza, il Capo dei Mulini, il Rotolo, la Sciara—will succeed in opening wide a fabulous and magic scenario where words and gestures cannot but have the religious elevation of the things that are essential to our human charity. (*LV*, 19–20)

That he finds a musical, auditory solution to this representational challenge is noteworthy, returning us to the beginning of this introduction, when the director underscores his desire to translate the rhythms of Verga's text cinematically. In its polytextuality, reference to textual rhythm (like the "spirit" of a text), and palimpsestic notion of Sicily in literature (from Homer to Verga), "Tradition and Invention" anticipated twenty-first-century tendencies in the study of adaptation, where scholars have moved past text-to-screen analyses that list the various media-specific capacities of literature (telling verbally) and film (showing visually). As Thomas Leitch has argued, traditional studies inevitably beget the same conclusion, that "it wasn't like that in the book," perpetuating dated notions that reading and writing be privileged over filming and viewing (Leitch 2003, 154). When such "traditional" studies began is significant. While Anglo-American scholars frequently remark that George Bluestone's 1957 book *Novel into Film* constitutes the seminal text for adaptation studies, European thinkers were already contemplating adaptation in the first years of the twentieth century. Anton Kaes observes a lively discussion about adaptation in German public debate as early as 1909 (Kaes and Levin 1987). Already in 1911, Arthur Schnitzler had prepared his novel *The Veil of Pierrette* for screen, and in 1913 he finished the script for Holger Madsen's film version of *Liebelei* (Tinazzi 2007, 11). In France, Paul Laffitte created La Film d'Art in 1908, a company that employed members of the Comédie Française and eventually produced the *Cahiers du mois*, in which studies of adaptation appeared as early as 1925 (Bragaglia 1993, 9). The year 1908 was when an Italian production house based in Milan, Saffi-Luca Comerio, produced adaptations of Manzoni's *The Betrothed* and Francesco Mastriani's *Buried Alive* (Ripari 2015, 159). Beyond thinkers like Canudo, over the course of cinema's first few decades, Italian writers from across the spectrum sought work in the "promised land" of cinema that would take Italian filmmaking through the crisis years of the 1920s and into the 1930s (Brunetta 2008, 27).

Adaptation did not lose its relevance during the transition to sound and the birth of the modern Italian film industry. With the fascist creation of the Venice Film Festival 1932 and Italy's hypermodern film studio (Cinecittà) and film academy (Centro Sperimentale di Cinematografia) in 1935, Italian cinema was on course to become a global player in international film production, partially fueled by literary-based films. Luigi Pirandello, Mario Soldati, and later Cesare Zavattini and Giacomo Debenedetti all migrated toward cinema in the form of screenwriting, where they benefited from the advent of the spoken word in the age of sound. These figures created not only adaptations but also original screenplays, displaying how literary films grew from the same processes as nonliterary ones. After World War II, adaptation was folded seamlessly into neorealism's "sudden flourishing in Italy of a mass practice of storytelling," and the film–literature relationship was one of the many ways scholars and critics attempted to define what was new about neorealism (Re 1991, 37). "It was a period in which the cinema had yet to be legitimate as culture and as art," remarked Carlo Lizzani, "And so we needed this literary ancestry . . . We were like castaways. Every one of us was searching for a handhold in literature" (Lizzani 1983, 108). From a nonexhaustive list of adaptations during neorealism, Mario Guidorizzi notes that of Italian films made between 1939 and 1955, 218 of about 1,200 films were adaptations (Guidorizzi 1983, 167). Despite the stalwart positions of those who rejected a cinema based on literature (Cesare Zavattini, Carlo Bo, Luigi Chiarini), many of neorealism's most iconic films relied on literary antecedents (Marcus 1993, 4–7).

Beginning with this neorealist moment, *Luchino Visconti and the Alchemy of Adaptation* examines how Visconti's adaptations meander from their sources in unexpected ways, moving downstream through the landscape of Italian cinema that they fed and were fed by. Alchemy, the powerful transformation of one thing into another through a mysterious process, refers to that "opening wide a fabulous and magic scenario" that appears in the conclusion of "Tradition and Invention." Incorporating literature and cinema, filmmaker and film industry, individual and nation was typical of Italian cinema from the early 1940s until the mid-1970s, where an interconnected ecosystem of creative exchange developed into one of the world's leading film industries. In this way, this book seeks to subvert monolithic notions of Visconti, who has often been celebrated for an intransigent adherence to realism, Marxism, or decadence, depending on the point of view. Reflecting on cinema through literature allowed Visconti to experiment with various techniques associated with literary authors while pressing the boundaries of cinematic representation. Rather than a means for transporting any tradition of literature to film, adaptation becomes a process by which Visconti laid cinema bare, exposing its essential features and arguing for its primacy among dramatic forms. As this book explores in all of its variety, adaptation was the central platform for the spectacle that was Visconti's art, where literary rhythms echoed through the sounds of cinema.

Part I

Neorealist Interiors in Word and Image

1

La terra trema (*The Earth Trembles,* 1948)

Inhabiting *The House by the Medlar Tree,* from Verga to Visconti

> And those people's dignified misery was beautiful, the sobriety of their poor houses, their wooden, handmade tools. I was extremely fascinated by their possessions, as was customary of certain ancient people, two houses, one on land, one on the water.
>
> —Franco Zeffirelli, assistant on *The Earth Trembles*

At the center of present-day Aci Trezza, a small hamlet on the northeastern coast of Sicily, stands the Museo Casa del Nespolo, or Museum of the House by the Medlar Tree, a modest museum with a lava-stone archway. Sporadically open to the public, the museum takes its name from Giovanni Verga's 1881 book, *The House by the Medlar Tree*, where the "house" refers to the home of the novel's main characters. The museum is split into two rooms that memorialize two authors: Verga, major exponent of Italian nineteenth-century school of literary realism, called verism, and Visconti, whose version of Verga's novel, *The*

Figure 1.1. Mara and Lucia gaze out from the window of the family home in *The Earth Trembles* (Luchino Visconti, 1948).

Earth Trembles, has been called the masterpiece of twentieth-century cinematic neorealism. The first room, the Visconti Room, offers a series of photographs, posters, and memorabilia that chronicle the location shooting of *The Earth Trembles* filmed in Aci Trezza in 1947 and 1948. The second, the Verga Room, reconstructs a typical living area where traditional fishermen described in the novel might have lived. Antique fishing tackle, cooking utensils, and furniture clutter a space that once included some of Verga's photographs and a collection of letters to the author's brother, Pietro.

In melding the literary with the cinematic, this museum constitutes a hybrid epitext, defined by Gérard Genette as "any paratextual element not materially appended to the text within the same volume but circulating, as it were, freely, in a virtually limitless physical and social space" (Genette 1997, 344). In Sicily, literary epitexts of this type are frequently housed in the former residences of authors or located at gravesites, birthplaces, or other locales related to the artists and their works. In nearby Catania, for example, Verga's former home has been converted into a museum, the Casa Museo Giovanni Verga, that pays homage to the writer by preserving the original features of his house. While lacking the extravagance of Gabriele D'Annunzio's palatial Vittoriale on Lake Garda or the secluded appeal of Francesco Petrarca's graceful home in Arquà, Verga's residence conveys a certain intimate elegance, with the visit centered around the author's library and study. These locations represent Italy's heritage industry, where tourist bureaus exploit the nation's reputation as the cradle of European art and beauty as an economic mainstay (Hom 2015). Visconti's homes are now a cinematic node in this network. His various personal residences have been converted from private homes to public institutions: the multiuse Villa Erba on the shores of Lake Como includes a museum, The Rooms of Luchino Visconti, dedicated to the director's infancy and youth; Villa La Colombaia, his summer residence on the island of Ischia, once featured a literary café along with the director's tomb; and Castello di Grazzano, the Visconti ancestral home just south of Milan, houses a park and a faux medieval village that can be visited by appointment.

As an architectural epitext, divided along cinematic and literary lines, the House by the Medlar Tree Museum materializes how adaptation intertwines film and literary legacies, with books and their cinematic versions, authors and auteurs becoming part of "a host of interlocking literary experiences" (Collins 2010, 119). While related to these sites rooted in the real biographies of literary and cinematic authors, the House by the Medlar Tree Museum is not the same rustic home described by Verga, nor is it the corresponding house where Visconti filmed *The Earth Trembles*, which was actually an amalgamation of three different homes (Mancini and Sciacca 1981). Like other museums, it is a simulacrum, contrived to resemble life as seen through the eyes of two artists. Mixing authenticity with fiction, the museum symbolizes the perplexing claims to reality and objectivity that underpin two of Italy's most significant -isms of the nineteenth and twentieth centuries: literary verism and cinematic neorealism. These realisms relied on a documentary-like approach to recording the experiences of Italy's poor, relating their humble, tragic stories through remarkable artifice that transformed truth into an aesthetic concept (Asor Rosa 1973, 11–12). Verga and Visconti shared in the paradox of realism, in which the representation of reality involves the mediation of replication, not the immediacy of transcription. As a model for the "new" Italian cinema, Verga was hallowed in two articles from 1941 published in *Cinema* by Mario Alicata and Giuseppe De Santis: "Truth and Poetry: Verga and Italian Cinema" and "Again Verga and Italian Cinema" (Alicata and De Santis 1941a, 1941b). *Cinema* featured contributions by some of Italy's foremost leftist intellectuals, whose essays called for a cultural renewal that was impossible to come by under fascism. Alicata and De Santis looked to Verga as a literary model for cinema, beckoning "a revolutionary art inspired by humanity that suffers and hopes" and championing adaptation as a means for creative renewal in cinema. For them, a proto-cinematic Verga exemplified the magmatic potential for a new Italian cinema, one that would become the gritty neorealism of the immediate postfascist age. In their essays, they outline which literary characteristics found in Verga might be most attractive to Italian filmmakers. Marcia Landy lists these as "the repetition, parataxis, formulaic patterns, the use of proverbial wisdom, and the limitations and deceptions of verbal languages so central to the melodramatic and operatic character of folklore" (Landy 1998, 112). Interestingly, Verga was also championed by the opposite political camp, with figures from fascism such as Giuseppe Bottai also finding Verga's literary representations of Sicily to be positive models for the renovation of Italian cinema (Semprebene 2009, 121).

Although *The Earth Trembles* is now considered as iconic a literary adaptation as any in Italian cinema, its linkages between film and novel are hardly uncomplicated. As noted by Franco Zeffirelli, Visconti occluded the connection between Verga's novel and *The Earth Trembles* for legal reasons. "If *The Earth Trembles*' direct derivation from *The House by the Medlar Tree* is not in the opening credits," Zeffirelli stated, "it is because Visconti was unable to obtain the rights from [Verga's] heirs" (Zeffirelli 1996, 28). Visconti always emphasized *The Earth Trembles* status as first a documentary film and second a literary adaptation: a displacement of adaptation similar to that of *Obsession*, his previous film (discussed in the next chapter). Critics followed suit, establishing the photography of landscape and the documentation of real-life Sicilian fishermen as the film's primary focal points. To address this questionable primacy of documentary over adaptation, I examine how Visconti filmed the family home through an analysis of lighting and mise-en-scène. The choreography of the Valastro family, shot in the carefully lit interiors of the house, betray the essential artifice underpinning Verga's novel, highlighting the Sicilian author's "invisible hand" through an adaptation that continually called attention to the artistic operation under way. The house stages the communication between Valastro family members and the community of Aci Trezza, whose petty grievances and rivalries doom the family to disintegrate. Seen together rather than in opposition, adaptation and documentary underscore neorealism's essential hybridity, one of the main stumbling blocks to defining neorealism that continues in the present.

Visconti and Political Neorealism before Gramsci: "The Creative Treatment of Actuality"

Prima facie, *The Earth Trembles* features all the telltale signs of an ethnological documentary, with Visconti declaring a documentary intent in the film's opening captions. The opening scroll establishes the authenticity of place ("The things represented in this film happen in Italy and precisely in Sicily in the town of Aci Trezza"), real people ("all of the film's actors were chosen from the inhabitants of Aci Trezza: fishermen, laborers, bricklayers, wholesalers, girls"), and the film's ideological interest in addressing social injustice ("The story that the film tells is the same one that, renewed for years and years, in every land where one group of men exploits another"): all hallmarks of documentary filmmaking (Visconti 1977). Captions give way to a direct-address voiceover that institutes an authoritative presence that guides viewers. Introductory captions and voiceover are key to contouring the documentary "voice" of *The Earth Trembles* that is fundamental to the documentary mode of filmmaking in general, where centering such a narrator orients the viewer to the unusual images on screen. Voiceover is "that which conveys to us a sense of a text's social point of view, of how it is speaking to us and how it is organizing the materials it is presenting to us. . . . Voice is perhaps akin to that intangible moirélike pattern formed by the unique interaction of all a film's codes" (Nichols 2012, 18–19). *The Earth Trembles* bears other characteristics from the documentary tradition. The technique of registering the antiquated methods and behaviors of a marginalized people representing themselves on screen was taken from Robert Flaherty's *Man of Aran* (1934), while the model of the didactic documentary, in which a film tells the "real" story of those downtrodden by the march of progress, indicates the influence of prewar works of John Grierson, especially the fishing-centric *Granton Trawler* (1934). Even the film's self-reflexive manner (discussed below) can be seen to evoke documentary filmmaker Dziga Vertov's *Man with a Movie Camera* (1929), which pushed the definitional boundaries of documentary by asserting the visibility of the filmmaking apparatus. These would be important precursors to what Alberto Cavalcanti would call the *documentario narrativo* or narrative documentary (also known as the poetic documentary) that were influential for the flourishing of Italian documentaries during the 1930s and were renowned for marrying documentary with fiction (Caminati 2012).

Visconti completed a number of documentaries during his lifetime, and in the interim between *Obsession* (1942) and *The Earth Trembles*, he collaborated on the collective resistance documentary *Giorni di Gloria* (*Days of Glory*, 1945). He also made a second documentary, *Appunti su un fatto di cronaca* (*Notes on a News Story*; see fig. 1.2) that appeared in 1953 as part of the series "Documento mensile." *Notes* exhibits the sights and sounds of the Primavalle district in Rome in an elliptical, abstract fashion, recounting the murder of a young girl, Annarella Bracci, that had appeared in newspapers.

Finally, Visconti is credited with *Alla ricerca di Tadzio* (*In Search of Tadzio*, 1970), a promotional short dedicated to the casting process of his 1971 film *Death in Venice*. Uncoincidentally, many features from the documentary tradition are fundamental to the broader neorealist project beyond Visconti's own filmography. Pairing "prototypes" of documentary and neorealism, Nichols writes: "some fiction films like Vittorio De Sica's *The Bicycle Thief* (1947), can also share these [documentary] qualities with *Nanook* without being considered a documentary at all" (Nichols 2001, 21–22). As indicated by the film's opening crawl, Visconti played up the

Figure 1.2. Inhabitants of Primavalle look out their window in *Appunti su un fatto di cronaca* (*Notes on a News Item*, 1953).

transparent, documentary qualities of *The Earth Trembles*, once claiming that his dedication to the struggle of the Sicilian fisherfolk was so steadfast that it allowed him to work without a script: "It is the life of these people—their difficulties—their struggle that ends always in loss—their resignation. What script? . . . one needs only follow the people, regard them with the camera" (Rondolino 2003, 201).

These documentary features cannot be separated from *The Earth Trembles*' production context, which intensified the stress on cinema's relationship with real life by pairing it with an Italian political reality. *The Earth Trembles* was partially funded by the Italian Communist Party (PCI) in the runup to the 1948 elections, aligning the film with their political program as a work of propaganda rhetorically engaged in forwarding the communist message of class struggle and solidarity. The film was to answer the PCI's call for unity between artists and the party that was made famous by the debate between Palmiro Togliatti and Elio Vittorini in 1947 over the proper rules of engagement that artists and intellectuals should respect in the arena of postfascist politics in Italy (Leavitt 2020, 157–58). This funding source tinged all subsequent interpretations of *The Earth Trembles*, causing it to be regarded as further evidence of Visconti's collaboration with the PCI. The party's revolutionary spirit was to be inscribed in the film's main character, 'Ntoni (Antonio Arcidiacono), a fisherman who together with his family, tries to topple a generations-old economic order of exploitation that had plagued their community. Rather than sell the family's catch to local wholesalers who artificially reduce prices for their own gain, 'Ntoni tries to transport his fish directly to market in nearby Catania, becoming an agent of historical change with hopes of wresting control of the means of subsistence from his oppressors. That the story ends in failure with the family ruined reinforces the Marxist character of *The Earth Trembles*. The much-cited 1960 essay, "Oltre il fato dei Malavoglia" ("Beyond the Fate of the Malavoglia") supposedly written by Visconti but likely penned under his name by PCI Central Committee member Antonello Trombadori, describes *The Earth Trembles* in terms of Antonio Gramsci, the thinker who exercised a significant influence over Visconti's career (Gundle 2000, 100): "The mythical key that, up until that point, I had enjoyed in Verga, was no longer sufficient for me. I felt the compelling need to discover what were the historical, economic, and social bases on which the southern drama grew, and it was with the illuminating reading of Gramsci that granted me possession of a truth that still awaits confrontation and resolution" (*LV*, 48–49). At the time, Gramsci was a touchstone for debates over how to remedy social and economic marginalization in the south. Framed by Gramsci's "Southern Question," but also inspired by Carlo Levi's novel *Cristo si è fermato a Eboli* (1945), this discussion among intellectuals, anthropologists, and documentarians shed light on the need to address the dire conditions of poverty in rural regions (Caminati and Sassi 2017, 366). The mention of Gramsci as a part of the ideation of *The Earth Trembles* is somewhat misleading. Gramsci's *Prison Notebooks* were not published before the filming of *The Earth Trembles*, and although Visconti had certainly been introduced to some of his ideas through his affiliation with prominent communist intellectuals, the extent to which he had read and digested Gramsci before filming is the subject of some debate. When filming began on November 10, 1947, Gramsci's *Prison Notebooks* had yet to be published in edited form, leading to what Lino Micciché calls the "mistake on 'gramscianism,'" in which many scholars inaccurately ascribed the Gramscian intertext to *The Earth Trembles* (Micciché 2006, 85 n.27). Guido Liguori, on the other hand, provides a reading of Gramsci's reception in Italy during this period and prior, one that might suggest Visconti's greater familiarity with the philosopher's works (Liguori 1996). Given Visconti's preference for fiction and relative distance from the socialist pamphlets of his communist comrades, there is some question as to how extensively Visconti studied Marxist texts, including those written by Gramsci. Pietro Notarianni once commented that "Visconti was not exactly an impassioned reader of Marxist texts, I mean, he was much more likely to read Proust" (*Per Luchino Visconti*, episode 6, 1987). This is not to reject Gramsci's influence on Visconti's later works or reduce the significance of his ideas on adaptations that followed the *Prison Notebooks*, *Senso*, or *Rocco and His Brothers*, for example. By conveniently establishing *The Earth Trembles* as the first Gramscian adaptation, scholars have tended to highlight the ideological rather than literary roots of Viscontian adaptation during neorealism, as well as Gramsci's influence on Visconti in general.

Although we will see that it was Verga (not Gramsci), who was the primary reference point for *The Earth Trembles*, one might locate this ex post facto establishment of a Gramscian influence in Visconti's intent at the time. That is, to produce a revolutionary text rooted in the actuality of Italy's recent experience of fascism, the war, and the antifascist resistance. An early treatment of *The Earth Trembles* titled "Promemoria su un film dai Malavoglia (ai giorni di oggi)" ("Memorandum on a Film of The House by the Medlar Tree Today"), written sometime between the end of World War II and the commission of *The Earth Trembles* by the PCI, highlights how the local story would be coded in the fresh events of contemporary history (*FV*, 6, 14, document 1). In this version, 'Ntoni returns home to Aci Trezza from the fascist battlefields in Greece embittered by his experience, the trauma he endured making his reentry into society impossible: "He no longer believes in anything. He ends up smuggling and in the mafia." 'Ntoni was to be offset by the positive character, Luca, who joins the CIL (the Corpo Italiano di Liberazione, an actual partisan force from the Italian resistance that operated along the Adriatic in 1944) and is killed. Thus, the saga would take Italy's wartime history as its springboard, with the "memorandum" remarking: "Therefore, all of the contradictions, the vexations and hopes that relate drift over this little population of a Sicilian village of fishermen, farmers, and artisans from 1943, '44, and '45." The subsequent plan for the film was to create three interlocking parts: the initial fisherman segment ("Episode of the Sea") set in a village outside of Catania, followed by a second section in Caltanissetta about a conflict between sulfur miners and owners ("Episode of the Sulphur Mine"), then a third dedicated to the clash between farmers and Mafia bosses ("Episode of the Land") (Micciché 1996a, 38–41). The various episodes would refer to recent history and signal current events affecting Sicilian communists after the war. The "Episode of the Land," for example, was designed to reference the massacre at the town of Portella della Ginestra that occurred on May 1, 1947, when eleven Sicilian peasants celebrating May Day were killed in a politically motivated, anticommunist shooting.

While film historian Lino Micciché has been one of the scholars who most emphatically established the textual affinities between *The Earth Trembles* and *The House by the Medlar Tree*, he also wrote that the film "initially had (almost) no literary referentiality," emphasizing that it was commissioned by the PCI for a documentary about the working conditions in Sicily (Micciché 1996a, 57). For Micciché, the project on *The House by the Medlar Tree* that Visconti had conceived at least since publishing "Tradition and Invention" in 1941 only came back into focus after initial treatments for a documentary on Sicilian workers were scuttled. A recent study on *The Earth Trembles* by Mauro Giori and Tomaso Subini takes issue with the Micciché's favoring of the film's documentary origins. Examining new documents from the Diego Fabbri Archive, the authors argue that a stubborn accentuation on the film's documentary beginnings reflects the ideological position of the PCI at the time, who partially financed the film and wanted it and Visconti to sit beneath their cultural wing (Giori and Subini 2014, 8). Giori and Subini observe that while Micciché argues that *The Earth Trembles* represents "an ideal relationship between film and literature" that is "an operation of 'critical reading' of a classic work . . . essentially ready for reinterpretation," he also establishes the idea, influential among scholars, that Visconti married the aesthetic of classical realism with the pre-election PCI political platform. On the contrary, these scholars demonstrate that Verga was always at the center of the film's ideation, highlighting the primacy of adaptation over documentary in the generation of the film.

The film's documentariness, in fact, has always been regarded with some doubt, given that it is overwhelmed by compositional beauty, which led some to deride it as "art for art's sake." In 1949, Glauco Viazzi listed some of the issues with the film that would be repeated by others: "pictorial formalism, the 'anti-commercial' length of the film, the snobbism of dialogue in Sicilian dialect, the absence of progressive political organizations and unions of the Italian people: these artistic defects weigh heavily on the film" (Bruni 1996, 168). In elevating the characters from their humble, earthly roots, Visconti was accused of trafficking in a "formalism of the wretched," in which he exploited the lumpen proletariat for aesthetic ends (Rosi 1979, 141). With *The Earth Trembles*, Visconti was first marked as the "formalist" neorealist, who conveyed a cold, distant vision of the people and place that bordered on false artifice. This formalism was negatively associated with intermedial references, among which *The House by the Medlar Tree* was just one extracinematic source. "Forced into poses alla Modigliani or wedged vigorously into frames alla Rembrandt," wrote Gian Luigi Rondi in 1951, "the real fishermen of the Sicilian coast barely managed to be characters: they became pallid figurative compositions in which real life failed to deliver a breath of truth" (Bruni 1996, 170). Rather than connect the filmmaker with the world he depicted, the voiceover only further distanced Visconti from his material, either by demonstrating an essential separation between dialect and standard Italian (Sitney 1995, 75–76) or by serving as an instrument of clarification that did "violence" to the film (Nowell-Smith 2003, 44).

The Home in *The House by the Medlar Tree* and the Aesthetics of Fragmentation

Adaptation and documentary are hardly opposites, and an adaptation is no more a reproduction of a text than a documentary is a reproduction of reality. Adaptors of literature and documentarians make a series of aesthetic and thematic choices (Barnouw 1993). To appreciate *The Earth Trembles* as a docu-fictional adaptation, one need look no further than the filming of the family house to witness how the actual environment of postwar Aci Trezza was combined with settings and characters from *The House by the Medlar Tree*. As Mario Zangara recognized, the house represented a point of intersection between book and film, where Visconti cinematized the economic concerns so central to Verga's novel (Zangara 1953, 36–37). In the novel, pecuniary motivations are expressed by a chorus of narrative voices who tell the story of the Toscano family, called I Malavoglia, who secure a loan to acquire a load of lupin beans. Their boat, *The Providence* is wrecked in a storm at sea and the family loses its valuable cargo and its pater familias, Bastianazzo. Without any means for economic survival, the Malavoglia default on their debt and have their house repossessed. These factors precipitate a split among the Malavoglia family members, who either die off or leave the community altogether. The fluctuating fortunes of the family in connection with their property can be seen in *The House by the Medlar Tree*'s beginning chapters, where the ancestral home is a source of pride for the family and scorn from their neighbors. The opposition between family and community is vital to the novel, introduced in chapter 1 through the family home, symbol of the family's sustained prosperity and stability (Verga 1964, 7). By chapter 2, their enduring fortune becomes the source of gossip, revealing an underlying calumny circulating among other denizens of Aci Trezza. Verga refers to how neighbors are "outside like snails in the rain," who "know what I eat," and he uses a complex series of proverbs to highlight this tension between family and neighbors (Verga 1964, 23). After their boat is sunk in chapter 4, the discussion immediately turns to the value of their house, with characters La Vespa and Zio Crocifisso weighing in on its worth in chapter 5 and circling in for its repossession in chapter 9, when the family is forced to leave and relocate to the adjacent town of Aci Castello.

In his preface to the novel, Verga highlighted the distanced artistic mode he was undertaking: "This story is the sincere and dispassionate study of how the first anxious desires for material well-being must probably originate and develop in the humblest social conditions" (Verga 1964, 3). This separation between author and text was echoed in Verga's most famous manifesto on literary verism, the preface to *L'amante di Gramigna* (*Gramigna's Lover*, 1880) in which he underscored the human origins and nature of his storytelling, as well as his intent to provide a "human document" that would be interesting to those readers of the "great book of the heart" (Verga 1979, 59–60). The stress on documentation was part of Verga's materialism, or the belief that human nature is determined by social realities. How this socially determined nature was expressed constitutes the truly revolutionary quality of Verga's art: the peasants themselves narrate these conditions in their own voices, dialogically structuring the network of social groups in which they find themselves. To construct this polyphony of narrators required that Verga create a language to textualize oral culture, a language that was comprehensible to a broad readership, yet one that likewise conserved some of the regional authenticity of its narrators. What separates Verga from the French naturalism of Zola is the introduction of a free indirect style that melds autonomous author with individual characters, bringing an unruly collection of voices under the yoke of authorial control. Leo Spitzer described this as a "systematic filtration of his narration . . . by way of a chorus of semi-real, popular speakers" (Spitzer 1979, 294).

Visconti's choice to maintain the regional dialect from Aci Trezza might be perceived as a distancing from the purified, manufactured language of *The House by the Medlar Tree*, but the dialect in the film was hardly unmediated. Franco Zeffirelli, a Tuscan who worked as an assistant on the film, described the intricate process of translation that brought speech to screen. Visconti chose dialogue from the novel, writing dialogue in Italian. Zeffirelli would render the Italian into the local dialect, then Visconti would coach the actors on how to recite. To do so, Zeffirelli claimed to have learned the Sicilian of Aci Trezza in less than a month (Agnese Giammona, the woman who played Lucia in *The Earth Trembles*, commented, "Zeffirelli pretended to know Sicilian better than we did"; Bacon 1998, 35). In an interview from 1959 with Jacques Donial-Valcroze and Jean Domarchi, Visconti described his aesthetic fascination with the sonic qualities of their language, which he sought to cinematize: "It is an extraordinary language; a language that has *images*"(*LV*, 73). As noted by Stefania Parigi, the dialect in the film was as aesthetic as it was authentic: "Thus the closure, the archaism, the intranslatability for Visconti become sites of aesthetic fascination" (Parigi 1996, 141). Rather than a direct documentation of the actual dialect, recorded from its authentic speakers, interventions into dialogue and acting reflect Verga's original crafting of speech and situation.

As in the novel, these voices speaking in dialect in the film frequently discuss finances and the harsh economic realities of life in Aci Trezza. Mirroring how the book's characters are organized along lines of financial well-being (Crocifisso) or failure (Alfio Mosca), Visconti estab-

Figure 1.3. The Valastros in the courtyard.

lishes the rich-poor dichotomy by pitting the Valastros (his name for the Malavoglias of the book) against the wholesalers Raimondo, Lorenzo, and Nino. The wholesalers are depicted almost as caricatures of evil, seen enjoying a plentiful meal in their spacious and well-lit dining room while they scheme to thwart 'Ntoni and his family. The airy visual openness of this modern space contrasts the spartan, undecorated interiors of the house by the medlar tree.

The cinematography of these and other interiors in the film benefited from the considerable talents of Aldo Graziati, also known as G. R. Aldo, or simply Aldò, who was hailed for his ability to profile dramatic peaks and valleys through lighting and landscape. Aldo established himself as a still photographer and cameraman in France in the late 1930s and early 1940s, and after his cinematography on *The Earth Trembles*, he gained international renown with award-winning work on director Augusto Genina's *Cielo sulla palude* (*Heaven over the Marshes*, 1949) and *Othello* (1951) by Orson Welles. His career was tragically cut short in an auto accident during the shooting of Visconti's *Senso* in 1953. Of Aldo's various works,

Heaven over the Marshes is similar to *The Earth Trembles* in terms of its rural setting, attention to family dynamics, concentration on the struggles of life in the Italian provinces, and its approach to lighting. *Heaven over the Marshes* was based on the true story of Maria Goretti, who was sainted for protecting her virginity during a fatal attack that befell her in 1902. As in *The Earth Trembles*, where the sea nurtures and thwarts the Valastros, nature in *Heaven over the Marshes* is a dangerous provider. The Pontine marshes become a malignant habitat that afflicts the family father with malaria and inflames the passions of her assailant, Alessandro, who murders Maria for resisting his sexual advances. *Heaven over the Marshes*, like *The Earth Trembles*, features lighting that balances the naturalism of exterior and interior spaces with a self-conscious expressionism. To illuminate Maria's mortally wounded body at the end of the *Heaven*, for example, Aldo brightens the dark interior of the house with what appears to be natural light, giving the impression that she was felled just beneath bands of sunlight trickling into the room. When Maria is later seen lying in a hospital bed, the room is lit by a solitary candle that casts shadows of her mother and the nurse against the walls. This naturalism dissolves in the subsequent shots, when lighting is used to cast deep shadows that symbolize the dark circumstances of Maria's mortal wounds. When the lighting source shifts from a lateral position, ominously projecting shadows on the wall, to an overhead one, key lighting bathes her face in an angelic glow, and the tone of the film transitions from the horror of the attack to the comforting elevation of the departing soul, lifted into the light of paradise. For Augusto Genina, this was part of Aldo's experimentation. "He did not follow formulas, had no system, followed his inspirations, each time working with light and shadows in different ways . . . He did screen test after screen test, lighting and darkening so that his acute and expert eye found or did not find that small piece of negative that he was looking for" (Genina 1979, 197).

In his article dedicated to *Heaven over the Marshes*, André Bazin lauded how Italian filmmakers broke free of any objective, documentarian orientation in telling their "true" stories:

> But it seems that in the last few years, more and more plastic composition has become the rule. This has become a way of integrating into realism a vivid and ornate theatricality, which is no less characteristic not only of Italian film but also of Italian artistic sensibility in general. . . . In *The Earth Trembles* (1948), for instance, one sees very well how Luchino Visconti . . . strives to create a necessarily grand

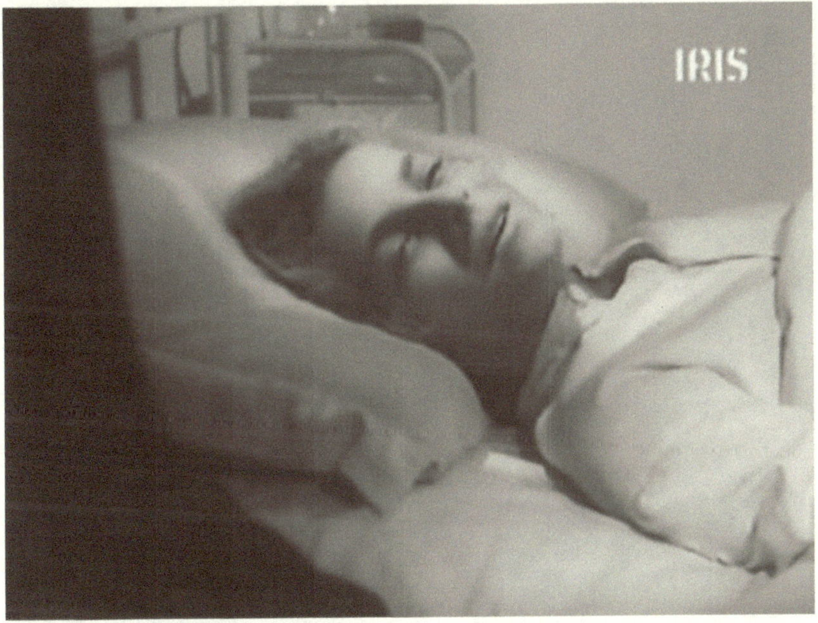

Figure 1.4. The deathbed of Maria Goretti, *Il cielo sulla palude* (*Heaven over the Marshes*, Augusto Genina, 1949).

> synthesis between the most rigorous verisimilitude, on the one hand, and the most plastic composition, on the other, a plasticity that necessarily completely transforms the verism. (Bazin 1997a, 89)

The coexistence of naturalism and expressionism and the illusion of natural lighting is especially evident in the sequences in the Valastro family home in *The Earth Trembles*. Lighting allows for an increased plasticity of the house, shot in dimensions that strip away this sense of good luck and portend the fragmentation of the family to come. The home is first pictured from the outside, with a high-angle shot showing Mara (Nelluccia Giammona) crossing the courtyard, a small oil lantern in her hand. As in the use of the candle in *Heaven over the Marshes*, the projection of this lighting source on her face creates shadows as she walks along, giving the illusion that the diegetic lighting source is the only one operating in the shot. As she opens the front gate, artificial lighting suddenly appears: she is spot-lit with high key lighting that forms a wide concentric circle around her and the entryway that she is framed by.

Figure 1.5. Mara at the house by the medlar tree, *The Earth Trembles* (Luchino Visconti, 1948).

As quickly as it appeared, the spotlight is extinguished as she turns toward the house, allowing for the dim glow of the lantern to return. This effect maintains the illusion that the illumination is achieved within the film, a tactic that continues to be used throughout: characters open doors and windows strategically to allow light in, then close them to shut light out. Illumination seems to enter from multiple directions, complementing the overall picture of a multigenerational family functioning in unison at the beginning of the film. This is made explicit when Lucia points out the individuals in the family portrait hanging on the wall that will reappear toward the end of the film, where the family's toil is juxtaposed against the "tacky artifice" of the photograph (Marcus 1993, 41–42). The complexity of lighting extends outside as well. In the nighttime scene on the sea, illumination is initially provided by the large fishing lamps on the bow of each boat while the voiceover comments: "The lamps come and go across the black sea." Framed by the voiceover ("And the hard work continues"), this scene marks the film at its most documentary: the diegetic lighting source, along with the sounds of the fishermen's voices and the attention to the details of their work (they haul in nets teeming with fish; they row) render exterior spaces at their most naturalistic. As the lamps recede to the background, however, horizontal key lighting shines on the men's faces in the foreground to better illuminate their conversation.

From the beginning of the film, lighting coordinates the film's distinct mise-en-scéne to address the permeation of the family by the meddlesome community members who will ultimately accelerate their downturn. The harbor is introduced as the central place of work, and early on we see the Valastro men laboring to repair their nets, haggling with the wholesalers over the price of fish, and preparing their boat for the next day's catch. This workspace is underlined by a voiceover that highlights the generational quality of the Valastro work. There is no clear-cut separation between professional and domestic spaces, with work entering into every sector of the Valastro family existence, including the private family home. The initial shots of the outside of the house are accompanied by a counterperspective that conveys the exterior spaces of the courtyard from the interior rooms. Rather than one continuous space, the effect is to underscore a certain fragmentary location, separated by doors and windows and the lighting zones they produce. Following the film's shadowy incipit, there is a remarkable brightness to the first section set in the house, analogous to the positive hues of Verga's chapter 1, where the home is pictured in rock-solid stability that promises to bring romantic fortune to the Malavoglia family. This attention to the family's sunny romantic destinies are introduced with subsequent shots of 'Ntoni's visit to Nedda (Rosa Costanzo) and with Mara's window-side conversation with Nicola (Nicola Castorino) later on; two of the film's three main romantic pairings suggest how fortunes at sea are tied to romantic potential on land. Windows provide direct access to the Valastro women, who remain at home, and through their contrasting composition, we see how Visconti succeeds in describing two divergent relationships based on social class. Mara is coaxed to the window by Janu singing a love song (in *The House by the Medlar Tree*, it is sung by the character Rocco Spatu), then Nicola comes to visit with her, the wall of the house separated by the windowsill supporting a basil plant. This is a meeting of equals, with the pair shot horizontally, Visconti framing them along the same plane. The portrait-like composition of Mara posed in the window is later coupled with the long shot of the nighttime street, where Nicola, solitary and forlorn, is subtly lit from the nighttime shadows at the center of town. This horizontal balancing of the Mara/Nicola duplet is the opposite of the visual construction applied to Lucia (Agnese Giammona) and Don Salvatore (Rosario Galvagno), the local official whose sexual dalliance with Lucia is part of the Valastro family's decline. Don Salvatore is repeatedly shot peering into the window from a low-angle shot with the women below, as if to underscore their social and economic inferiority and the predatory and dominant position of the male figure. The bedroom is also the setting for Lucia's fairytale, where her naive vision of courtly love is shattered by Salvatore's more base intentions. In this case, the porosity of the house via the window reveals the negative interactions between family and community.

That the house is portrayed as a permeable space easily infiltrated by light, sound, and especially the peering eyes of others, is significant for Visconti's representation of a community that Verga defined by petty jealousy and calumny. Here, Visconti provides a self-conscious vacillation of point of view that shifts from 'Ntoni to his neighbors. In the scene where the family joyously returns from Catania after having mortgaged their house, a shot through the open window follows 'Ntoni as he exits to conduct a jocular conversation with his neighbor, Giovannina, who gives him a good ribbing. When asked if he is happy, he responds, "Si, sugnu contentu, ca nun mi rromperò cchiù 'a schina pi ll'autri, e lavorerò pi mmia, uora" (Yes, I'm happy because I won't break my back for others and will work for myself now), to which she replies with a proverb: "U mummu ca è tunnu, cu acchiana e cu va a funnu!" (which translates roughly to: "The world is round, some rise to the top while others sink to the bottom!") (Visconti 1977, 105). The next set of shots pans across the rooftops, up to another neighbor, Vincenza, sweeping on her balcony. Vincenza voices the exchange of gossip that is natural to their town: "'Ntoni! Viri ca 'i vicini su' comu i canali d'u tettu! Ca si dùnunu" ('Ntoni! Look at your neighbors who are like the tiles on the rooftop, where water passes from one to the next), to which Giovannina replies: "Cumari Maria! 'U sapiti 'Ntoni? Tuttu ca canta, tuttu ca rridi, a tutti ca sputa" (Lady Maria! Did you hear about 'Ntoni? He does nothing but laugh, jeer, and spit on everyone). This verbal exchange is coordinated with a visual one that alternates between observation and being observed. This juggling of perspectives is rendered explicit when we see a subjective shot from 'Ntoni's point of view (the camera peers

Figure 1.6. Shot of Ntoni's feet looking up at his neighbor in the window.

over his shoulder with his shoes in the foreground; see fig. 1.6) looking up at his neighbor playing the flute.

This series of shots, which Vito Zagarrio notes add a notable, over-the-shoulder "voyeurism" to the sequence, underscore the visual and aural scrutiny that the family subjected to (Zagarrio 1996a, 125). Here the correlative to Verga's free indirect style gains cinematic footing in an early example of experimentations with subjective perspectives that were already evident in the opening sequence of *Obsession* but became more prevalent from *White Nights* (1957) onward. Visconti again contours the family home to be a place that is surveilled from the outside through the subjective shots of the house toward the middle of the film, when members of the bank arrive to inspect the property under foreclosure. We see a complex set of viewpoints from inside and outside the house, from the houses of others. As the bank officials arrive, we see the house from inside the house of a neighbor (see fig. 1.7), the camera placed behind her as she opens the shutters, matching her view as she peers out.

Figure 1.7. The Valastro home from the viewpoint of their neighbor's window.

These subjective shots of the Valastro neighbors accompany the more objective approach to portraying community members, who are often visualized engaged in publicly shaming the family. The pitiful return of the wrecked fishing boat is met with both pity and jeers; the angry neighbors who defend Lorenzo against 'Ntoni's attack to shouts of "it was your arrogance that was your undoing!"; to the final sequence of the "ship's baptism" when the community laughs as 'Ntoni is ostracized for being off his rocker (they call him *testa malata* or "sick in the head"). The fragmentary composition of the house, never seen as a whole but continually split into adjoining rooms, foreshadows the rupture of the nuclear family that occurs with the loss of the home. This fragmentation underscores how the units of the Valastro family are simply smaller tiles in the mosaic of the Aci Trezza community. Without a doubt, this is a response to *The House by the Medlar Tree*'s use of multiple voices and situating of the family in the broader context of the book's insular community.

Like the present-day museum, split into adjoining rooms to celebrate literary and cinematic authors who stand shoulder to shoulder in its cramped floor plan, the house is filmed to become a central point of contact between literary and cinematic versions, one that highlights a multiplicity of perspectives offered by the duality of adaptation. Book and film interact continually. Introducing this complex array of character perspectives offers additional layers to the documentation of the family drama taken from *The House by the Medlar Tree*, where by splicing adaptation with documentary, Visconti created issues for the film's definition as one or the other. Deviating from while also honoring the literary text at the basis of the film beckons toward the sort of ambiguity and mystery that progressively came to define Visconti's poetics of adaptation. Indeed, Visconti's hybridity, seen in other adaptations, was also neorealism's, itself a crossroads of reality and fiction (Minghelli 2008, 47). Home to symbolic and material elements, the filming of the house in *The Earth Trembles* crystallizes the film's ethical and aesthetic treatment of its subjects, presenting a complex of documentary and adaptational textures in relation to the real world and its literary reflections. That Visconti would narrate Verga's story in a set of voices from within and without the filmic narrative indicates the director's interest in questions of cinematic narration and perspective that continued in the next set of adaptations, where the community of narrators from Aci Trezza is replaced by the distinct female narrators of *Senso* and *White Nights*. Yet this emphasis on perspective was also fundamental to the film that came before *The Earth Trembles*, *Obsession*, where viewpoints from an American hard-boiled novel were adapted to an Italy in the final throes of fascism.

2

Ossessione (*Obsession*, 1942)

In from the Outside: Literary Interiors in Neorealist Exteriors

I don't know another way to define this type of film, if not neorealistic.

—Mario Serandrei on *Obsession*

Visconti often downplayed the novel *The Postman Always Rings Twice* as a textual source for his first film, *Obsession*. Despite clear connections with the book, he relegated Cain's hard-boiled novel to the lowly position of a narrative "pretext," emphasizing its relative triviality in *Obsession*'s screenwriting phase. Speaking of *Ossessione* in 1965, Visconti noted

> There was no close relationship with any narrative . . . other than the anecdotal trace that I spoke of: the novel by Cain. But anything else might have served the same purpose. We wanted to begin with Verga. Forced to silence Verga, we would have moved forward with a narrative pretext: a news story, for example, if the newspapers had reported it. Rather, it was the way the anecdote was carried out that was important. I remember the long discussions we had: we wanted to make a portrait of Italy. (*LV*, 105)

Figure 2.1. Opening credits, *Obsession* (Luchino Visconti, 1942).

Although not one to always extoll each and every influence, Visconti was rarely so apprehensive in acknowledging a literary author whose work underpinned one of his films. The reference to Verga, an important source for *The Earth Trembles*, is also perhaps overstated with regard to *Obsession*. The variety of Verga works (in particular *I Malavoglia*, *Jeli il pastore*, *Artisti da strapazzo*, and *L'amante di Gramigna*) were a few of the many literary sources he sought to adapt in this early period before *Obsession* was filmed. Among many others, Visconti had been workshopping Alain-Fournier's *Le grand Meulnes* (1913), Melville's *Billy Budd* (1924), Dumas's *La Dame aux camélias* (1848), O. Henry's *The Furnished Room* (1906), and Sherwood Anderson's *I Want to Know Why* (1921) during those years (Giori 2018, 31–42). These titles demonstrate the importance of French and US authors alongside the more recognized Italian figure of Verga during a formative period defined by the vacillation between literature and cinema (Rondolino 1997). Nevertheless, with *Obsession*, Visconti felt he had to strip *The Postman Always Rings Twice* of its US nationality to tell his more native story of life in Italy under fascism and to make a film that was "absolutely Italian" (*LV*, 104). Mario Alicata, who worked on the film, also discounted the novel's significance, recounting Visconti's desire to Italianize Cain's book by emphasizing landscapes:

> Luchino proposed to "remake in Italian" *The Postman Always Rings Twice* that he had seen translated into French. . . . We all read the book, some more than others. Then, together, we isolated the central theme: a beautiful woman, the wife of an old, ugly husband, falls in love with a young man who happens across their shop, and then the insurance, the murder, and their accidental death while fleeing. And together we began to work, with collective contributions to the question of the Italian surroundings, with Luchino figuring in heavily on the choice of landscape. (Visconti 1971, 15)

While Italian intellectuals under fascism often looked to US authors, creating a "myth of America" that was crucial to opposition of the totalitarian regime, Cain attracted a variety of stereotypes (commercialism, artistic inferiority, etc.) negatively associated with the United States (Ricci 2008, 130). That Visconti's statements evince some snobbery against the pulp American writer is unmistakable, demonstrating an early and influential dismissal of a "low" cultural form at the basis of one of his films. As in the case of *The Earth Trembles*, there was a legal reason the director and his collaborators might undersell the sourcing of *Obsession* (Liehm 1986, 328). First published in the United States in 1934, *The Postman Always Rings Twice* did not appear in Italy until 1945, ten years after its publication in France, although it had materialized in serial form in the pages of the magazine *Panorama* in 1940. Visconti was given a copy of a French translation of the novel by Jean Renoir that he shared with Giuseppe De Santis, Mario Alicata, and Gianni Puccini (Rondolino 2003, 113). But he never acquired the rights to adapt it. Consequently, *Obsession* became the subject of a prolonged legal dispute with the producers of the French version of *The Postman Always Rings Twice*, *Le dernier tournant* (*The Last Turning*, Pierre Chenal, 1939). In 1946, Gladiator, a French financier, initiated a case for plagiarism against Visconti and Industrie Cinematografiche Italiane (ICI), the producer of *Obsession*. The case was not concluded until June 25, 1956, when Visconti was cleared of all charges by the Tribunale di Milano (Micciché 2006, 30 n.10).

Another reason Visconti and generations of critics that followed might mute the position of *The Postman Always Rings Twice* was *Obsession*'s status as the first work of neorealism. As mentioned previously, neorealism was a moment in film history lasting roughly from 1940 until the mid-1950s, and it hinged on the figure of the militant filmmaker who reasserted the concreteness of reality by focusing on the lived experience of suffering Italians. Directors of this period were seen to exert a neorealist optic connected to the historical moment in films like *Obsession*, *Sciuscià* (*Shoeshine*, Vittorio de Sica, 1946) and *Roma, città aperta* (*Rome, Open City*, Roberto Rossellini, 1945). Representing the downtrodden victims of fascism and the casualties of World War II, these works expressed the arduous process of national and psychic rebuilding suited to addressing the moral exigencies of a war-torn nation. Holding up a mirror to society, what Gian Piero Brunetta called the "mirror of the collective soul," neorealist cinema paired audience desires and anxieties with those seen on screen: "In this period," Brunetta opined, "the public is both recipient and protagonist of the films that were made" (Brunetta 2006, 8). Furthermore, neorealism marked a historic break from more than twenty years of fascist rule, when Benito Mussolini's regime was believed to have used cinema as part of its ideological state apparatus. With neorealism, "We have passed," Cesare Zavattini wrote, "from an unconsciously rooted mistrust of reality, an illusory and equivocal evasion, to an unlimited trust in things, facts, and people" (Zavattini 1974, 217). Such a trust in material things bred a position against literature-based cinema in the early years of neorealist theorizing, where adaptation became associated with the calligraphist films of the period, many based on literary models that supposedly evoked fascist escapism and a preference for form over content. Neorealists condemned adaptations such as *Piccolo mondo antico* (*Old-Fashioned World*, 1941) and *Malombra* (1942) by director Mario Soldati, films based on works by author Antonio Fogazzaro that looked back to nineteenth-century literary models instead of forging into new territory of the real. "The calligraphers' use of adaptation," Millicent Marcus observes, "thus provided a model of how literature served Fascist ends in indirect and therefore more insidious ways than did the unabashed filming of such obvious nationalist-imperialist vehicles as *Scipione l'africano* (*Scipio Africanus: The Defeat of Hannibal*, Carmine Gallone, 1937)" (Marcus 1993, 6). As demonstrated in chapter 1, when Italian intellectuals later came around to the idea of filming literary antecedents, they looked to the national figure of Verga, not a foreign writer like Cain.

In a general climate where adaptations were viewed as politically suspect, interpreters of *Obsession* overlooked traces of literature to accentuate the photography of Italy itself. Giuseppe De Santis found the Italian surroundings in the film to be essential for constructing "an atmosphere of absolute immediacy and verisimilitude" (De Santis 1985, 30), which according to Umberto Barbaro, would transmit "A piece of Italy that had never before been seen in our films" (Barbaro 1976, 507). Encapsulating this national landscape was a challenge taken up by Giorgio Bassani who, while working on an Italian translation of *The Postman Always Rings Twice*, declared the difficulty of "translating that landscape, searching to see it in Italian" Bassani (Villa 2008, 247). The primacy that critics allotted to local landscapes as proving grounds for the film's authenticity has endured in *Obsession*'s now voluminous critical bibliography, indicating how landscape has become central to the theoretical framework of Italian neorealism as a whole. For many, what made neorealism different from the cinema that came before it was exactly how it reconfigured such outside spaces and repositioned humans in their environment. In *Obsession*, this included the reorientation of bodies, both female (Past 2008) and male (Duncan 2000; Van Watson 2002; Giori 2017). These arguments for landscape, emphasizing how Italian locations were crucial to chronicling an Italian story, suggest how national borders were erected around *Obsession* and neorealism from early on, creating a problematic perimeter for as international an artist as Visconti. "It was hardly necessary," Cesare Pavese famously quipped, "to leave Europe to become, as they say, neorealists" (Pavese 1953, 292). Interesting, then, is the international appeal of *The Postman Always Rings Twice*, a novel that has been adapted to screen, stage, and radio around the world. Tay Garnett's 1946 adaptation, *The Postman Always Rings Twice*, starring Lana Turner and John Garfield, was the first Hollywood version, followed by Bob Rafelson's 1981 adaptation by the same name, with Jack Nicholson and Jessica Lange leading a steamy screenplay penned by David Mamet. Filmmakers from Hungary, Malaysia, and Germany have all taken turns adapting Cain's novel to cinema. *The Postman Always Rings Twice* was brought to theater in London in 2005 and in Moscow in 2008, to opera in 1982, and to radio in 1991 and 2013. As mentioned in the preface, Visconti's film version had its own stage adaptation in London (2017) starring Jude Law and Halina Reijn. This surfeit of interpretations across media indicate how the book's erotic marrow, located at the core of every adaptation, holds an appeal that stretches beyond the restrictive Italian borders that Italian critics placed around *Obsession*.

Only a very unimaginative notion of adaptation would demand that *The Postman Always Rings Twice* dominate interpretations of *Obsession* and overshadow its context in Italy of late fascism or its position at the threshold of neorealism. Yet the attention to landscapes rather than Cain's book conjures a rather intriguing limitation on adaptation: one that begs further investigation. Outside of the many textual equivalencies found by comparing film to book, a brief examination of *Postman* as the basis of *Obsession* will reveal how Visconti used the book to shape the film's atmosphere, in which various interior spaces round out the psychological development of the main characters. This is the atmosphere of noir, mixing themes from French existentialism and American hard-boiled fiction into the perhaps contradictory category of the "neorealist noir" (Wood 2007, 240). Without enumerating every literary particle transferred from *Postman* to *Obsession* (for side-by-side comparisons of text and film, see Micciché 1977, 147–52), in what follows, I examine how internal spaces (the *osteria*, the Ancona boarding house, the prostitute's Ferrara quarters) channeled locations from Cain's novel, complimenting national landscapes with literary interiors. A posteriori, *Obsession* marked Visconti's anointment as a progenitor of Italian neorealism and his identity as an outsider, whose experience in cinema was inaugurated while assisting Jean Renoir in France, not in Italy. Mixing the dangerous suffocation of domestic life with the safe harbor for sexual dalliance, literal transferences from book to film, such as the characters (Frank/Gino, Cora/Giovanna, Nick/Bragana), were accompanied by more figurative ones: elements such as the dangerous "black widow," the problem of a hardened male antihero; and themes like prostitution, violent eroticism, and a moral decline that leads to physical or spiritual death. This examination unearths a tension in neorealism between indigenous and foreign influences that marked both Visconti and the status of literary adaptation in Italy in the decades that followed his first film.

The Invention of Landscape(s), from Italy to France

In a 1941 essay, Giuseppe De Santis lauded Alessandro Blasetti and Mario Soldati along with Jean Renoir for their distinct approaches to landscape, employed to illuminate interior feelings through exterior motifs. "Everything plays a role . . . in determining the drama of the characters: equally the figurative motifs and those invested by the interior motivations expressed by the actors. These motivations are emotions that a human being cannot express. That is what Renoir seems to suggest to us; so it is necessary to use the things that surround him to express these emotions" (De Santis 1941, 262–63). After the war, this linkage between human and environment became fundamental to neorealism's revolutionary aesthetic, celebrated for bringing about a sea change in cinema's capacity for conveying verisimilitude and truth. In equalizing background and foreground, neorealism broke from classical narrative film, where settings served an entirely narrative function. As András Kovács notes, a neorealist film presents "a narrative form in which the hero is wandering through a multitude of different spaces that express his existential or psychological situation. What counts here is not what is happening with the hero at those locations but what he sees or hears there" (Kovács 2007, 254). Cesare Zavattini presented the perceptions of this wandering, nomadic figure in his theory of *pedinamento* or surveillance, in which the neorealist camera stalked alongside the protagonist to provide spatial and temporal "facts" of their situation (Margulies 2002, 220–22). In *Obsession*, such surveillance can be illustrated by Gino's peripatetic adventure through the Po Valley, an itinerant Italian flaneur whose perambulations transport him beyond the cityscape and into the barren countryside. This neorealist emphasis on topographies of the nation was made famous by the anecdotal tale of Vittorio Mussolini, the dictator's son and head of the film journal *Cinema*, whose viewing of *Obsession* led to an outburst of "This is not Italy!" The enchantment with the outsides marked the critical history of *Obsession* immediately, where over the course of the ensuing decades, scholars repeatedly commented on how exteriors visually summon inner states in the film. Pierre Sorlin, for example, called *Obsession* a "living picture of the Italian provinces" (Sorlin 1979, 190), and Antonio Costa remarked that it offered "a kind of archaeology of Italian landscape within the institution of cinema during the first years of the 1940s" (Costa 2010, 137). In her book, *Landscape and Memory in Post-Fascist Film*, Giuliana Minghelli examines *Obsession*'s outside spaces as frontiers of meaning. She writes: "Haunting is the spectral dimension of dwelling and, in the world of [*Obsession*], the only form of inhabiting possible. It is within the framed landscapes that punctuate the unfolding of the story—within their 'deep surface'—that this desire for a place emerges allegorically as a repressed and subversive historical desire" (Minghelli 2013, 30). The phantasmic features that Minghelli identifies in *Obsession*'s dreary landscapes link the space of desolate expanse to the place of the Po Valley, whose historical dimension are veiled but not completely hidden by the blurry horizons that reoccur in the film (Steimatsky 2008, xx).

Figure 2.2. Giovanna walks along the desolate beach.

Within this discussion of neorealist exteriors, *Obsession* was acclaimed as "the invention of the Italian landscape," its geographic or topographic framework guiding interpretations of the film (Costa 2010, 137). To all of these interpreters, neorealist films were seen to brim with a general topophilia, where "excessive topographic specificity" (Gorfinkel and Rhodes 2011, xix) of landscapes extended to cityscapes as well, especially in and around Rome (Shiel 2006).

This emphasis on Italian geographic specificity does not necessarily suit a figure like Visconti, whose antifascism and background in cinema began outside of Italy in the years leading up to *Obsession*. From 1932, when he left Milan, until 1937, when he returned to Italy, Visconti traveled to England, Greece, Tunisia, France, and the United States, among other places. During this period of wandering, Paris was where he undertook his first substantial experience in cinema, as third assistant and costumer on Renoir's *Partie de campagne* (*A Day in the Country*,

1936). A few years later, he collaborated with Renoir on the film *Tosca* (1941). When war broke out, Renoir was forced to leave, entrusting Visconti and Carl Koch to finish the project (Blom 2017b). As noted by Visconti's various biographers, his apprenticeship under Renoir contains a crucial political element that the director would refer back to. He once described his sojourn in Paris as his own "road to Damascus," triggering his conversion to communism through contact with members of France's Popular Front: "When I was in Paris in 1936, to work in the cinema . . . I was kind of an imbecile. Not a Fascist, but unconsciously affected by Fascism, colored by it. . . . I knew nothing, understood nothing—where politics were concerned my eyes were as tightly shut as a newborn kitten's. But the friends I made there opened my eyes. They were all Communists, card-carrying Communists" (Stirling 1979, 45). Romanticizing this Marxist-Pauline conversion occluded the other, no less significant homosexual awakening that took place during this same time (Giori 2012, 48). It also overshadowed his work on the film *A Day in the Country*, an important prototype for postwar film adaptations of literature. A short film, *A Day in the Country* tends to be regarded as a minor note when compared with Renoir's full-length works such as *Les bas-fond* (*The Lower Depths*, 1936), *La Grande illusion* (*Grand Illusion*, 1937), *La Marseillaise* (1938), *La bête humaine* (*The Human Beast*, 1938), and *La règle du jeu* (*The Rules of the Game*, 1939) which established the director as one of the premier French filmmakers of the era. *A Day in the Country* is based on the 1881 short story by Guy de Maupassant titled "Une partie de campagne" (A Country Excursion) about an interclass love affair set in the French countryside. It was never completed owing to poor weather conditions for shooting and was recut to a forty-minute length, then released in 1946. The resulting featurette tells the simple story of shopkeeper Monsieur Dufor, who takes his wife, mother-in-law, daughter, and her fiancé to the countryside outside of Paris. The outdoor spaces frame the romantic encounter between the petit-bourgeoise Henriette and the local rower, Henri, whose brief riverside tryst is halted by oncoming rains. Their intertwining emotional arc is mirrored in the surface of the river, seen in the film's opening shot as sunny, serene, and teeming with life, then becoming dark and tempestuous, pelted by raindrops that interrupt their lovemaking. Flashing forward to years later, Henriette, now married, visits the same location, and she encounters Henri once again. They acknowledge being haunted by memories of that delightful afternoon, then go their separate ways. The final shot of the eddying river provides a seamless conclusion, with Renoir completing the visual transfer of Maupassant's watery locus amoenus.

Numerous commentators have remarked on the film's properties as a literary adaptation, recognizing how Renoir cinematizes Maupassant's ironic tale lyrically, giving material form to the literary story by creating multiple planes of cinematic movement in the breezy natural surroundings of the riverside setting. André Bazin was first to recognize *A Day in the Country* as an innovative model for adaptation, and the film makes an appearance in his seminal essay, "Adaptation, or the Cinema as Digest" published in *Esprit* in July 1948. Bazin identified it as a film that departed from the notion that adaptation be understood as a simple translation from book to film: "It is faithful to the spirit of Maupassant's short story at the same time that it benefits from the full extent of Renoir's genius. This is the refraction of one work in another creator's consciousness. And there is not a person who will deny the beauty of the result. It took somebody like Maupassant, but also someone like Renoir (both of them, Jean and Auguste), to achieve it" (Bazin 1997, 42). Rather than a direct processing of one medium into another, Renoir's film, in Bazin's view, was a refraction in which author and filmmaker partake in the same work with "two media making a whole that was not reducible to the sum of its parts" (MacCabe 2011, 5–6). As he would elsewhere, Bazin shifts the focus away from an adaptation's fidelity to a literary original, instead outlining Renoir's relationship with Maupassant's text as one that presented "the equivalence in meaning of the forms." In his essay "Adaptation," Dudley Andrew also took up *A Day in the Country* to similar ends. He notes how engaging with the interrelations of two media enables a filmmaker to maintain the "fidelity to the spirit" as well as the tones and rhythms of the original:

> That tale, "A Country Excursion," bears a transcendent relation to any and all films that adapt it, for it is itself an artistic sign with a given shape and value, if not a finished meaning. A new artistic sign will then feature this original sign as either its signified or its referent. Adaptations claiming fidelity bear the original as a signified, whereas those inspired by or derived from an earlier text stand in a relation of referring to the original. (Andrew 1984, 96)

Bazin and Andrew ignore any notion that Renoir's film might be superior or inferior to Maupassant's story, placing the fidelity discourse aside to focus on what is transmitted by both. Each suggests the relationship between book and film is one of unity, based on a filmmaker's ability to express a certain style present in the literary model. For Andrew, Renoir's adaptation altered the development of film styles across the globe. He argues that *A Day in the Country*'s style was fed by Zola's literary naturalism of the early twentieth century, anchoring a chain of influences from literature to cinema that in Italy continued in what Andrew calls Visconti's "naturalist impulse," which he transported to *Obsession* and *The Earth Trembles*. Conversely, the cinema also influenced literature. "Naturalist fiction helped cinema develop its interest in squalid subjects and hard-hitting style," Andrew notes. "This in turn affected American hard-boiled novelists like Cain and Hammett, eventually returning to Europe in the film styles of Visconti, Carné, Clouzot, and others" (Andrew 1984, 105).

The exchange of styles, flowing together across national and artistic borders, was fundamental to what Andrew defined as the "sociology of adaptation," in which literature and film are viewed as intersecting cultural practices. Bazin saw a similar exchange, placing the critic in a central role for appreciating these film–literary intersections:

> If the film that was made of Steinbeck's *Of Mice and Men* (1940; Lewis Milestone) had been successful [. . .], the (literary?) critic of the year 2050 would find not a novel out of which a play and a film had been "made," but rather a single work reflected through three art forms, an artistic pyramid with three sides, all equal in the eyes of the critic. The "work" would then be only an ideal point at the top of this figure, which itself is an ideal construct. The chronological precedence of one part over another would not be an aesthetic criterion. (MacCabe 2011, 6)

Bazin's equilateral triangle makes for a rather elegant model for appreciating adaptation across media. But it also demonstrates the position of the critic in constructing such models, in grasping the exchanges between film, literature, and the other arts and explaining them to others. Neorealism is the apotheosis of the critical construct, built up in the years that followed the actual phenomenon by critics and scholars who continue to hazard definitions of this moment in Italian cultural history. In overemphasizing *Obsession*'s representation of the "real" Italy, critics of the film during neorealism did not appreciate how the adaptation of an American text was at least partially responsible for the conveying this Italian reality, demonstrating how the discourse on adaptation of certain texts had yet to achieve much status in Italian culture at the time. This position contrasts with current scholarship on the neorealist phenomenon, where Italian directors and writers are understood to have borrowed from a global network of film and literary cultures (Ruberto and Wilson 2007).

When Renoir gave Visconti the translation of *The Postman Always Rings Twice*, he hinted at an appreciation of American hard-boiled fiction that was typical in France, where readers of the 1930s liked "their Americans exotic, violent, and romantic" (Naremore 1998, 23). Indeed, the US author, transmitted through the French director, indicates an extra-Italian origin of *Obsession* that was viewed with suspicion (O'Rawe 2010). To some, the philosophical and moral outlook presented by authors such as Cain, Dashiell Hammett, and Raymond Chandler was key to French existentialism and a certain "noir" sensibility that was growing in literature and film of this era. Albert Camus, for example, was inspired by Cain's *Postman* when he wrote his novel *The Stranger* (Nothomb 2009, 113). Although many of these authors' books were adapted into some of the most famous titles of Hollywood film noir, the directors of those adaptations were European, solidifying noir's transatlantic connection. German émigré filmmakers like Fritz Lang, Robert Siodmak, Billy Wilder, and Edgar G. Ulmer operating in Hollywood in the 1930s inserted a European sensibility into some of the most iconic American noirs of the postwar era. They used the stylistic lighting and mise-en-scène of German expressionism, where distinct diagonals and horizontal lines delineated the off-kilter moral geometries of individual characters. Stark chiaroscuro illuminated the morally ambivalent private detectives as they hunted equally immoral femme fatales in the seedy enclaves they inhabited. The focus on the US cityscape in much of Hollywood film noir of the 1940s was also evident in French poetic realism of the 1930s, another key influence on *Obsession* (Wood 2007, 239). Renoir's *The Lower Depths* and *The Human Beast* sit together with a set of French films starring Jean Gabin and featuring similar themes and sensations as their noir descendants. Marcel Carné's *Le Quai des brumes* (*Port of Shadows*, 1938), *Hotel du Nord* (1938), and *Le Jour se léve* (*Daybreak*, 1939); Julien Duvivier's *Pépé le Moko* (1937); and Pierre Chenal's *Crime et châtiment* (*Crime and Punishment*, 1935) all feature the fatalism, alienated characters, misogyny, and urban background that was later associated with film noir. "Stylistically," writes Ginette Vincendeau, "Poetic-realist films are undoubtably 'noir.' The gloom of the city streets and canal banks is illuminated by shiny cobblestones and pierced by mist-shrouded lampposts and gleaming nightclub signs" (Vincendeau 2007, 26). Connections to French existentialist literature and poetic realism are relevant to Visconti, and not just because he spent so much time in France in the 1930s. Before his adaptation of Camus's *The Stranger* in 1967, Visconti had adapted Jean-Paul Sartre's *No Exit* to the Italian stage in Rome (Teatro Eliseo, October 18, 1945). *Obsession* is highly suggestive of Sartre's early existentialist thought, with visual conventions like the roadway incipit, the dark tones and shadows, the sense of bleakness and alienation combining with the film's overall narrative structures (a crime of passion, flight from justice, death) and figures (the drifter, the femme fatale). In his classic essay on the film noir, Robert Porfirio (1996) reads noir's "black vision" as coming directly through hard-boiled fiction, not European existentialism. *Obsession*, however, would have benefited from both sources, presenting a hybrid European hard-boiled existentialism. In the next chapter, I discuss how Visconti's adaptation of Dostoevsky's *White Nights* reverberates with existentialist themes, with the romantic dreamer spearheading themes of fantasy, fate, and disillusionment.

There is a final commentator on adaptation in *A Day in the Country* worth mentioning. That is Seymour Chatman, who in his 1980 article on Renoir's film examined how the filmmaker found creative solutions to visualizing descriptions from Maupassant's text. He points specifically to the sequence in which the female character is seen enjoying herself on the outside swing where, according to Chatman, Renoir transmits the mixture of innocence and seductiveness that underpin this character's description in Maupassant's tale. "Since seductiveness, like beauty, is in the eye of a beholder, Renoir requisitions Rodolphe's point of view to convey it. It is not Henriette so much as Rodolphe's reaction to Henriette, even on first seeing her, that shall establish her seductiveness and not only in his mind but in ours, because we cannot help but look on with him" (Chatman 1980, 133). Chatman goes on to describe how this appropriation of Rodolphe's point of view is matched by various other male gazes present in this scene ("pubescent peekers in the hedge, the seminarians, Rodolphe, and the older priest"), and of course there is the film's spectator as well.

Figures 2.3, 2.4, 2.5. Various perspectives on the swinging girl in *Partie de campagne* (*A Day in the Country*, Jean Renoir, 1946).

Public, Private, and Places in Between

Such play with gendered perspective is also at the heart of *Obsession*, where Visconti manipulates conventional male cinematic points of view in scenes set in the film's interior spaces. He does so to convey the loneliness, despair, alienation, and moral and psychological confusion from *The Postman Always Rings Twice*. One of the most perceptive readings of *Obsession*, by Derek Duncan, points to Visconti's dramatic twist on the traditional male gaze, where instead of attaching the camera to a heterosexual male viewpoint, Visconti places Gino in the viewfinder, laying the groundwork for a destabilizing objectification of the male protagonist. "It is in their effect on the spectator," Duncan notes, "that Girotti [the actor playing Gino] and his vest are most disturbing for they constitute improper objects of desire in a medium that depends on the stability offered by the heterosexual, male gaze" (Duncan 2000, 103–4). This is most obvious in the scene when Gino initially arrives at the restaurant and meets Giovanna. Dramatic tension is constructed by Gino's face being withheld from the camera's view, followed by the over-the-shoulder shot of Gino looking at the seated Giovanna. What begins with the shot-countershot of their faces regarding one another sets up juggling viewpoints, foreshadowing the construction of erotic desire and exploitation throughout the film.

The opening pages of *Postman* read: "They threw me off the hay truck about noon. I had swung on the night before, down at the border, and as soon as I got up there under the canvas, I went to sleep" (Cain 1992, 3). Frank's voice is typical of the hard-boiled narrator: he describes the hard-scrabble life of the penniless drifter searching for opportunity on the road in a vast, flat, desolate expanse of the Southern California desert. Through him, we encounter both the nondescript identity of the roadside diner ("It was nothing but a roadside sandwich joint, like a million others in California"; Cain 1992, 3) and its remarkable inhabitants: Cora and her husband Nick, called "The Greek." In the film, the opening shot from the interior of the truck's cab wipes to reveal a stationary truck on an open roadside. Two men exit the cab, their actions extraneous to the plot, the camerawork inscribing a sense of authenticity in its view of the roadside location. The opening sequences of film and novel both foreground an essential contrast between road and restaurant, exterior and interior. This interplay will be part of what Pierre Sorlin has observed as *Obsession*'s "rigid" symmetrical structure (Sorlin 1979). The road is associated with the male drifter: in the book, Frank is returning

Figures 2.6, 2.7, 2.8. Gino (shoulder), Giovanna, Gino's face (*Obsession*).

from a sojourn in the Mexican border town of Tijuana, while in the film, Gino later describes his circuitous search for work across northern Italy. The characters thrive at the margins of this liberating expanse of nature, where they maximize the potential for freedom.

When the drifter meets the married female counterpart, the open road terminates at an enclosed destination, occupied by the alluring woman who is herself walled in by conventions of her social standing as wife. Cora in *Postman* and Giovanna in *Obsession* wade through the drudgery of marriage and work, trapped in the vortex that eventually pulls in the male characters, whose attempts to flee their seductive grasp are destined to fail. "Rather, it is a series of escapes and returns, along a road that seems to promise a future," Minghelli notes, "while only delivering a spatial and temporal– that is *historical*—suspension between a spectral home (the burdened inheritance of the past) and a city full of equally spectral hopes" (Minghelli 2013, 37). Cora and Giovanna declare their imprisonment in the kitchen to be the result of economic desperation and prostitution. Cora recounts how she traveled to Los Angeles after winning a beauty contest in Iowa, then was forced into restaurant work: "Then two years of guys pinching your leg and leaving nickel tips and asking how about a little party tonight" (Cain 1992, 14–15); Giovanna describes how she staved off desperation by "being invited to dinner by men." Part and parcel of this economic element is the concept of marriage-as-toil, and from the outset both women are identified as units of labor. In the film, Visconti symbolizes this drudgery in an expressionistic shot of Giovanna, slowly falling asleep among a sea of dirty dishes (see fig. 2.9). De Santis noted the marked painterliness of this scene: "Do you remember the scene when Giovanna eats alone in the inn's kitchen, surrounded by all those dishes in need of washing? Is it not a portrait by Modigliani?" (De Santis 1985, 29). Giovanna cringes at Gino's innuendo-laden suggestion that she is a "good cook," marking kitchen work as menial. The kitchen reveals the transactional nature of an unhappy marriage. It is an oppressive atmosphere (seen most clearly in the sweaty nighttime conversation between Bragana, Gino, and Giovanna) endured by female characters for the promise of financial stability.

The symbolic confrontation between Eros and Thanatos throughout *Postman* is formally highlighted in two bedroom sequences in *Obsession*. In place of Cora and Frank's initial sexual encounter, marked by a passion bordering on sadism ("I took her in my arms and mashed my mouth up against hers. 'Bite me! Bite me!' I bit her. I sunk my teeth into her lips so deep I could feel the blood spurt into my mouth"; Cain 1992, 11), Visconti

Figure 2.9. Giovanna in the kitchen among a pile of plates.

responds with ellipsis, staging only the aftermath of Gino and Giovanna's original tryst. The scene is formally complex and displays a mise-en-scène that joins realism with expressionism: the messy, unmade bed is framed by a series of mirrors that capture the desperation, tenderness, and miscommunication that mark their postcoital conversation. The camera works slowly from Gino's naked torso to Giovanna's face, pictured in the mirror beneath exaggerated lighting effects: a band of light carefully illuminating her expression, with chiaroscuro highlighting her face and Gino's back as it emerges from the shadows. The two speaking figures are splayed on the bed, its stable, horizontal lines interrupting the two bodies in motion. This horizontal line cants diagonally when Giovanna seats herself in the corner with the dark shadow behind her as she explains her sexual frustration at being married to an older man. The constructedness of the scene is most obvious when the mirror on the armoire swings open, occluding the two characters and ominously revealing Bragana's clothing.

The darkly lit restaurant, an interior place marked as locus of transgression, links to a second erotic encounter when Gino travels to

Ancona in search of work. Here Visconti complicates Frank's departure in *Postman* when he leaves the diner in hopes of moving on with his life and leaving Cora behind. Visconti introduces the "Spaniard," a wayfarer who takes Gino under his wing. This development announces the film's antifascist subtext most clearly, the designation making reference to the republican side of the Spanish civil war. The Spaniard's dialogue expresses a socialist worldview and approach to brotherhood, money, and exchange, and he has been seen as a queer proxy for the entire *Cinema* group's political insurgency (Fabbri 2019), introducing a candid homoeroticism from the "pickup" in the train to their lovers' tour through Ancona (Micciché 2006, 53). In the context of the film, the sexual potential of the Gino/Spaniard coupling seems more significant than the Marxian subtext and is made noticeable in the dialogue between the characters sharing a bed in the boarding house. The Spaniard first jokes with the boarding house owner about sharing a bed with Gino ("we won't ruin your matrimonial sheets"), then discusses hunger and appetite, followed by admonishing Gino for thinking so much about a woman. Chatman (1980) observed that the camerawork in *A Day in the Country* channeled the male viewpoints from Maupassant's story; here, Visconti's camera lingers on the Spaniard's eyes, which are fixated on Gino's body while he devours chicken wings, licking his fingers suggestively, then as he prepares a cigarette between his lips while Gino is stretched next to him in the bed. Their discussion of freedom is subordinated to a visual tracking of Gino's movements in the room that underscore the Spaniard's sexual desire. His longing look at Gino's displayed body under matchlight has long been the source of this eroticized reading, with Van Watson noting similarities to a previous scene with Giovanna (Van Watson 2002, 182).

How to transmit the atmosphere of moral and existential darkness of Depression-era Southern California from *Postman* to the Italy of late fascism constituted a challenge for Visconti. In his seminal essay, "Dickens, Griffith, and the Film Today," Sergei Eisenstein considers affinities between English writer Charles Dickens and US filmmaker D. W. Griffith. Although the essay largely focuses on a critique of Griffith's use of montage, seen as inferior to Eisenstein's and that of other Soviet filmmakers, it also contains some rather intriguing observations on the relationship between writing and filmmaking across space and time. Equating Griffith's use of close-ups to the tea kettle that opens Charles Dickens's 1845 novella *The Cricket on the Hearth*, Eisenstein notes parallel techniques of characterization through atmosphere:

> Certainly, this kettle is a typical Griffith-esque close-up. A close-up saturated, we now become aware, with typically Dickens-esque atmosphere, with which Griffith, with equal mastery, can envelop the severe face of life in *Way Down East* [1920], and the icy cold moral face of his characters who push the guilty Anna (Lillian Gish) onto the shifting surface of a swirling ice break. Isn't this the same implacable atmosphere of cold that is given by Dickens, for example, in *Dombey and Sons*? The image of Mr. Dombey is revealed through cold and prudery. And the print of cold lies on everyone and everything—everywhere. And atmosphere—always and everywhere—is one of the most expressive means of revealing the inner world and ethical countenance of the characters themselves. (Eisenstein 1963, 199)

Thus, Eisenstein outlines how Griffith analyzed the moralism of provincial American life in 1920 by adopting Dickens's novelistic approach, designed to reveal the interiority of his Victorian-era English characters. This chilly atmosphere, most obvious in the ice floe sequence mentioned by Eisenstein, can be recognized elsewhere in *Way Down East*, like in Anna's first encounter with her rich relatives in Boston, where the towering geometries of doors and thresholds gives a sense of restriction and austerity.

Just as Griffith forwards the icy atmosphere that figured Dickens's characters, Visconti conveys the dark viscera of the protagonists from *Postman*, with interiors staging nostalgia and regret, invoking a pastness that does not adhere to the presentness required (in theory) of a neorealist film. Rather than away from it, *Obsession* travels through Cain's text, marking off interior spaces as sites for an emergent—if incomplete—subjectivity. These inside spaces and places demarcate zones of loneliness and angst that was characteristic of American hard-boiled fiction, unearthing a European, Sartrean inflection on choice, freedom, and ultimately a thwarted search for meaning that appears in later Visconti films. In doing so, the American book becomes a model for Visconti's cinema, presenting domestic spaces that stage straight and queer couples' doomed potential, enclosing and disclosing the illusion of dream, the reality of fatalism, and the conceivability of evil that were part and parcel to *Postman*. *Obsession* can thus be appreciated as a particularly good realization of Cain's world, reasserting categories of subjectivity and the erotic from these international sources into an Italian social and historical reality that became hallmarks of Viscontian adaptations to come. One can fit Cain in a group of authors from across that world that fed Visconti's early creative endeavors in the years before and after the war. Cain's novel, along with the existentialist thread, served as notable counterpoints to the national discourse on Italian neorealism that continued to emphasize cinematic exteriors of Italy. In the next chapter, I demonstrate how adaptation helped transition Italian cinema from the neorealism of the 1940s into its next chapter of the 1950s, where Visconti continued to look beyond the borders of Italian literature and film.

3

Senso (1954) and *Le notti bianche* (*White Nights,* 1957)

Voice and Body: Books through Stars of the Screen

> *Senso* is the first of his films that explicitly recalls a literary text: but it was only a "minor" work that couldn't cast any shadow over him and that he could use as he wanted without protest.
>
> —Italo Calvino

In the mid-1950s, Visconti made two melodramas that, like *The Earth Trembles*, were based on nineteenth-century fiction: *Senso* (1954), an adaptation of Camillo Boito's novella from 1883, and *White Nights* (1957), based on a short story by Fyodor Dostoevsky written in 1848. In terms of scale, these films could not be more different. *Senso* marks the first of the director's great historical films, extraordinary for its sprawling vision of northern Italy during the twilight of the Italian unification, known in Italy as the Risorgimento. Against *Senso*'s vast orientation across Italy's spatial and temporal map, *White Nights* is regarded as one of Visconti's "minor" works, presented in the narrow confines of a studio set. Although both films are seen as allegorizing a key moment of postwar Italian history, they are often linked in terms of their departure from neorealism.

Figure 3.1. Alida Valli in *Senso* (Luchino Visconti, 1954).

Senso is considered a landmark film for the debate over literary and film realism that it provoked, a dispute that contains important points for the question of adaptation in the postneorealist age. Of *Senso*'s more famous naysayers, Cesare Zavattini denounced the film's historical spectacle for breaking with neorealism's "historicity of the present" (Zavattini 1975, 890). Zavattini condemned *Senso*'s theatrical nature that evoked, once again, a fascist-era form of cinema and illusion. Luigi Chiarini also rejected *Senso*'s spectacular form that he opposed to a neorealistic content, smearing Visconti's film as a negation of neorealism as pure formalism, "destined to make the mode of representation prevail over the substance of the thing represented" (Chiarini 1975, 884). For these critics, *Senso* forwarded an overly complex intertextual grid of literary, painterly, and operatic allusions, from a detached, aristocratic perspective (Lerner 2007, 344 n.1). In defense of the film, Guido Aristarco famously noted that *Senso* marked a step away from neorealism, seen as "chronicle," toward realism, which he regarded as "narrative": a binary that had been bandied about in Italian intellectual circles at least since *Roma, città aperta* (*Rome, Open City*, Roberto Rossellini, 1945) (Leavitt 2013). Aristarco saw *Senso* as an analogue to Honoré Balzac's nineteenth-century novels, where the narration of complex historical trajectories replaced the description of "purely material phenomenon" (Marcus 1986, 172–73). Aristarco recognized *Senso* (as he would later *Rocco and His Brothers*) as something akin to the historical novel as studied by Hungarian theoretician György Lukács (Aristarco 1960, 3).

Although Aristarco's interpretation of *Senso* is interesting in terms of literature and cinema, it does less to help us understand *Senso* as an example of literature in cinema. In fact, Aristarco was at the forefront of those who marginalized Boito's source text in their interpretations of the film. Other than Giorgio Bassani, who defended Boito and his novella (Boito 1945; Villa 2008, 241–49), Aristarco was like those who had denigrated James M. Cain's *The Postman Always Rings Twice* as a source for *Obsession*. He regarded Boito's "frivolous novella" as little more than a pretext for the film (Aristarco 1969a, 9). Italo Calvino would concur, describing Boito as Italy's "little Maupassant" and the novella as a "minor work" (Calvino 1995, 1904–5). Boito as source was also overshadowed by *Senso*'s other intermedial references, obviously to Verdi and Italian lyric opera but also to painting, as in the re-creation of Hayez's *Il Bacio* that Lux used to promote the film (Blom 2017a, 27). Beyond questions of literary and cinematic realism that the debate over *Senso* introduced, an analysis of the film with *White Nights* reveals a new development for Viscontian adaptation in which voiceover transmits a literary antecedent through a female star. These literary voices indicate a psychological realism generally associated with the post-1949 films by Antonioni and Rossellini and later the works of Fellini. These directors were criticized by Marxist interpreters for ranging too far from the "materialist" realism offered by Visconti's works of the era that were regarded as more consistent with the tenets of neorealism (Wagstaff 2007, 412). In studies of film adaptations, voiceover narration is frequently categorized along literary lines, with either the "authorial" (third-person omniscient, outside the diegetic space) or "character" (first person, interior to the diegesis) types of voiceover being present. In this way, voiceover is seen as yet another apparatus for balancing literary words with cinematic images. However, I argue that voicing literary words through a female star augmented all of the theatricality, emotion, and excess that were consistent with the Italian film melodrama of the 1950s. However literary these voices may be, they become inseparable from the actress. As Mary Ann Doane argues, "The voice is not detachable from a body which is quite specific—that of the star. In the cinema, cult value and the 'aura' resurface in the star system" (Doane 1980, 36). In *Senso*, voiceover reinserts Boito's erotic tale of romance and betrayal in the dramatic arc of Italian history, heralding the theme of political betrayal already underlying Italian actress Alida Valli's star persona. *White Nights* uses voiceover to transfer narration from the male dreamer in Dostoevsky's story (Mario in the film) to the female foreigner, Natalia, played by Austrian actor Maria Schell, whose own stardom was constructed by roles in other prominent adaptations of the era. That the beholders of these "literary" voiceovers were those of female stars points to a rather captivating exchange between literary text and stardom, adaptation and blockbuster film, that will be discussed further in part II.

Discussions of Visconti and voiceover inevitably reach back to *The Earth Trembles*, in which interpreters established a didactic function of voiceover that helped guide spectators who could not understand the antiquated dialect spoken by the film's characters. This informative function is consistent with a reading of *The Earth Trembles* as a documentary, where an omniscient narrator structures the film from the outside. Others interpreted voiceover in *The Earth Trembles* in a different way, with Lisa Rosen pointing to Millicent Marcus and Geoffrey Nowell-Smith as believing that this clarifying function betrayed the film's realist program, introducing another avenue for Visconti's aestheticism that did "violence" to the film's documentary-like qualities (Rosen n.d.). For Stefania Parigi, who views such artistry in a positive light, voiceover was simply a constituent component of the film's overall soundscape that, when assembled, was an essential part of the film's overall "aesthetic fascination" (Parigi 1996). Mario Serandrei highlighted the importance of postsynchronization in this and other Visconti films (Serandrei 2014, 350). In two films that followed—*Bellissima* (1951), and the episode *Anna Magnani*, part of the portmanteau film *Siamo donne* (*We, The Women*, 1953)—Visconti demonstrated an evolution of his use of voiceover that coincided with the casting of actress Anna Magnani (see fig. 3.2). (To these, one might add a third film that features the prominent use of voiceover, *Appunti su un fatto di cronaca* [*Notes on a News Story*, 1953], a short documentary discussed further in chapter 7.) With Magnani, female narration and voiceover helped reconcile the realist-aesthetic divide seen by critics of *The Earth Trembles*, moving the discussion toward questions of celebrity, the Italian film industry, and a star system capable of creating and maintaining a network of international screen divas. In *Bellissima*, Visconti presents themes of stardom and stage motherhood to take to task neorealism and Italy's new culture of cinema burgeoning in and around the Roman film studio Cinecittà.

Figure 3.2. Anna Magnani, the concerned screen mother in *Bellissima* (Luchino Visconti, 1951).

The short film *Anna Magnani* elicits questions of female celebrity in the key of neorealism, albeit with an emphasis on stage and song. Neither film is an adaptation, but both were written by Cesare Zavattini and share an approximate story world in the performance milieu of Rome around 1950. This was a period in which Magnani's stardom was at its peak as the Italy's most recognized female star, and Visconti claimed to have pursued *Bellissima* based solely on Magnani's participation (Micciché 2006, 198 n.16). Casting Magnani to represent Rome as the epicenter of performance, these films foreshadow the meta-performative and meta-cinematic mise-en-abyme that figured centrally in *Senso* and *White Nights*.

Unfolding around Cinecittà, *Bellissima* presents Magnani as the ambitious stage mother Maddalena, who accompanies her daughter (Tina Apicella) to compete in a radio contest for "the prettiest girl in Rome," whose winner will be cast in star director Alessandro Blasetti's (played by the actual director) next picture. Maddalena is equally purveyor and victim of the story: she convinces herself that acting will provide a better future for her child, then is swindled by the scoundrel Annovazzi (Walter Chiari), who offers empty promises of promoting her daughter in exchange for money. Maddalena is repeatedly shown narrating from within the film's diegetic texture, first when she persuades her husband of their daughter's dramatic potential, then when she offers a brief autobiographical account to Annovazzi. The film concludes with a histrionic exhibition of description, with Maddalena lamenting how she was enchanted by the beauty contest's illusion of upward mobility and became intoxicated by the exciting world of cinema. Without emphasizing direct address such as voiceover, *Bellissima* fits Maddalena's narrated stories in its own, peering behind the curtains of Cinecittà to portray the lives of those in its orbit. Laying bare the Italian machine of celebrity in this way brings Magnani's performance as Maddalena further into relief, doubling back on the system that elevated the actress to superstardom.

This world of performance is disclosed with a similar degree of straightforwardness in *Anna Magnani*, the episode of *We, the Women*. Zavattini had to convince Magnani to take this role, pleading that without her, it felt like a table missing a pair of legs (Hochkofler 2013, 160). As a whole, *We, the Women* is based on behind-the-scenes encounters with some of the era's most celebrated film divas in Italy (Alida Valli, Anna Magnani, Isa Miranda, Ingrid Bergman), who all play themselves. In the episode directed by Visconti, Magnani immediately reinforces her position as narrative focal point by narrating her story through voiceover: her voice recounts a tale from ten years before, when she was fined for transporting her dog in a taxi. The bulk of the episode captures Magnani engaged in a drawn-out argument with the taxi driver, and then the police, with whom she repeatedly spars over the illogical rules governing the movement of canines in vehicles for hire. What begins as a tour-de-force in exasperation becomes a seminar in artistic professionalism when Magnani performs a stirring version of "Com'è bello fa' l'amore quann'è sera" at the episode's conclusion, a song she sings delightfully while gazing directly into the camera. This direct address, visually and audibly breaking the fourth wall, indulges the spectator in the musical talents and physical presence of their star, whose performance is registered in intimate close up that, as Marcus provocatively suggests, presents a "micro-genealogy" of Magnani's entire career (Marcus 2002, 44). Together, *Bellissima* and *Anna Magnani* encapsulate Magnani's crafting of a unique film career based on a screen persona that blended a common, unspectacular beauty with a fiery Mediterranean mien, a persona that symbolized the new postwar Italy (Gundle 2007, 123–124). Magnani was particularly valued for her acting's raw quality, said to close the gap between representation and real life. As O'Rawe notes: "Critical discussion of Magnani has revolved around her passion and authenticity, and related tropes of spontaneity, instinct, and the animalesque, and Magnani is best known for her roles in postwar Italian cinema that harnessed these qualities" (O'Rawe 2017, 158). Whether in the accounts recited by the character Maddalena in *Bellissima* or by the actress in *Anna Magnani*, both voices express the actress's intuitive, impassioned nature, ideal for her roles in melodramas. Indeed, *Bellissima* portrays maternal pathos at its most desperate and overwrought, while *Anna Magnani* distinguishes lines separating an actress's everyday frustrations from her sublime talents on stage. Once seen pejoratively, melodrama has been taken up in recent studies arguing for its rich vein in Italian cinema. During the 1950s, melodramas attracted massive audiences at a time when Italians frequented the cinema more often than people of any other nation (Morreale 2011; Cardone 2012; Bayman 2014). Fueled by the antagonisms and contradictions, Italian melodramas pitted good versus evil and featured characters dominated by passion and self-sacrifice (Brooks 1995, 42). For Visconti, the diva was the keystone to the film melodrama: "That which fascinates me the most is the character of the 'diva,' this unlikely being whose role in today's spectacles is ripe for reevaluation. In modern mythology, the diva incarnates the rare, the extravagant and the exceptional" (Visconti 2008, 37). Visconti projects two other remarkable diva voices in *Senso* and *White Nights*—voices that are, uncoincidentally, adapted from the literary works they sourced.

Senso: Boito and Valli, Betrayal and History

One of the most famous Italian stars during the late 1930s, Alida Valli, left Italy in the 1940s to pursue her career in Hollywood with producer David O. Selznick. Selznick sought to craft Valli's star persona in the mold of other European transplants to Hollywood, such as Marlene Dietrich or Ingrid Bergman, promoting her only by her last name "Valli," a tactic he had used with Greta Garbo (Gundle 2012). Valli's absence from Italy in the years of neorealism, though an opportunity to bolster her international fame in Hollywood, had negative consequences for the development of her national cachet. During that time, Magnani, Sophia Loren, and Silvana Mangano successfully yoked their talents to neorealism's artistic prestige, becoming icons of Italy's "natural" feminine beauty who thrived well into the 1950s (Small 2014, 116–17). Unlike these actresses, Valli carried a burden that weighed on her postwar celebrity: the taint of fascism. Having trained at the Centro Sperimentale di Cinematografia, the Roman film school created under fascist fiat, Valli's rise to stardom in six films made under director Max Neufeld between 1939 and 1940 coincided with the upsurge of Italian filmmaking under the fascist regime, which under the direction of Luigi Freddi and the General Directorate for Cinema, controlled the film industry as a state-owned enterprise (Ricci 2008, 67–68). Valli's status among prewar female stars was solidified when she was cast in *Oltre l'amore* (*Passione*, Carmine Gallone, 1940) and *Apparizione* (*Apparition*, Jean de Limur, 1943) alongside Amedeo Nazzari, at the time Italy's most bankable male lead (see fig. 3.3).

Although some have viewed Valli as one of many mediocre ingénues of fascist cinema, Valli was clearly more than a young, pretty face preferred by the regime. A rising star in Italian cinema of the late 1930s, she was the first Italian actress to receive what was called the *scrittura hollywoodiana* (Hollywood contract), a five-year contract with Italicine that paid 5,000 lire a month (Pellizzari and Valentinetti 1995, 39). This association with the fascist film industry had serious consequences for Valli after the war, when she was plagued by rumors linking her to high-ranking fascist officials, with some claiming she was a spy and others that she had had sexual relations with Mussolini's son (Gundle 2012, 566). Valli herself once claimed only to have begun to comprehend fascism's meaning in 1941 (Valli 1979a, 41). Government documents recovered in 2012 demonstrate Valli's status as a person of interest by US intelligence services: "According to an organizational chart filled out by the 'Special Police Unit' of the Ministry of the Interior of the RSI (the Italian Social Republic) . . . a certain Alida Valli was confidante to the squad's head, Giuseppe Bernasconi. This group was dedicated to espionage, counterespionage against anti-Fascists, Communists, and also Jews" (Paliaga 2012, 28). These same records reveal that Valli had been the victim of a mistaken identity, "erroneously identified with another woman in Bergamo who looked like her," but the effect on her reputation and career was significant. When she applied for a visa to begin working in Hollywood with Selznick, her application was initially rejected. She noted that her detractors attacked her by way of poison pen: "Hundreds [of letters] had arrived at the US consulate to 'inform' that I had been friends with all of the men in Mussolini's family, the father, sons Bruno and Vittorio and grandsons, and that contemporaneously (some affirmed 'contemporaneously,' others said 'in the interim') Alfieri, various minor members up to Goebbels, and some from the German SS" (Valli 1979b, 107). Her denials and the exculpating government reports aside, the

Figure 3.3. Valli and Nazzari in *Oltre l'amore* (*Beyond Love*, Carmine Gallone, 1940).

mark of fascism did not disappear easily, even following her to Hollywood, where a 1948 article in the *Los Angeles Examiner* read "Il Duce Ex-Mistress Sought in Los Angeles" (Gundle 2012, 574).

When Valli returned to Italy in the early 1950s, the suspicions continued. As late as 1964, she was defending herself against claims of collusion with the regime: "It is time to put an end to it: I never saw *Il Duce*, not even on the storied balcony!" (Falcinella 2011, 45). Yet suggestions that Valli had been compromised by fascism made her an ideal fit for the role of the traitor Livia in *Senso*, originally slated for Ingrid Bergman (Granger 2007, 157). In *Senso*, Livia's adulterous relationship with Austrian officer Franz Mahler melds marital infidelity with treason against the nascent nation of Italy. Visconti politicized Boito's novella by filtering it through Antonio Gramsci's perspective on Italian unification, popularized by the influential publication of Gramsci's *Prison Notebooks* that began in the late 1940s. Therein, Gramsci explained Italian unification in the late nineteenth century as nothing more than a royal conquest, not a popular movement, "a failed revolution" in which the Savoy leaders in Piedmont expanded their territory to become head of a new Italian constitutional monarchy. According to Gramsci, unification had been romanticized in history books as a moment of collective uprising, not a case of class conflict where the rich used independence to perpetuate their power over the poor. By structuring the interpretation of the Risorgimento as a failed revolution along the lines of Italian melodramatic tradition, the film epitomized Gramsci's notion of the national-popular: a "liberating" cultural form that combines intellectual and subaltern classes, synthesizing high and low (Subini 2005, 51).

Visconti originally intended to foreground this interpretation through the duplicitous Livia from the novella and the addition of his own character, her cousin Ussoni (Massimo Girotti), who was to represent the popular revolutionary spirit suppressed by the monarchs. Early treatments of the film written during 1953 opened *Senso* in Verona following the Battle of Sadowa (1866). Livia was to be first introduced in the hospital where she had been denounced as a spy: "It so happened that a nurse in the female ward denounced the presence of an undesirable to the Italian soldier; of a spy that everyone believed was Austrian because there was little doubt she had been with the Austrians" (*FV*, 7, 24, 5, 8). This opening remained at least through the second draft of the screenplay, which opens with Franz's (then called Hans) execution, followed by Livia's screams and the dialogue introducing the flashback that would initiate the film: "I met him in Venice a few months before." In the novella, Boito also frames his story with a flashback, beginning with Livia who, approaching middle age, reflects on her treacherous past while gazing at herself in the mirror: "Every action, every word, and especially every indignity from that trying period of my past was etched in my mind" (Boito 1883, 262). In this incipit of a secret memoir in which she confesses the misdeeds of her youth, Boito's Livia provides the story's historical and geographical coordinates. She recollects events that took place sixteen years prior in Venice in July 1865, referring directly to the wars for Italian independence when she describes how her lover was killed "in one of the battles of '59, I can't remember which." By inserting a political conscience and making Livia keenly aware of the ramifications of her acts for the formation of Italy, Visconti was seen to have dramatically deviated from the literary source in his adaptation. Millicent Marcus remarks that "A comparison of Boito's Livia with Visconti's reveals how the filmmaker has transformed a static, ahistorical character into a typical one, in Lukács's sense of the word, embodying the salient conflicts of her era and exemplifying the process by which the old order passes into the new" (Marcus 1986, 178). For Calvino, Boito's character lacked depth and was driven solely by sensuality: "His Countess Livia is a woman who bases her entire life in sensuality, an extremely surface, instinctive, bourgeois and Venetian sensuality that takes her to passion and revenge as if on the natural growth of a wave" (Calvino 1995, 1899).

Eventual cuts by Italian censors successfully reduced *Senso*'s Gramscian rereading of unification history. In one excised scene, the royal military leader refuses to include Ussoni's reactionary forces, to which Ussoni replies: "Let's speak frankly, Captain. The order that you have transmitted to me reflects the repugnance of the entire army for the revolutionary forces, beginning with General Lamarmora. It is clear that they want to exclude these forces from the war" (Marcus 1986, 168). Visconti originally wanted to conclude the film with Livia fleeing through a group of prostitutes and drunken Austrian soldiers, one who cries out "Viva l'Austria!" (Visconti 1979, 327). After the scenes with Ussoni were cut and the historical character was reduced, more space was given to the story of Livia's unbridled passion and her egotistical pursuit of personal romantic fulfillment. While certainly not erasing the historical emphasis, the cut version of *Senso* granted Boito's Livia a more pivotal role in structuring the film narrative. This can be observed through a brief analysis of the voiceover, which takes on Livia's first-person perspective from the novella, offering her personal confession of betrayal (Marcus 2001, 291). When the voiceover is first heard, just after the raucous incipit and following Ussoni's challenge of Mahler to a duel, Livia establishes herself as the narrative anchor: "Everything began that evening. It was the twenty-seventh of May." Doing away with the flashback structure from earlier versions of the script and Boito's novella, the film uses the voiceover instead to indicate the opposing sentiments—love or country—that will guide her throughout. "I had a strange foreboding . . . of what his departure might mean . . . for me" (Visconti 1970a, 120). At times, the voiceover is redundant, adding little to the scenes on screen. For example, take the wanderings of Franz and Livia through nocturnal Venice (see fig. 3.4), when the voiceover speaks: "We walked together for a long time, along the deserted streets. Time had stopped. There was only the secret pleasure I felt in listening to his talk, in hearing his laugh . . . and listening to the sound of our footsteps echoing in the silent city." While Livia's understanding, guilt, and ultimate regret are absent in Boito, they are voiced in the film ("And now I felt almost a sense of shame. How could I have spent the whole night out with a man I didn't know, an Austrian, an officer? I was an Italian woman, and married"; Visconti 1970a, 128). The theme of the woman controlled by passions remains: "One afternoon as I waited for him in vain in that room, for the first time I realized, in terror, that I was no longer in control of my feelings . . . as I'd imagined!" (Visconti 1970a, 132).

Figure 3.4. Livia and Franz in Venice, *Senso*.

With this, Livia introduces the theme of decay and inevitability that will contour the film's overall structure of downward spiral. While in Aldeno, she remarks: "I was tied to him forever now. For his sake I'd forgotten . . . betrayed the men who were fighting. I was trying to make my dreams come true, to end my suffering"; later, "I decided to leave . . . at dawn . . . before the area around Aldeno was occupied by the patriots . . . before the Italians could get to Verona. I knew I was leaving my home . . . and my people . . . forever. And yet I felt no remorse or sadness."

For Visconti and his collaborators, censorship altered the film to such an extent as to render much of the film's message of royal betrayal almost unintelligible. Yet by placing Boito's first-person narrator in the body of Alida Valli, Visconti preserved some of his original intent to foreground political and historical betrayal, so relevant given Italy's recent history of fascism, especially as Valli was still compromised by an association with the regime. *Senso* launched Valli's career into its next phase, in which the actress continued her prolific and engaging work in Italian cinema and elsewhere. Now preferring the first-person, embodied star as a narrator to the third-person, "detached, authoritarian, male" narrator of *The Earth Trembles*, Visconti motions toward an experimentation with perspective and point of view that will become evident in *White Nights* and the films that follow it (Youdelman 1988, 9).

Narrating *White Nights,* from Him to Her

Filmed in the crowded confines of Cinecittà, *White Nights* takes a step away from the grand, comprehensive vision of *Senso*. Deriving its basic plot from Dostoevsky's story of the same name, *White Nights* follows bachelor Mario (Marcello Mastroianni) as he falls in love with young foreigner Natalia (Maria Schell), who eventually spurns him for a man she has met a year before. The film was a coproduction under the name of Cinematografica Associati, a group made up of screenwriter Suso Cecchi D'Amico, producer Franco Cristaldi, Marcello Mastroianni, and Visconti. By all accounts, the original idea for a Dostoevsky adaptation came from Emilio Cecchi (Rondolino 2003, 376). On one hand, the choice to situate the film in Livorno rather than the more St. Petersburg–like Venice seems to suggest a reference to the working-class milieu of neorealism. As Carlo Testa remarks: "Leghorn, too, has canals, sufficiently less splendid to have made it ideal for the director's purposes" (Testa 2002b, 37).

On the other hand, Visconti uses the city to highlight the intersection between film and theater, underscore the artifice of cinema, and emphasize illusion rather than reality (Rondolino 2003, 378–79). An elaborate set of Livorno was built in Cinecittà's Studio 5, replete with canals, bridges, and a main thoroughfare. The director claimed that the decision to create a set rather than shoot on location was an economizing one, although the ruinous costs the construction incurred tend to counter that suggestion (Hennessey 2011, 161). Throughout, Visconti creates an unreal, fabricated *theatrum*, a self-evident studio reproduction, bathed in expressionistic lighting and alive with dramatic special effects of sudden wind, fog, an almost comically unrealistic sunset, and even falling snow. The few areas that reoccur (the bridge [see fig. 3.5], the central ruins, Mario's room in the boarding house) take on various symbolic values and provide locatable fixtures to background the developing emotional states of the characters. The central bridge materializes the conflict between reality and illusion, separating Mario's bachelor reality, shown in his humble living quarters, from Natalia's fantasyland, populated by a fairy tale grandmother and dreams of a knight in shining armor (Nowell-Smith 2003, 98).

That this conflict would be staged in such a spatially delimited area might be viewed as relatively curious in cinema, since the filmic space is theoretically infinitesimal (Bazin 1974, 284). Lino Micciché notes how

Figure 3.5. Mario and Natalia on the bridge (*White Nights*, Luchino Visconti, 1957).

Visconti was the first to introduce the *kammerspiel* or "chamber film" concept to Italian cinema, using a small cast filmed in an enclosed set repeatedly in films like *The Job* (1962), *Sandra* (1965), and *Gruppo di famiglia in un interno* (*Conversation Piece*, 1970) (Micciché 1996b). The idea of the chamber film came to Visconti by way of theater. The concept of theatrical intimacy was succinctly outlined in the introduction to August Strindberg's *Miss Julie*, a play that Visconti had incubated for some time and finally realized in January 1957, the same year as *White Nights*. In his preface, Strindberg emphatically called for an increased closeness with audiences to address what he saw as a widespread sense of stagnation in modern theater (Strindberg 1983, 75). Such aesthetic smallness and attention to gesture and detail was also an important component in Cesare Zavattini's neorealist theorizing, where he promoted a kind of aesthetic compactness. Zavattini believed that when the camera focused on the smaller elements of existence, it illuminated how cinema privileged the relationship between art and life (Wagstaff 2007, 80). One might witness the same sort of visual reduction in *White Nights*, although to different ends. Condensing the cinematic space allowed Visconti to experiment with lighting to create different effects in ways that suggested cinema's capacities for expressionism, not realism. In addition, the introduction of elements of theater and opera (the characters attend a performance of *The Barber of Seville*) suggest a broader intertextual field of reference, and the shift toward an exploration of internal psychological conflicts instead of the exteriority of social conditions points back to Dostoevsky's novella. Such estrangement via theatrical performance would be similar to the use of opera in *Senso*.

Visconti's casting of Schell to play Dostoevsky's mysterious Nastenka (Natalia in the film), introduced a key metamorphosis between text and adaptation, as well as a critique of the source text's narrator. The narrator in Dostoevsky's story is the male figure, whose agony and longing are made evident from the beginning: "A strange anguish had tormented me since early morning. I suddenly had the impression that I had been left all alone, that everyone was shrinking away from me, avoiding me" (Dostoevsky 1961, 7). Although this could well be the voice of Mastroianni's character, Mario is soon decentered from the film's frame and its narration by Natalia. This is visible in Natalia's flashback, an example of Viscontian technical bravura that has only partially been appreciated. The scene depicts a conversation between Mario and Natalia in the rubble-strewn streets of Livorno at the moment she tells him the story of meeting the man whose return she awaits. She offers to explain her strange behavior, stating that "Mine is such a boring story." After describing her Slavic origins, the camera follows the two figures through the streets as her voice shifts into voiceover, telling him about a strange boarder (Jean Marais) who came to rent a spare room in her family's home. Without cutting, the camera pans left from a medium shot of her seated outside on the street directly to the interior of her grandmother's home, seamlessly transitioning from present to past to frame a scene from her memory. This perspective into her past exists in an ambiguous territory of memory, illusion, and dream that drive the entire plot from Mario's first encounter with her through the film's conclusion. That the voiceover is Natalia's also significantly replaced Dostoevsky's male narrator with a female one. "From that day on, I used to die every time I heard some noise in the entrance hall. I'd think, 'There he is.' . . . Sometimes when I was sure he wasn't home, I'd go up to his room with the excuse of doing some housework" (Visconti 1970b, 33). This voiceover is contrasted with a notable silence of the character (as opposed to narrator) Natalia during a fifteen-minute flashback sequence in which she takes a trip with this man and her grandmother to the opera (see fig. 3.6). When the extradiegetic music cuts to the diegetic music of their night at the opera, Natalia's silence amplifies her position outside the scene being depicted, where the sounds of the other voices and music accompany her movements within

Figure 3.6. A night at the opera (*White Nights*).

it. Such a strategy augments the theatricality of the scene significantly, adding a crescendo of melodrama that concludes only when flashback and filmic present collide when the lodger is replaced by Mario.

Attention shifts to performers and performances, underscoring the focalizer Natalia/ Schell whose "literary" voice becomes part of the cinematic text. In her appearance as a flaxen-haired foreigner ("of Slavic origin" she says at one point) whose parents have disappeared, Schell cuts a uniquely melodramatic figure of the foreigner from the pages of Dostoevsky. Young in appearance and childlike in her movements, she is a modest, pre-ball Cinderella, whose suffering under the watchful eyes of surrogate mothers, along with dreams of escape through marriage to a distant "prince," exhibit a fairy tale quality. Visconti highlights Natalia's non-Italian origin by casting the Austrian Schell, marking an interesting twist on Dostoevsky's dark Nastenka. Schell achieved fame in European film circles of the 1950s, garnering a special mention at the Cannes Film Festival of 1954 for her role in Helmut Käutner's *Die letzte Brucke* (*The Last Bridge*, 1954), and the Volpi Cup for Best Actress in René Clément's *Gervaise* (1956) at the Venice Film Festival of 1956. Schell was in high demand during this period, with Visconti claiming that they needed to speed along the production of *White Nights* because she was under contract for only a short time (Hennessey 2011, 169). Moreover, *White Nights* was just one of many literary adaptations Schell was cast in after *Gervaise*, an adaptation of Zola's *L'Assommoir.* Her subsequent role was in another Dostoevsky adaptation as Grushenka in Richard Brooks's *The Brothers Karamazov* (1958), and she starred in Alexandre Astruc's *Un vie* (*One Life*, 1958), based on a story by Maupassant. In *White Nights*, Schell's fair complexion and foreign identity increase the fantasy persona of her character. She is no simple dream girl but an exotic embodiment of the female foreigner, capable of inciting strange reactions in the local men, as in the beginning when two hoodlums on a motorcycle menace her with catcalls. (The ironic nature of her character is announced by her name, "Natalia" and its resemblance to "Italia.")

This interplay between native and foreigner in *White Nights* is further crystallized by the meta-cinematic appearance of the Italian actress Clara Calamai, who played Giovanna in *Obsession*. The utopic vision of romantic fulfillment that Natalia energetically pursues stands in contrast with the gritty realism of Calamai's aging prostitute, whose disillusionment resists every possibility that happiness is forthcoming. Schell is rendered all the more foreign when paired with Calamai, an actress who exudes an unmistakably Italian identity and represents an important reference point for Visconti's cinema and neorealism. Calamai becomes a visual motif of the faded, destitute beauty of neorealist cinema in an age that required something more than documentary realism to be relevant. For Visconti, dream, not reality, took center stage in this new, postneorealist path. In an interview published in the *Cahiers du cinéma* in 1959, he notes: "I must say that I attached myself to this little story—grand in Dostoyevsky, small in my film—specifically for the possibilities for evading reality that it offers, for the contrast between awakening in which everything is unpleasant and those three nighttime hours spent with that girl who becomes a bit of a dream, something unreal, almost impossible. It was this game that attracted me" (*LV*, 71). That Maria Schell was transformed into the narrator of this cine-literary narrative points to how adaptation highlighted the constructed nature of the film, indicating Visconti's movement away from the real, toward the fantastic.

Visconti's First Super Spectacle

Senso represents a move toward large-scale filmmaking that characterized most of the rest of Visconti's career. In a letter dated August 26, 1953, editor, screenwriter, and one of Visconti's most trusted collaborators, Mario Serandrei offered some comments on *Senso*'s screenplay.

> All three of the films you have made thus far have been important, at a high artistic level, and have had a decisive influence on the direction of cinema: they are the pure expression of progressive art cinema. What is missing, however, is the great popular success. One must break through to strike the broad public. Successes with your progressive minority, critics and friends, are not enough to allow you to continue to create, to be able to have another 100 million [lire] at your disposal. Obviously, I am not recommending that you betray your ideals as man and artist, but I think you could line your hammer with a little felt. . . . Dear Luchino, I know that you have hands that know how to change stones into diamonds. I am sure that again this time you will make a film that will take the breath away from your critics. But I would like this to be the moment of a great popular success. That success that will enable you to make even more important films. (*FV*, 1, 300, 1, 2)

Serandrei's letter is prophetic, and with *Senso*, Visconti finally did break through to popular audiences. In the next part of the book, I turn my attention to the blockbuster adaptations of the 1960s: *Rocco and His Brothers*, *The Leopard*, and *The Damned*. All three feature-length films were coproductions that shattered records for ticket sales and attendance during a time in which Italian cinema took advantage of the situation in Hollywood, which between 1958 and 1968 entered into a phase of steep decline (Quaglietti 1980, 207–8). By contrast, Italy's film industry was gaining steam, producing 129 films in 1960 and 200 in 1961. As Barbara Corsi notes, already in 1961–1962, seven of the ten highest-grossing films on Italy's screens were Italian (Corsi 2012, 73). Following in the footsteps of *Senso*, *Rocco and His Brothers* was a megahit in Italian box offices, second only to *La Dolce Vita*. Likewise, *The Leopard* became a popular and critical hit in 1963, and *The Damned* attracted enormous audiences in Italy and abroad in 1969. So began Visconti's blockbuster phase. Inaugurated with *Senso*, this phase featured greater financing, bigger sets, more international stars, and an overall sense of scale that was on par with big-budget productions from Hollywood of this or any era. In histories of Visconti's cinema, scholars have struggled to balance the satisfaction of popular audiences, normally linked with escape and entertainment, with the aesthetic and political rigor with which Visconti's films were associated. To rectify this split, I demonstrate how these films mix literary texts with cinematic genres, marrying them beneath the amorphous category of the *superspettacoli d'autore*, or "auteur super-spectacles." In *Rocco and His Brothers*, the boxers from the pages of Giovanni Testori's *Il ponte della Ghisolfa* (*The Bridge of Ghisolfa*) are transformed into icons of the Italian boxing movie. In the case of the iconic historical film, *The Leopard*, we will see how the artistic "aura" that Walter Benjamin saw as fading through technology of photography is transformed by Giuseppe Tomasi di Lampedusa's best-selling book and Visconti's blockbuster adaptation. In *The Damned*, Shakespeare's *Macbeth* structures a salacious Nazi film. All three films present adaptation as a conduit, in which literature was just one source flowing into the many tributaries of the cinematic.

Part II

The Super-Spectacle Adaptations

4

Rocco e i suoi fratelli (*Rocco and His Brothers,* 1960)

Passion and Pugilism in Visconti's Boxing Film

J'ai fait de la boxe!

—Actress Annie Girardot on the set of *Rocco and His Brothers*

A BRIEF SUMMARY OF BOXING in *Rocco and His Brothers* (1960) is a necessary starting point for addressing how Visconti adapts the boxing material from Giovanni Testori's *Il ponte della Ghisolfa* (*The Bridge of Ghisolfa*). After arriving and establishing themselves in Milan, four of the five Parondi brothers search for work to support each other and their mother, Rosaria. Rocco, Simone, and Ciro gravitate to a local boxing gym frequented by Vincenzo, the one brother already established in Milan. There, nefarious promoter Morini identifies Simone as a potential talent, offering to transfer him to a superior facility where he will be groomed by trainer Cerri. When Simone's commitment and potential are questioned after a humiliating loss, Cerri recruits Rocco to take his place. Following a violent altercation between Simone and Morini, Rocco commits to an exploitative contract to pay off Simone's

Figure 4.1. Boxing in *Rocco and His Brothers* (Luchino Visconti, 1960).

debts. Rocco rises to the status of national champion; Simone, destitute, murders the prostitute Nadia and is betrayed by Ciro to the police. The film concludes with a shot featuring the youngest brother, Luca, touching a series of posters promoting Rocco's next bout.

In a 1960 interview, Visconti downplayed the significance of boxing in *Rocco*, rejecting any association with the generic boxing film: "Discouraged because they cannot find work, anguished, the boys end up becoming boxers. But, certainly don't say 'Visconti is making a film about boxing.' This is nothing more than an exterior, accessory element; and at the same time a symbol of physical violence. When faced with their difficulties, the boys capitulate, one after the other" (*LV*, 77). Elsewhere, the director asserted boxing's metaphorical status as analogous to the fishermen's labor from Verga's *The House by the Medlar Tree* and therefore symbolic of the proletarian struggle he treated in *The Earth Trembles*: "There [*The House by the Medlar Tree*] 'Ntoni and his family, in the struggle to survive, to liberate themselves from their material obligations, attempt the 'loading of the lupines' enterprise: here, Rosaria's sons attempt pugilism: and boxing is the 'loading of the lupines' from *The House by the Medlar Tree*. Thus, the film is related to *The Earth Trembles*—that is my interpretation of *The House by the Medlar Tree*—making it almost a second episode" (Rondolino 2003, 398). In the context of what has been described as Visconti's signature mode of adapting literature through the prism of Gramsci's philosophy, each ill-fated enterprise triggered the disintegration of the nuclear family. In *The House by the Medlar Tree*, 'Ntoni's ship sinks, and with it, the solitary piece of capital held by the Valastro family; in *Rocco*, Simone's failure to advance in boxing signals his and the Parondi family's decline (Testa 2002a, 8). This deterioration includes Rocco, whose success in the ring is clouded by being compelled to fight to pay off his brother's debt.

The privileged link with *The Earth Trembles* crystallizes four key coordinates guiding readings of the film, introducing a critical quadrivium—political engagement, neorealism, literary adaptation, melodrama—that overwhelm any other potential reference points for *Rocco*. Beginning with the film's ideological foundations, the comparison with *The Earth Trembles* helped establish *Rocco* as a direct, militant engagement with social and political exploitation. This principle of engagement, *impegno* in Italian, stipulated that Visconti deploy a political (Italian Communist Party) and theoretical (Gramsci) set of weaponry to denounce the ills of contemporary Italian society. As in the case of *The Earth Trembles*, *Rocco* was criticized for its formalism, pitting Visconti's politics against his aestheticism. Considering the tension between the political and the aesthetic in *Rocco*, Sam Rhodie inquires, "Visconti, a committed political artist, in the very act of underlining political meanings in his fictions, came close to affirming a faith in art against contemporary reality. . . . Could it really be argued that an escape into Art and Beauty as enduring values with which to accuse the present was an advanced progressive politics?" (Rhodie 1992, 31–32). Second, the link with *The Earth Trembles*, a canonical contribution to neorealism, introduced questions of transparency and documentariness to the discussion of *Rocco*. Its registration of southern migrants in northern cities was seen as channeling *The Earth Trembles*'s documentary charge to address a more recent social problem and reality (Brunetta 2006, 74–80). Third, evoking his famous adaptation of Verga's *The House by the Medlar Tree* when he suggested that *Rocco* was another "verghian" chapter in his filmmaking, Visconti once again matches himself with the Italian literary tradition of verism. Finally, in its focus on "the irresolvable conflict between social/familial/gender demands and individual desires," *Rocco* motions to the melodramatic mode that had become a Visconti signature (Pravadelli 2017, 241). All four of these elements fit neatly into the director's profile as a realist, making *Rocco* a continuation of the neorealist trilogy that had anointed him as "the apostle of the Italian road to realism."

Visconti insisted that boxing was just one operative device for expressing the realist tones of immigrant Milan: "In my film I want to provide a portrait of the human condition of these people . . . with a glimpse, I would like to show the world of boxing, that morass of deaf and powerful interests, a genuine mechanism of gangs that exploit the struggles of the athletes and the enthusiasm of the crowds . . . the moral sadism of this environment will be added to that of the big city" (Giori 2011a, 204). In this light, the brothers' toil in the ring stood for the social and political crisis facing millions of southerners, with Visconti shedding light on the "true" conditions of the immigrant plight, opening a window onto "the everyday reality."

Not all interpreters of the film moored *Rocco* to Verga's novel or politically engaged neorealism. Some recognized similarities between the boxing milieu of *Rocco* and the cinematic underworlds of Hollywood films of the period. Italo Calvino wrote in *Cinema Nuovo* in 1960: "The issue of inserting the masses from underdeveloped regions into big cities was at the basis of one of cinematographic narrative's most illustrious traditions: the American *gangster* film. Visconti's film, in its best parts, takes up, deepens, and aggravates the language of images and rhythm and lights and bitterness of the metropolitan saga from the *gangster* film" (Gremigni 2009, 252–53; original emphasis). Calvino's mention of the Hollywood gangster film introduces a generic point of reference that was also picked up by others. His early questioning of the discourse on the Italian notion of political engagement or *impegno* began around the same time he was commenting on *Rocco* (Antonello and Mussgnug 2009, 11). Vito Pandolfi acknowledged affinities between the boxer-brothers, Rocco and Simone, and cinematic boxers of Hollywood origin:

> From Hollywood productions, certain films on boxing and their backstories are not missing (because in reality, despite the recalls to Gramsci, [*Rocco*] also joins these). But which other incisiveness and humanity can there be than from the old *Champ* with Wallace Beery and Jackie Coogan to *Someone Up There Likes Me*, even if Visconti aspires to a more complex vision, dense with meaning. (Pandolfi 1961, 24)

Pandolfi refers to King Vidor's *The Champ* (1931) as a classic Hollywood boxing film, while *Somebody Up There Likes Me* (Robert Wise, 1956) was an example of a something more proximate to *Rocco*. Of course, Pandolfi hedges against labeling *Rocco* a boxing film. He lauds *Rocco*'s relative density ("dense with meaning") in contrast with presumably more conventional, less intellectual Hollywood products. So does Andrea Cappabianca in his book on the international boxing film, *Boxare con l'ombra* (2004), where he carefully differentiates *Rocco* from the typical boxing film. Cappabianca positions boxing in the critical dyad of realism and melodrama, essential pillars of Viscontian auteurism: "Obviously, Luchino Visconti's *Rocco and His Brothers* is not a film about boxing. It is an auteur work, placed at the very viscontian junction between realism and melodrama, and at the same time, one that posits a sociological document (one filtered by fiction) of the Italian situation of that period" (Cappabianca 2004, 154). He goes on to contend that Italy never created a boxing genre to call its own, reaffirming that *Rocco* was more indebted to neorealism than generic categories: "In Italy, the boxing film will never become a real *genre* (or subgenre), but is, once again, in touch with the neorealist lesson" (Cappabianca 2004, 147). By denying any contamination with the boxing genre film, Visconti, Pandolfi, and Cappabianca seem to agree: *Rocco* should be regarded as anything but a "boxing film."

With the exception of Giori (2011a), the most comprehensive study of the film, canonical approaches to Visconti's cinema have done little to address boxing's central position in *Rocco*. In a politically engaged communist director, Italian critics considered traces of generic formulae to be "forms of compromise" that were ideologically unacceptable (Antonello 2012, 176). Instead, *Rocco* was seen as another articulation of the verisimilar where "realism and authorial expressivity . . . will be the means whereby the art film unifies itself" (Bordwell 1979).

Rather than denigrate the presence of generic markers in art films, other critics have recognized their creative potential, and not just in Hollywood films. As Braudy notes:

> When we perceive the function of vampire-film conventions in *Persona* or boxing-film conventions in *On the Waterfront* as clearly as we note the debt of Kurosawa's samurai film to American westerns, or that of the New Wave films to American crime films of the 1950s, then we will be able to appreciate more fully the way in which films can break down the old visions between elite and popular art to establish, almost unbeknown to aesthetics and criticism, a vital interplay between them. (Braudy 1984, 113)

Contrary to the director's representation of the sport's relative insignificance, boxing and the boxing film were key points of reference for *Rocco* from its inception. The first version of the screenplay concluded with Rocco's dramatic death in the ring, victim of injuries suffered in a previous bout. When asked about the film's subject prior to the extensive screenwriting phase, Suso Cecchi d'Amico responded, "I don't know much. I do know that there are five brothers and that boxing has something to do with it" (Rondolino 2003, 394). Of the film's 695 shots, 136 represent training and prize fights featuring Rocco and Simone in the ring, and a further 98 display fisticuffs between southerners (the brawl following Simone's first bout), Rocco and Simone (their drawn-out fist fight following Nadia's rape), or Simone and Morini (who come to blows after Simone rebuffs Morini's sexual advances). All told, roughly a third of the film's duration is dedicated to scenes in the locker room, training and fighting in the ring or boxing gym, or reproducing physical altercations of a decidedly pugilistic nature. More recently, a copy of the film was sold in Italian newsstands together with an issue of the sports newspaper *Tuttosport*, included as promotional material marketing *Rocco* as an Italian boxing film (Foot 1999, 211). The film's legacy is also tied to its status as a model for films like Martin Scorsese's *Raging Bull* (1980) (Holden 1993). The sport presumably would figure centrally in the planned remake of *Rocco* for RAI television, originally set to begin shooting in 2014. Luca Argentero, fresh off his role as boxer Tiberio Mitri in the TV miniseries *Tiberio Mitri: il campione e la miss* (*Tiberio Mitri: The Champion and the Beauty Queen*; see fig. 4.2), was to star as Rocco in a four-installment series to be produced by Guido Lombardo and Carlo Bixio of Publispeil (Urbano 2010).

Crucial to the notion that boxers were fundamental to the adaptation is that *Rocco* was the first Visconti film based on an original idea, not a literary source or a Cesare Zavattini script (like *Bellissima* and the episode of *We, the Women*). Yet to call *Rocco* a nonadaptation would be misleading, pointing to the multiform ways literary texts entered Visconti's poetics. The world of boxing, for instance, was a key feature of Testori's collection of stories, a fundamental (if frequently overlooked) literary source for *Rocco*. Testori's work was one of multiple literary texts that Visconti used in preparing *Rocco*. Elements of Arthur Miller's *A View from the Bridge*, Verga's *The House by the Medlar Tree*, Mann's *Joseph and His Brothers*, and Dostoevsky's *The Idiot* all combined with the immigration story as foundations of *Rocco*'s complex narrative (Giori 2011a, 101–38). The film itself was seen as an attempt to find a cinematic equivalent to

Figure 4.2. *Tiberio Mitri: Il campione e la miss* (*The Champion and the Miss*, Angelo Longoni, 2011).

the literary novel, what Visconti called "a great cinematographic novel" structured in five episodes that might be seen as chapters or acts of a tragedy (Pistoia 2008, 37). Although the boxers and their settings may have been drawn from the various texts Visconti's work refers to, I assess how boxing stretches from the literary content of Testori's *The Bridge of Ghisolfa* to the cinematic context of the immigrant boxer. While Visconti falls short in documenting the experiences of real southern immigrants in their encounter with Milan, he successfully creates cinematic ones based on a literary source. His boxers carved out the familiar narrative pathway of the immigrant fighter omnipresent in national and international boxing films of this period (Hennessey 2016, 221–26). This attention to boxing, real and represented, is not arbitrary. In the years leading up to *Rocco*'s release, the sport was becoming a widespread leisure activity for diverse audiences around Italy. "Both Fellini and Visconti," Pierre Sorlin observes, "demonstrated the spread of new forms of entertainment: music-hall, dance-hall and, above all, sporting competitions" with sports becoming "the big fashion of the 'miracle years,' a passion common to all classes" (Sorlin 1996, 118). That boxing's popularity was reaching new heights around the time of the 1960 Summer Olympic Games in Rome was not lost on Visconti. In 1960, references to neorealism and Visconti's political engagement were used to defend the film, first from censors and later from its snub by Italy's cinematic establishment (Foot 2000). Today, associations with neorealism and *impegno* condition thoughts on nonnational, "popular" cultural and cinematic elements of *Rocco*, burying them beneath more firmly established interpretative paradigms.

From Adaptation to a Grammar of the Boxing Film

In discussing the mixture of literary with other sources at the heart of *Rocco*, Mauro Giori ties the film to other Visconti adaptations. "The procedure adopted by the director does not differ in substance from that which he followed in adapting novels and novelle: it is a matter of a voracious overlapping of disparate sources that were, above all, but not exclusively, literary ones" (Giori 2011a, 101). As we will see, *The Damned* (chapter 6) and *Sandra* (chapter 7) were also hybrid adaptations that balanced a number of literary resources. In these cases where a single literary source did not provide any overarching structure, I argue that cinematic categories (the boxing film for *Rocco*, the Nazi film for *The Damned*, the *giallo* and gothic for *Sandra*) were increasingly significant, becoming fusing agents for combining disparate materials. Of the literary determinants for *Rocco* listed above, Testori's text was the most acknowledged and most contested literary source. While *The Bridge of Ghisolfa* is the only literary source identified in the film's titles, various contributors downplayed its significance in the creation of *Rocco*'s screenplay. Yet, *Rocco*'s immigrant dream of advancement through boxing is introduced immediately in *Il ras* (The Boss), a story (actually two) from *The Bridge of Ghisolfa* that helped inspire the cinematic boxers in *Rocco*: "Born a slave, you'll die a slave. Hopes? All bull, illusions in your head, fool that you are" (Testori 1985, 183). Interested in boxing, Cornelio Binda joins the boxing club Box e Atletica, where he meets Duilio Morini, a local champion who takes Cornelio under his wing. At first positive, characterized by an attraction that is both homosocial and homoerotic, their relationship later sours, with Morini avenging his battle against Cornelio in the ring by dishonoring his sister, Angelica. In *Rocco*, Visconti links the atmosphere of the boxing ring with some of Testori's main characters from "The Boss" and other stories. Simone especially reflects characters Ivo, Cornelio, Attilio; Nadia is like Gina, Wanda, and Enrica; Morini is based on Duilio Morini and G.M. Although various pieces of dialogue in the boxing setting (the discussion of nicotine in the teeth, for example) are transported verbatim from "The Boss," other storylines appear, like those from "Cosa fai Sinatra?" (What are you doing, Sinatra?), "Il resto dopo" (The Rest Later), "Pensieri nella notte" (Thoughts in the Night), where the brotherly conflict between Attilio and Dario is mirrored in the drama between Simone and Rocco. When Attilio finds out his brother is seeing Gina, a girl with whom he had a brief relationship, Dario beats him and rapes the girl in what will become one of the most controversial scenes in the film. Despite the many alterations Visconti made, the fact that he transports the basic structures from Testori's stories is undeniable.

With these direct linkages to *The Bridge of Ghisolfa* in mind, it should be noted how *Rocco* reflects many ways immigrant boxers have traditionally been represented in Italian and Hollywood cinema, emulating how cinematic and literary conventions can be combined. Boxing films often encapsulate the immigrant aspirations to overcome material difficulties through athletic achievement, bolstering *Rocco*'s depiction of the poor southern family's arrival in Milan. Fortunes in the ring set Rocco and Simone on separate yet interlaced pathways of rise and fall. Boxing is consistent with the most customary reading of the film, which identifies three narrative macrosections: (1) the Parondi arrival in Milan; (2) the family members' successful and failed attempts to integrate into their new industrial environment; and finally, (3) the disintegration of the traditional family at the end of the film (Canova 2000, 177–80). On one hand, this arc suggests the typical, tragic degeneration characteristic of Visconti films. On the other hand, boxing as a potential and especially dangerous avenue for upward mobility exposes a clear junction between this Italian immigrant story and the boxing film species. As Woodward explains: "Boxing has a long history as a route out of poverty, which has not only been seized upon by individuals but also recognized by government, for example through the provision of boys' clubs, gymnasia and the development of provision in schools. More recently sport has become a target of interventions which seek to promote social inclusion and new versions of citizenship" (Woodward 2007, 17). What ties the fighting in the ring to the thread of the immigrant story is Nadia, the prostitute who introduces the Parondis to boxing, then becomes romantically involved with both boxers before being raped and murdered by Simone. Her rape foreshadows the climax of the film. Nadia's graphic murder outraged censors, who eventually disfigured the scene, as well as some audience members who allegedly came out in droves to "protest their indignation" (Biagi 1960, 3). Nevertheless, Nadia effectively sutures the boxing story with the immigrant saga, introducing boxing as a potential means for economic gain. When she meets the Parondis in their basement apartment, she sees a newspaper clipping of Vincenzo dressed as a fighter, then recounts the tale of a boxer she knew who struck it rich. Objectively, the prostitute is a counterpart to the boxer; for hire, she initially personifies the competitive spirit for accumulating wealth and redemption through physical toil, epitomizing values of boom Italy that *Rocco* critiques. Nadia later makes these parallels between prostitution and boxing plain, describing both as working "for passion" (Hipkins 2006).

Pairing the figure of the strongman with that of the prostitute—Samson to Delilah—is a motif in a variety of boxing films, the boxer's

Figure 4.3. The prostitute and the boxer: Nadia and Simone.

female complement recurrently defined as either saint or seductress. Nadia in this role echoes the noirish women in *Rocco* and other Visconti films (consider Giovanna in *Obsession* and "the prostitute" in *White Nights*, both played by Clara Calamai), unmarried women who portend danger or death for male characters.

By promoting the fantasy of boxing as a means to material gain, Nadia is also associated with Morini, the corrupt manager whom Rocco and Simone encounter early in the film. This gangster-promoter figure had a clear precursor in Hollywood boxing films of the 1930s. Morini personifies the pitfalls dotting boxing's illusory path to fame and riches, and his speculation on the Parondi brothers is both financially and physically predatory. He fronts the money to gamble on Simone's future victories in the ring, then to extort sex; finally, he signs Rocco to an extended fighting contract as collateral for Simone's robbery (Bolongaro 2014). This avatar of moral and financial corruption is omnipresent in Hollywood boxing films of the 1930s such as *Kid Galahad* (Michael Curtiz, 1937), *The Crowd Roars* (Richard Thorpe, 1938), *Golden Boy* (Rouben Mamoulian, 1939), *Body and Soul* (Robert Rossen, 1947), and *The Set-Up* (Robert Wise, 1949) from the 1940s, and figures in the backstory to many films of the 1950s, such as *On the Waterfront* (Elia Kazan, 1954), *Somebody Up There Likes Me* (Robert Wise, 1956), and *The Harder They Fall* (Mark Robson, 1956) (Grindon 2007, 405).

The chain of causation illustrated here demonstrates *Rocco*'s difference from typical *film d'art*, with Simone playing out the relatively conventional storyline of the boxer's rise and fall. Here, the boxer shows early promise and success, only to fade into physical and moral decline. After Simone's opening victories, defeat sets him on a path of progressively more serious crimes, from petty theft to rape to murder. He is humiliated when he learns that Rocco will supplant him in the ring and with Nadia, motivating Nadia's rape and Rocco's beating. Unlike Ciro, whose distancing from his family is executed through a mastery of his new environment as a skilled worker, Simone is absorbed into the city's criminal underworld, taking Nadia with him. To gird the authenticity of this dark environment, real boxers and trainers from the world of Italian professional boxing were cast in the film: "Moreover, other than Fiermonte, numerous authentic boxers took part in the filming: from Choca to Rocco Mazzola, from Bruno Fortilli to the manager Barravecchi, one of the veteran creators of champions" (Carancini 2010, 99). Visconti inserted these real-life boxers to conjure the unvarnished world of boxing and supplement an engrossing realism. Teeming with the visual data of the material boxing world, the gym's spatial integrity is aided by

Figure 4.4. Scenes in the boxing gym.

the appearance of actual boxers, buttressing the interpretation of *Rocco* as a sociological portrait (see fig. 4.4).

Other boxing films made in Italy between the early 1940s and 1960 also featured professional boxers. Primo Carnera, a heavyweight champion from the 1930s, appeared in *Harlem* (Carmine Gallone, 1943), a film that borrowed dramatic devices from the earlier Hollywood production, *Kid Galahad.* Specific to Visconti's film, the figure of Rocco was based loosely on Italian champion Rocco Mazzola, a boxer from Potenza who also made an appearance in *Rocco.* Many of the film's other fighters had successful film careers in Italy. Middleweight Enzo Fiermonte starred in *L'ultimo combattimento* (*The Last Fight*, Piero Ballerini, 1940) and *Il campione* (*The Champion*, Carlo Borghesio, 1943), then directed and played the protagonist in *L'atleta di cristallo* (*The Crystal Fighter*, 1946), before being cast as one of the "real" boxers in *Rocco.* A more prominent boxer-actor to participate was Tiberio Mitri, known as "the Tiger of Trieste." Mitri became Italian middleweight champion in 1948, European champ in 1949, and contended for the world championship belt against "Raging Bull" Jake LaMotta at Madison Square Garden on July 12, 1950, losing in a fifteen-round decision. In 1950, Mitri married Fulvia Franco, a former Miss Italia and screen actress. Their relationship was dramatized in the TV film *Tiberio Mitri: il campione e la miss* (*Tiberio Mitri: The Champ and the Beauty Queen*, 2011), one of a few recent boxing films like *Tatanka* (Giuseppe Gagliardi, 2011) and *Acqua Fuori dal Ring* (*Ring of Water*, Joel Stangle, 2012) set in Italy. Shortly after his marriage, Mitri began acting in popular Italian films, first in Mario Soldati's swashbuckling adventure *I tre corsari* (*The Three Pirates*, 1952), then as a boxer in *Era lei che lo voleva!* (*It Was She Who Wanted It!*, Marino Girolami and Giorgio Simonelli, 1952) starring Walter Chiari and Lucia Bosè. He worked in boxing films like Vittorio Duse's melodrama *Il nostro campione* (*Our Champion*, 1955) and *Un uomo facile* (*The Defeated Victor*, Paolo Heusch, 1958). These fighters symbolized the sport's rising popularity in Italy, where other than the dominance of the European Lightweight belt from 1940 until 1946, Italian boxers controlled multiple European weight classes in the 1950s and 1960s. A crescendo of favorable results culminated in 1960 with the Rome Summer Olympic Games, where under the tutelage of coach Natalino Rea, Italian boxers put on a commanding display, winning three gold medals, three silver medals, and one bronze medal.

Boxing was not limited to dramatic films but also appeared in various Italian comedies of the 1950s, such as *Al diavolo la celebrità* (*A Night of Fame*, Steno and Mario Monicelli, 1951), and *I soliti ignoti* (*Big Deal on Madonna Street*, Mario Monicelli, 1958), and two later spoofs of *Rocco* from 1961–62: *Rocco e le sorelle* (*Rocco and His Sisters*, Giorgio Simonelli, 1961) and *Walter e i suoi cugini* (*Walter and His Cousins*, Marino Girolami, 1961). Notwithstanding these boxing films and the sport's increased national relevance, the notion of an Italian boxing film has always been met with skepticism. *Harlem*, for example, encountered critical rancor in Italy, with Antonio Pietrangeli lambasting director Carmine Gallone for trying to re-create a Hollywood film (Pietrangeli 1943, 34–35). The enforcement of national boundaries that surround a film like *Rocco* has been a formidable barrier to comparing the film's Italian story of internal migration to generic categories. This is intimately tied up with the marriage between cinema and national identity and how neorealism and its auteurs were privileged in their representations of the Italian national character (Noto 2011, 31–32). The ex post facto process of defining genres and cycles evenly pits the Hollywood boxing film against more nationally bound, Italian categories such as neorealism. In *Rocco*, Viscontian realism combines various "regimes of verisimilitude," obliterating the imagined wall between Hollywood and Italian types of cinema (Neale 1990, 47).

The choice to include the professional boxers to augment the spatial authenticity of the boxing settings—the gyms, theaters, dressing rooms—was based on information gathered during an intense anthropological study of Milan and its outskirts by Visconti and his collaborators. This localized vision gained new prominence with the excision of the film's planned prologue, set in the southern region of Basilicata, that would have opened the picture far from its Milanese center. Visconti traveled to Basilicata in December 1959 to photograph and experience the land from which *Rocco*'s characters were escaping. He intended the landscape to foreground the family's geographical roots and southern identity (Megale 2003, 14). The first version of *Rocco*'s screenplay opened with a view of Basilicata's rocky shore, Rocco and Simone depositing their father's coffin into the sea. Simone remarks, "If you had died during the winter, we would have brought you to be buried in Bernalda where there is a cemetery. Now there's mud and landslides everywhere and no roads to be found. You always feared dying in winter" (Megale 2003, 32). This rural setting would have created a pictorial link to the seascape in *The Earth Trembles*, conjoining *Rocco* to Visconti's neorealist masterwork.

Basilicata and the southern coordinates were abandoned in the final screenplay, and Milan became the determining model for locations and characters. "We spent countless hours in gymnasiums," Suso Cecchi d'Amico recounted, "I spent a year in them, and I don't like boxing. Gradually, the subject took shape" (Schifano 1990, 313). Unearthing the unknown areas of Milan and its periphery was an arduous process, and research for the film was recorded meticulously through a collection of photographs, of which forty-four were boxing scenes taken in both Milan and Basilicata (Megale 2003, 31). The importance given to reflecting the city's actual boxing spaces was not limited to featuring professional boxers in boxing scenes or choosing authentic-looking shooting locations. It also extended to the bodies of the actors. In preproduction, Renato Salvatori and Alain Delon were subjected to extended physical training (Carancini 2010, 99). Such physical transformations are typical of boxing films, the most famous examples being Robert De Niro's dramatic weight gain while filming *Raging Bull* and, more recently, Jake Gyllenhaal's sculpted frame in *Southpaw* (Antoine Fuqua, 2015). As we will see, the limited transmutation of Delon's body to resemble that of a professional athlete was one reason critics gave for questioning his casting in the role of Rocco.

Rocco and His Brothers: Arthouse or Italian Blockbuster?

Rocco continued Visconti's shift toward large-scale filmmaking that appealed to a wide audience inaugurated with *Senso* that prevailed in select big productions such as *The Leopard* and *The Damned*. Unlike other auteur films of the era, *Rocco* found audiences beyond Italy's urban centers. Discussing the popularity of the film outside Italy's main cities, Vittorio Spinazzola remarked: "The film's fortune was, for the most part, granted by audiences in the periphery and the provinces: the popular spectator. Thus, Visconti had finally communicated with that type of audience that is closest to his heart . . . two years later, he would definitively consolidate his prestige as man of spectacle resorting to the traditional means of the Hollywood superproduction: *divismo*, color, scenography, mass movements, all in the service of a cinematic rendition of a bookstore *bestseller*" (Spinazzola 1969, 310–11). *Rocco* introduced the social nature of a Visconti film to large swaths of the Italian populace, creating a dialogue with new spectators who engaged with his films in multiple ways. The letters that Italian workers wrote in response to *Rocco* challenged notions that popular audiences in Italy were essentially passive (Gremigni 2009, 254–66). In an interview with Aristarco cited in chapter 3, Visconti addressed the changing landscape of Italian film tastes at the time, remarking how audiences were bridging the gap between the movie theater and the arthouse (Gremigni 2009, 248). How *Rocco* triangulated with film audiences on one hand and the Italian film industry on the other represents a relatively unexplored area in our understanding of the film's distribution and reception. The same can be said for how a loose Visconti adaptation interacted with genre cinema. These lacunae stem from privileging the numerous high-cultural components of Visconti's works that the director himself underscored in interviews, published articles, and public statements. Furthermore, intimations of the popular clash with Visconti's identification as the unofficial filmmaker of the Italian Communist Party, an institution hardly receptive to Italian popular culture (Gundle 2000, 99–105).

Judging from the film's large box-office receipts, Visconti's individual indictment of the state of immigrant Milan blurred with its status as a form of entertainment and a consumerist product of the Italian film industry. Yet even before its debut, *Rocco*'s preproduction phase reveals a considerable debt to direct contributions from the Titanus production house's hired hands, pointing to the film's origins as a collective effort with Visconti as only one of many contributors. Screenwriting on *Rocco* was an exhausting process, involving numerous contributions from writers and producers across the duration of about a year. It created a large paper trail demonstrating that a variety of narrative elements were introduced and then jettisoned in later drafts (Giori 2011a, 33–48). The final version was a collection of individual sections, with Suso Cecchi d'Amico responsible for the character Simone, Enrico Medioli for Ciro, and Pasquale Festa Campanile and Massimo Franciosa for Vincenzo and Rocco. Visconti wrote the scene at the Idroscalo. The various participants in stages of the film's production context are also noteworthy. *Rocco* began as a Vides project under producer Franco Cristaldi, who funded the initial screenwriting by Visconti, Vasco Pratolini, d'Amico, and Medioli. When disagreements arose, Cristaldi passed the film to Goffredo Lombardo and Titanus, who brought in Campanile and Franciosa to collaborate on the screenplay. Other than Nicola Badalucco, who contributed to *The Damned* and *Death in Venice*, this was the only time Visconti expanded his usual team of writers. Campanile and Franciosa had previously worked in the comic vein of the "pink neorealism," screenwriting films like Mauro Bolognini's *Gli innamorati* (*Wild Love*, 1955) before gaining notoriety for their highly successful triptych of Titanus films by director Dino Risi: *Poveri ma belli* (*Poor, But Beautiful*, 1956), *Belle ma povere* (*Beautiful, But Poor*, 1958), and *Poveri milionari* (*Poor Millionaires*, 1959). Their identification with the world of commercial Italian cinema was not a mark in their favor, and Campanile and Franciosa admitted to being received coldly when they first arrived to work on *Rocco* (Pergolari 2008, 66–67).

Rocco was not the first boxer Campanile and Franciosa created. They previously wrote the 1957 boxing comedy *Il cocco di mamma* (*Mamma's Boy*, Mauro Morassi), about a gadabout boxer, Aldo, who falls madly in love with Laura, then must prove his dedication by being disfigured in the ring. Aldo's willingness to sacrifice himself is not unlike Rocco's, who fights only to pay Simone's debts. These writers were comfortable working within the Titanus production context, and many Campanile and Franciosa screenplays forwarded that Italian dream of advancement that is evident in *Rocco*, albeit through a comic, optimistic mode. These were consistent with a certain Titanus model that was prevalent at the time (Pergolari 2008, 61–62). Campanile and Franciosa, both from Basilicata, were initially brought in to help with the authentication of the Parondi characters with a prologue to be set in their native region, and they were tasked with matching literary "abundancy" with local flavor (Pergolari 2008, 65). This delegation of writing responsibilities and piecemeal process of screenwriting fits uncomfortably with assertions that *Rocco* was the product of Visconti's complete control, problematizing a traditional identification of the auteur as the film's creative mainspring. Enrico Medioli asserted that audiences perceived artistic harmony, not a patchwork: "I don't think the audience realizes that different hands have been working on the script. Besides, the one who creates the unity is the director" (Bacon 1998, 106). Still, Geoffrey Nowell-Smith insinuates *Rocco*'s troublesome evolution as an auteur film. He first establishes Visconti as *Rocco*'s primary visionary ("The building up of the story was contributed to by various hands, but the ultimate control at every stage rested with Visconti himself"), only to acknowledge the limits of this characterization: "As a result changes have taken place in the structure of the film which Visconti perhaps did not fully foresee and which he would not necessarily recognise as having taken place" (Nowell-Smith 2003, 124–26).

More recently, Visconti's identity as a neorealist auteur has placed the director on the wrong side of an energetic trend in Italian film studies that has portrayed the study of neorealist filmmakers as passé, even counterproductive to the field (O'Leary and O'Rawe 2011). Many directors of his ilk have been cast in a negative light, seen as patriarchs who have consumed a surfeit of scholarly attention, overshadowing less canonical figures and popular forms of cinematic production.

Addressing the issue of the popular in Visconti's works, Michèle Lagny underscores an essential contradiction at play: "To speak of Visconti in terms of popular culture seems simultaneously obvious and absurd" (Lagny 1997, 241). In her reading of *Rocco*, which considers the high-low counterbalancing as the engine of Visconti's creative machinery, Veronica Pravadelli writes: "Visconti's dual nature is the result of his ability to combine intellectually challenging narratives drawn from a whole array

Figure 4.5. Luca touches the poster promoting Rocco's match.

of literary and artistic sources, with highly spectacular *mises-en-scène*, or, in other words, to merge strategies of art cinema with those of popular cinema" (Pravadelli 2017, 233). This high-low blend attracted enormous audiences in the boom years after the peak of Italian viewership in the mid-1950s, a period when blockbuster films were tending toward national products and away from nonnational ones (Corsi 2012, 73). This phase has been called the "watershed years in the history of consumption," when Italian films were meeting the desires of Italian audiences as well as those of international spectators beyond European borders (Brunetta 1991, 87; Forgacs 1996, 275).

Although interpretations of *Rocco* generally couch boxing in purely metaphorical terms, the sport, both cinematic and literary, represents a constituent part of Visconti's textual apparatus—one that is additive, not detrimental to more established categories such as neorealism, adaptation, political engagement, and melodrama. A comprehensive look at his career reveals a director who resourced a wide range of artistic forms and features, from literature to cinema, high to low. This was especially the case in the 1960s, when *Rocco*'s amalgamation of literary and cinematic boxers set a course for some of the largest-scale films of the era. Following in the footsteps of *Senso*, the grandiose historical film *The Leopard* continued the trend of recasting literary works into Italy's biggest film productions, demonstrating how adaptation and genre combined to bring financial and critical prestige to the Italian film industry. Both the gothic *giallo Sandra* and the Nazi film *The Damned* evidenced the multiform ways Visconti's works of this decade increasingly mined transnational cinematic forms to bring adaptations to massive audiences.

5

Il Gattopardo (*The Leopard*, 1963) and *Il lavoro* (*The Job*, 1964)

Wedding Bestseller with Blockbuster

> The worldwide success of the novel upon which the film is based, the names of the director and the actors, and the three and a half billion [lire] spent on production ("in Hollywood," [Burt] Lancaster commented, "they would have spent half that") justify the interest and the curiosity that preceded the premier of Visconti's most recent film. The ladies finally wanted to see those clothes worn by [Claudia] Cardinale that Visconti had ignored the budget for: six-hundred thousand lire for a dress that was worn for ten minutes seems so much, but for the director of The Leopard, noted for his desire for authenticity, these are trifles.
>
> —Dino Bondi, March 28, 1963

The epigraph is from a film review published the day after the 1963 premier of Visconti's *The Leopard* in Rome. The reviewer highlights the national fascination with this cinematic event, suggesting an array of audience uses and gratifications orbiting this

Figure 5.1. Cover of Feltrinelli's Italian-language version of Giuseppe Tomasi di Lampedusa's novel *The Leopard* featuring Burt Lancaster and Claudia Cardinale from the film *The Leopard* (Luchino Visconti, 1963).

glamorous Italian "super spectacle." *The Leopard*'s excessive budget, star director and actors, ornate costuming, massive sets, and epic scale on par with the largest of Hollywood blockbusters of the age all seemed to be requirements dictated by the novel it was adapting. Just five years before, *The Leopard*, a historical novel by mysterious Sicilian author Giuseppe Tomasi di Lampedusa, had become the greatest bestseller in Italian history, published to popular acclaim and critical debate that shaped expectations for the film. Although Visconti and his collaborators at the Titanus production house embraced the novel's notoriety in the promotion of the film, its publisher, Feltrinelli, also jumped at the chance to use the adaptation to advertise the book. In figure 5.1, the confluence of book and film is demonstrated by the paperback cover. Thus, *The Leopard* became a prime instance of the ways publishing and screen industries can exist in a relationship of interdependence (Murray 2008, 9). Author Leonardo Sciascia once noted how Lampedusa's description of Angelica in the book seemed cinematic. The book's cinematic qualities, Sciascia appears to suggest, assured *The Leopard*'s essential adaptability. He observed that the writer had originally created her as an "entirely cinematic apparition, for which the spectator automatically confers the traits of imperious beauty and mystifying manners of an Ava Gardner" (Forgacs 2010, 32).

Today, the novel is still remembered for its mass-cultural success, becoming "one of the three or four books of the postwar period that destroyed the barrier between masterpiece and masses on a global scale" (Orlando 1998, 10). Published in 1958 and winner of the Premio Strega in 1959, *The Leopard* went through fifty-two editions in its first few months on its way to becoming one of the greatest events in the history of Italian publishing. The novel tells the story of Prince Fabrizio di Salina, a Sicilian noble who witnesses Italy's tumultuous birth, beginning with the arrival of Giuseppe Garibaldi and his troops, who began the conquest of Italy with an invasion of Sicily in 1860. Lampedusa embodies Italy's progress toward independence in the marriage of Fabrizio's nephew, Tancredi, to the beautiful but ill-bred Angelica, the ancient nobility being absorbed by Italy's upstart bourgeoisie. Feltrinelli, already triumphant after its publication of Boris Pasternak's Nobel Prize–winning *Doctor Zhivago* in 1957, decided to take a risk on Lampedusa's novel after it had been spurned by Mondadori and Einaudi. What is now known as *il caso Gattopardo*, or "The Leopard Case," refers to the public debate in which Italian intellectuals on the left were split over the novel's ideological footings (Lucente 1984; Guerriero 2008; Forgacs 2010). Critics like Mario Alicata, Guido

Aristarco, Pier Paolo Pasolini, and Elio Vittorini declared glaring flaws in the novel, claiming that it lacked depth and failed on a basic level to embody the kind of political engagement that a historical novel should have. Vittorini claimed that novels must "renew our relationship with history and re-establish one with nature" and "provoke the reader to accept or reject what they represent," something that *The Leopard* simply did not do (Marcus 1993, 48). The *Leopard*'s historical setting among the Sicilian nobility led Vittorini to denigrate Lampedusa for reproducing a literary form that was artistically retrograde. Others critiqued the novel as a work that focused solely on the concerns of the ruling class, with Sciascia claiming that *The Leopard* presented only the aristocratic standpoint of its author and not that of the Sicilian people (Sciascia 1996). Similarly, Mario Alicata believed that Lampedusa failed to take into account the broader brushstrokes of history and their effects on any social class outside his own, making *The Leopard* out to be a work of restoration that novelist Alberto Moravia would claim to be a politically conservative success of the right (Caputo 1975). With his adaptation of *The Leopard*, Visconti found himself portrayed similarly to his fellow aristocrat Lampedusa, and to this day, the latter period of the director's career is characterized by many critics as that of an artistically detached noble. In an echo of denunciations that had plagued *Senso* a few years before, Visconti was labeled an aesthete and a traitor to the militancy of the neorealist cause. Crafting a lavish historical melodrama out of *The Leopard* with star actors raised the ire of former critics like Zavattini and Chiarini, who thought Visconti's keen eye for detail and unmistakable style reduced the film's moral strength (Marcus 2001, 282).

Like *Senso*, *The Leopard* is now appreciated for cinematizing an analysis of Italian unification set down by Antonio Gramsci. Visconti is admired for transforming Lampedusa's Prince Fabrizio into an observer on the political transformism taking place, beholding how the land-owning class allied itself with the revolutionary cause to maintain its grip on power. As Goffredo Fofi remarked, "The film *The Leopard* 'corrected' the novel *The Leopard*, applying analyses and intentions upon it, superimposing them while, in some ways, consenting to its pessimism" (Fofi 2013, 8). Yet initial accusations of class, conservatism, and commodity levied against a period drama conjure the cinematic category of the "heritage cinema," an oft-reviled film form in which political conservativism was matched by the ornate surfaces of historical adaptations. Coined in the 1980s, the term *heritage cinema* was applied to British period dramas that were often (but not necessarily) adapted from literary classics or novels and plays set in the past. For example, three E. M. Forster adaptations, *A Room with a View* (1985), *Maurice* (1987), and *Howards End* (1992), directed by James Ivory and produced by Ismail Merchant, are some of the most referenced heritage films. The British heritage film was traditionally criticized along ideological lines, where it was seen as a stylized genre that transformed bourgeois and upper-class cultural values into national ones. Meticulously re-creating the surfaces of the past and lavishing attention on rural landscapes, heritage films were thought to reflect Margaret Thatcher's conservative political project that sought to profit from British history and traditions by commercializing the nation's heritage industry. Made for the export market and consumed by potential visitors from abroad, the heritage film invited the passive, fascinated gaze of a tourist. As Claire Monk notes, "the nature of the ideological critique implied that the spectator's positioning in relation to this non-human period spectacle was passive. Certainly there was no suggestion that the heritage-film spectator might exercise an active gaze, or experience a sense of mastery or agency (however illusory); rather, the period spectacle was conceived of as acting on the spectator. Whether or not the heritage-film's real audiences were predominantly female, this projection of a staggeringly passive, textually determined spectator positioned them as feminized" (Monk 2011, 21). Alan O'Leary, who has also connected Visconti with the Italian heritage film, notes how a combination of the touristic with the feminized gaze can be observed in Michael Radford's 1994 film, *Il Postino*, writing how "we get a tourist gaze on Italy superimposed on and equivalent to the gaze on the woman," where such films are "seen to commodify Italy's appeal—its lifestyle and landscape, the olive skin of its people—for the export market" (O'Leary 2013). For Rosalind Galt, three Italian films from the 1990s, *Cinema Paradiso* (1988), *Mediterraneo* (1991), and *Il Postino* were remarkably similar to the British heritage film in their approach to melodramatized landscapes of history. Rather than a specifically touristic gaze, however, Galt views the dramatic imagery of these films as "imbricated with the social logic of Italian political loss and thus interpellate the spectator not as a tourist but as a subject in mourning" (Galt 2002, 168).

Without a doubt, the critiques of *The Leopard* novel and film were likewise based on a certain suspicion of their popularity and potential for a mass market in Italy and abroad. The bestseller status and popular readership of the novel bolstered its reputation as a literary commodity (Lucente 1984, 228) that would transfer to Visconti's film in a variety of ways (Anile and Giannice 2013a, 225–44). Clearly the popular audience was associated with escapism already discussed in terms of the conservative end of the ideological spectrum. The same could be assumed of those spectators of the heritage film. *The Leopard*'s overt politics of the left, a position that has historically assumed a more active spectator, would seem to disqualify it from heritage film associations. Yet there are intriguing similarities that are worth exploring further. The meticulous detailing of nineteenth-century interiors, its foregrounding of a new "classic" of Italian literature, the cast of international stars, the film's melodramatic register, and the arid landscape filmed in widescreen suggest an intent to transmit something more than a Gramscian historical analysis. Such emphasis on the beauty of historical reconstruction, decor and decoration, illustrate an impulse to stylize that is not so different from what Andrew Higson observed in the British heritage film, where a critical standpoint was displaced by a fascinated one. If one is to make a more specific connection between *The Leopard* and the British heritage film, it might be in its intended audience and that audience's taste in authorship. As Higson notes, "Heritage films operate very much at the culturally respectable, quality end of the market. . . . They are discussed in terms of an authorship that, at least in the case of the literary adaptations, is doubly-coded—in terms of both film director and author" (Higson 1993, 110). The same can be said of engagements with *The Leopard*, illustrated by some early reviews in Italian newspapers, written in the days following the film's Roman premier in March 1963, where audiences and film critics accorded a special importance to the book–film, author–director relationships. Many reviewers highlighted the film's fidelity to either the letter or spirit of Lampedusa's text. Giovanni Grazzini, for example, noted that "There is a nice saying that even when a film is based on a novel, it must be judged solely on its cinematic values, but when that novel is "The Leopard," one of the most clamorous successes of Italian publishing, then what everyone asks is whether the betrayed writer rolls over in his grave, or sends a thankful greeting to the director who won him new admirers" (Grazzini 1963, 9). This image of the dead author, enjoying a faithful film of his book from beyond the grave, appeared elsewhere, with one reviewer suggesting that "if Giuseppe Tomasi di Lampedusa could see the film that Luchino Visconti made from his novel 'The Leopard,' he would not find anything substantially different from his own narration" (*FV* 14, 140). These observations are unexpected given the many remarkable differences between film and book outlined below, in which Visconti clearly politicized Lampedusa's work (for the most complete reading of the film as a political adaptation, see Anile and

Giannice 2013). Glaring infidelities notwithstanding, interpreters tended to focus on the film as a celebration of the book rather than a departure from it. Another reviewer stated that "more than a translation, [Visconti] provides a deep valorization," adding that "Other than a few divergences in the interpretation of historical events, Luchino Visconti remained rather loyal to the original story while also transfiguring its spirit and poetry cinematically" (*FV* 14, 140). This notion of a faithful adaptation brought other readers back to Visconti's status as an auteur whose super spectacles operated on the same scale as even the largest Hollywood production. Pietro Bianchi called *The Leopard* an "Italian *Gone with the Wind*" that was "more brilliant, more authentic, but also accessible to the regular spectator of Hollywood films," interpreting the film as an accurate adaptation of the book that was, simultaneously, undeniably Viscontian. "Transferring 'The Leopard' in stupendous, fascinating and languid images," Bianchi continued, "Luchino Visconti remained substantially faithful to the novel. But above all, faithful to himself, taking the opportunity to pick up a dialogue that began from 'Senso' " (*FV* 14, 140).

By underscoring the film's relationship to the book, critics and scholars alike highlighted the art and practice of adaptation, which with *The Leopard* achieved a new legitimacy in postwar Italian culture. In the last chapter, I examined how neorealism continued to cast its long shadow into the 1960s, when *Rocco and His Brothers* was interpreted with a critical accent on its ontological connection between cinema and reality. With *The Leopard*, a Visconti adaptation was finally celebrated rather than obscured as such, espousing a truly hybrid cine-literary experience that became increasingly important in both critical and popular reception of the Visconti adaptations that followed. Establishing *The Leopard* as a transitional text conforms to the dominant reading of Visconti's career as separated into two basic phases: the realist, Gramscian phase from *Obsession* to *Rocco and His Brothers*, and the decadent, Proustian phase from *The Leopard* to *The Intruder*. In his book *On Late Style: Music and Literature against the Grain*, Edward Said referenced this Gramsci-Proust pairing to contemplate the intersection between art and commerce, author and auteur, novel and film, bestseller and blockbuster invoked by *The Leopard* (Said 2006, 97). He outlined how the accessibility of historical novel and historical film among a national and then international audience demonstrates how readers became spectators and vice versa. Said's observations point to an engagement with a broad group of spectators who are either directly or indirectly familiar with a book being adapted. In the context of adaptation, this is what Linda Hutcheon calls a "knowing audience," in which spectators were acquainted with novel and film, shifting back and forth from adapted text and adaptation to appreciate the film adaptation *as* an adaptation (Hutcheon 2006, 120). Even spectators who had not read the book experienced a certain "conceptual flipping back and forth between the work they know and the work they are experiencing," having known about features of the novel circulated by Italian media in the period before the film (Hutcheon 2006, 139). For Thomas Leitch, this vacillation between written and visual included an "obsession with authors, book, and words" that we can observe as fundamental to enjoying *The Leopard* as an adaptation, as spectators derive pleasure from comparing the film with their earlier textual experiences (Leitch 2008b, 112). Simone Murray examines how this fluctuation is key to the cultural and commercial success of both novel and film, "Firstly, loyal readers of an acclaimed novel are important chiefly as key, opinion-setting early adopters, whose positive responses to a film adaptation can be used as a launching pad for a broader distribution and publicity campaign. . . . In the second phase of producers' strategy, fan approval can be used as a basis for critical and reviewer praise at key festivals and in the build-up to the awards season" (Murray 2012, 133). That Hutcheon's knowing audiences actively reconstruct film and literary works, generating meanings from both literary and cinematic stories, points to an intersection between constructivist film theory and adaptation theory, where spectators participate in an active interpretative venture (Redmon 2015, 260–62). This spectator is the opposite of the passive viewer thought to frequent popular genres like the historical and heritage films. This is crucial for contemplating the reception of a film like *The Leopard*, where audiences sought the unique pleasure offered by literary adaptation's essential duality.

Marriage, Present and Past: Matrimony and Transaction in *The Job*

Marriage, Visconti claimed, was the organizing principle of Lampedusa's *The Leopard* that he hoped to transfer to film: "The marriage contract between Angelica and Tancredi roots a number of points of view" (Visconti 1963, 25). In both book and film, the marriage between the noble Tancredi and the beautiful Angelica (fig. 5.2), daughter of Calogero Sedàra, an up-and-coming member of the Sicilian bourgeoisie, represents a transaction between old and new.

Angelica will receive an aristocratic title, endowing her family with all of the prestige therein, while her husband, Tancredi, will obtain a

Figure 5.2. Angelica, the face of postunification Italy.

considerable dowry to fuel his political ambitions in the freshly unified Italy. Marriage is equally as central to the narrative presented in *The Job*, an episode of the portmanteau film *Boccaccio '70* (1961) filmed just prior to *The Leopard*. Visconti visually connects the two works in *The Job*, in which we see a German translation of Lampedusa's book lying on the sofa during one scene.

The Job is based on Guy de Maupassant's short story *Au bord du lit* (*On the Edge of the Bed*), a satire about the count and countess of Sallure, who come to an agreement they find financially and sexually satisfying. To the count's criticisms that the countess is flirting with another man, she responds with terms of a potential contract. Rather than support his various mistresses, who come at a considerable cost to their family, the count will instead pay her a hefty sum in exchange for a "little debauchery." In doing so, she argues, he will be making a sound financial decision, keeping his money under his own roof while receiving the same benefits. Maupassant's story is mainly told through the dialogue between husband and wife, whose lively ribaldry constitutes the story's real enjoyment. *The Job* transports this running dialogue to film, capturing the conversation between Count Ottavio (Tomas Milian) and his young wife, Pupe (Romy Schneider), whose own agreement reflects that of the count and countess. Just as *The Leopard* displayed Prince Fabrizio in the ornate trappings of the nineteenth-century Sicilian nobility, *The Job* depicts the contemporary aristocratic world of Milan, introducing a world with which Visconti was personally familiar. Like they would with *The Leopard*, critics immediately made autobiographical connections between the director and his fictional aristocrats, noting the multiform ways the main characters seemed to speak for the director. Indeed, *The Leopard* and *The Job* mark a shift away from the street-level point of view of the lower classes that characterized *Obsession*, *The Earth Trembles*, *Bellissima*, and *Rocco and His Brothers*, to the palaces of the rich and highborn that were also featured in subsequent films from *Sandra* to *The Intruder*. Already in *Senso* a few years prior, autobiographical notes of a patrician worldview raised questions of subjectivity in an already complex cinematic network of reference and allusion.

The Job takes place entirely in the count's Milanese apartment, where he has assembled a team of lawyers in the opulently appointed library to strategize his response to an unfolding scandal. The count's private visitations to call girls has become public knowledge through the local tabloids. If his wife leaves him (as her father recommends), he will be financially ruined, exposing their marriage as one in which the count has peddled the prestige of his aristocratic title for the financial stability offered by his wife's family. "The real marriage is between you and Papa," Pupe remarks, "and as a matter of fact, he's the one who's gotten mad" (Visconti 1970b, 291).

By indicating the very public nature of the scandal that appears in the newspaper that the Count nervously reads and makes reference to, the film reflects on the Italian tabloid industry, also prevalent in films like *Roman Holiday* (William Wyler, 1953) and *La Dolce Vita* (Federico

Figure 5.3. Pupe regarding herself in the mirror from *The Job* (Luchino Visconti, 1962).

Fellini, 1960). In the film, the tabloid becomes one strand in a media web—telegrams, phone calls, letters, radio—that intrude on the characters' conversations and private moments, redirecting their movements throughout the apartment. Such disruptions are portrayed as modern inconveniences that exacerbate the split between husband and wife, already beset by the communicative challenges inherent to marriage (Pupe comments: "Don't think . . . that when I got married I had any illusions about breaking down the barriers of noncommunication. I knew perfectly well I'd be hideously alone"). These technological channels to the outside world invade the elaborate interiors of the apartment, its style and grandeur denoting an older way of patrician life. The elegant interiors, flush with antiquities and paintings, oppose the crass materialism of modern tabloid culture while lending authenticity of setting. For Visconti, the lavish items in the mansion and haute couture of the characters was no mere decoration but was fundamental to rendering the essence of their marital predicament: "These rooms, these sofas covered with turtle-dove velvet, this library of authentic, 19th century French oak, these abstracts by Domietta Hercolani, all that can be seen and is framed by Rotunno's camera, represents the world in which the main characters operate, a cold and precious world, deprived of that soul that Tomas and Romy pursue, but never manage to commit to" (Rondolino 2003, 425). The same "precious world" from *The Job* reappears in *The Leopard* in splendid historical fashion, pointing to a corollary approach to book-to-film transformation, where literary elements breathe new life in cinematic form. Suso Cecchi D'Amico and Visconti center *The Job* on two moments from Maupassant's story—the countess regarding herself in the mirror, and the count rising up to put his hands on the nape of her neck—that are reproduced in the sequence in which Pupe prepares for and then exits the bath. Their insignificant gestures, woven into the background of Maupassant's story, gain new prominence in their cinematic rendition ("That which in the literary original occupied a background position," Vincenzo Buccheri comments, "in the film passes decisively into the foreground; that which was decentered here becomes centered"; 2000, 190). This realism of this interior space is further complicated by Visconti's autobiographical references, which he inserts throughout the film. "Pupe" is the name Visconti used for Irma Windisch-Grätz, a Bohemian princess to whom he was briefly engaged in his youth. Pupe also comments on a meeting at La Scala with "Wally," a reference to Visconti's childhood friend Wally Toscanini, then makes reference to "the guys from Ghisolfa," signifying the work by Testori adapted to film in

Rocco and His Brothers (Rondolino 2003, 428–29). The director adds a tongue-in-cheek nod to his old friend Coco Chanel when Count Ottavio asks Pupe about her shirt, and she replies: "Chanel. It's old. More than a month." That this short film on an unhappy marriage would contain these autobiographical tidbits implicates Visconti's world in the satire. Hints of autobiography survived the transition from the Milanese aristocrat of *The Job* to the Sicilian noble of *The Leopard*, making *The Job* into something of a prologue to *The Leopard*. Presenting the main character (the aristocrat) along with the main theme (marriage between old and new) is further developed in the historical setting of the Risorgimento, adapted from Lampedusa's novel.

Readers at the Theater: History, Heritage, and Historical Films

In an interview with Guido Aristarco published in *Cinema Nuovo* in 1960, Visconti addressed the changing landscape of Italian film tastes, remarking how audiences were finally bridging the gap between movie theater and arthouse, entertainment and art:

> Aristarco: So, the public, like critics, has changed their attitude towards your work, becoming more sensible and mature? Without a doubt, this development has taken on various shapes over the past few years.
>
> Visconti: Until very recently, the public was amenable to any product, but most of all they wanted easy things that didn't cause alarm or fear or anguish, and fortunately that public is no longer present, or, better yet, is still present, but only partially. It seems to me that there has been an evolution in this regard, in the exploration of certain themes that are more pressing, more actual, and also emotions that are truer, deeper, and more sincere. (Gremigni 2009, 248)

The Leopard put its intent to reach this larger, more sophisticated audience on full display from the time Visconti took over the project from Ettore Giannini, whose screenplay was commissioned and then rejected by Goffredo Lombardo at Titanus. Ironically, Lombardo allegedly thought Giannini's *The Leopard* would be too expensive to make (Argentieri 2013,

360). On why Lombardo rejected Giannini's script, D'Amico commented: "[Giannini] had written a free adaptation of *The Leopard*, a sort of Sicilian fantasy much like his *Neapolitan Carousel*, while Lombardo wanted something that reflected the book that had also had a lot of success abroad" (D'Amico 1996, 107). *The Leopard* was an Italian-French coproduction between Titanus and Pathé that was distributed internationally by 20th Century Fox, who successfully lobbied to cast Hollywood star Burt Lancaster in the leading role. *The Leopard* was among other expensive Titanus productions during the early 1960s that ultimately led to the company's insolvency. Lombardo blamed Visconti's profligacy as the culprit for its failure, but others pointed to Robert Aldrich's epic *Sodom and Gomorrah* (1962) for Titanus's financial difficulties. Enrico Lucherini suggested that the Titanus failure was part of a broader crisis that included other films, such as Dino Brusati's *Disorder* (Anile and Giannice 2013b, 252). Titanus put its stock in such projects to meet spectator demands for film epics, or *kolossal*, that were then at their most popular with Italian audiences. In 1963–1964, *The Leopard* was one of the five top grossing films that were epics, including *Cleopatra* (Joseph L. Mankiewicz), *Lawrence of Arabia* (David Lean), *How the West Was Won* (John Ford), and *55 Days at Peking* (Nicholas Ray). Although not as relevant with mass audiences as these epics, adaptations also experienced a banner year in 1963, performing particularly well on the awards circuit. At Cannes, for example, *The Leopard* competed with several other notable adaptations, including *To Kill a Mockingbird* (Robert Mulligan), *Lord of the Flies* (Peter Brooks), *Whatever Happened to Baby Jane* (Robert Aldrich), and *This Sporting Life* (Lindsay Anderson).

Visconti helped energize historical films during these years, and *Senso* and *The Leopard* represent groundbreaking works that broke with a certain conservatism in cinematic representations of Italian unification (Casadio 1997, 11). Each was a key chapter in movies based on Italy's wars for independence, using nineteenth-century history to reflect on more recent events of fascism, the resistance, and the postwar order in Italy (Castello 1963; Sorlin 1980). *The Leopard* was part of an august subcategory of unification films—called Risorgimento films—that represented the events leading toward Italian independence in 1861 (Lasi and Sangiori 2011, 175–78). Garibaldi's 1860 Sicilian landing, called the Expedition of the Thousand, was perhaps the most mythologized moment of this unification process and was also depicted in Rossellini's *Viva l'italia!*, released just before *The Leopard* as part of Italy's centennial celebrations in 1961. As he had with *Senso*, Visconti began with a reading of Gramsci, made obvious by the film's critical reading of defeat in Italian history (Landy 1996, 128). As mentioned already, the publication of Gramsci's *Prison Notebooks* between 1947 and 1951 was an important event in reconsiderations of unification, fomenting a revolution of its own in Italian historiography. Gramsci believed that unification amounted to a passive revolution in which a new political order was established without significantly modifying existing social relations. Using the term *transformism*, Gramsci referred to the peculiar coupling between revolution and restoration that emerged during Italy's battle for independence, in which political opposition was co-opted into a governing union by established powers interested in stabilizing the new Italian state. To attach this pessimistic viewpoint on unification to *The Leopard*, Visconti started by condensing Lampedusa's timeline to bracket the film narrative between Garibaldi's landing at Marsala in May 1860 and the Battle of Aspromonte in August 1862. He excised chapter 5 (Padre Pirrone's visit to his village) and Lampedusa's final two chapters (chapter 7, dedicated to the prince's death in July 1883, and chapter 8 on the aged Angelica in May 1910), adding greater weight to the crucial beginnings of the unification period. Simultaneously, eliminating these chapters muted the nostalgic conclusion of the novel, which Lampedusa filled with regret and sympathy for the decaying aristocracy. However, the film conserved Tancredi's position as a central narrative axis point, stationed between the Bourbon past and the Garibaldian future. As Gregory Lucente remarks with regards to Tancredi's position in the novel, "in a way, then, Tancredi would seem to furnish an almost miraculous bridge back to the world, the mediation through which Don Fabrizio may at once retain the essence of his past and win the future" (Lucente 1978, 86). Lampedusa constructs an interior system of bisected allegiances to give attention to the historical contrast between past and future, while positioning Tancredi's modernity, versatility, and youthful ebullience as a counterpoint to Fabrizio's antiquity and static loyalties and the fatigue of his advancing age. In the film, the excision of Lampedusa's conclusion came with the significant addition of the Battle of Palermo, a historic battle for Sicily's capital, in a spectacular scene that does not appear in the book, bringing the details of history further into relief (fig. 5.4). Visconti captures this exciting moment of revolutionary triumph in all its martial glory.

With Tancredi leading the uprising, a Sicilian aristocrat is connected to the popular spirit of overthrow. When Tancredi pursues and then marries Angelica, he becomes an optimistic champion of the historical change that will stabilize his position in Italy's post-Risorgimento

Figure 5.4. Tancredi and the Battle of Palermo.

order. Uncoincidentally, Tancredi is the one who declares the novel's most famous dictum, "For things to remain the same, everything must change," a phrase that introduces a circular form that is taken up formally by Lampedusa in the first chapter of the novel, where the paradigm of circularity is introduced (Materassi 1972, 547). The marriage between Tancredi and Angelica soon makes Tancredi's break with the past permanent, and mingling his bloodline with that of the upstart house of Sedàra secures a pact with the future that seems to usher in Fabrizio's death. When Tancredi is pictured riding alongside his reactionary father-in-law at the end of the film, the alliance between bourgeoisic and aristocracy is bitterly consummated, the two listening approvingly to the gunshots that execute the same rebels with whom Tancredi was fighting just a short time before. Tancredi's transformation complete, Fabrizio slowly meanders away from Italy's future, in what Visconti called "a torturous and heart breaking meeting with the light of the dawn stars" (Visconti 1963, 26). As he did in *Senso*, Visconti viewed *The Leopard* through Italy's more recent experience with fascism: "Reading *The Leopard*, did you ever ask yourself if a man like Tancredi one day could have said yes not only to the repression of the revolt of '96, but even to Fascism? I posed this question to myself and must say that the light that Lampedusa shed on the affirmative response upset me" (Visconti 1963, 29)

That Visconti chose to stitch these historical, literary, and political intertexts together in the form of a large-scale costume drama returns to the question of adapting bestseller to blockbuster. The film version of *The Leopard* is dominated by the long ballroom scene in the Palazzo

Ponteleone that takes up a quarter of the film. The elaborate interiors of the palace and ballroom render history in a hallucinatory sequence of musical and visual repetitions, with the film scene becoming a microcosm for all of the dominant themes from the book including but not limited to the politics of the kingdom of Italy, the transformism of the new leading classes, the opportunism of the new landowning bourgeoisie, class skepticism, high-bourgeois and aristocratic materialism, and falling in love as an uncontrollable instinctuality (Micciché 1996b, 190). To fit this array of components in a single scene, Visconti vastly overdetermined the ballroom sequence in the economy of the film. Unlike in the novel, where the dance at Palazzo Ponteleone lasts approximately twenty pages (about one-twelfth of the book), the ball dominates 178 of the film's 725 shots, equaling 46 minutes of a 185-minute film, about a quarter of its running time (Bacon 1998, 91). Such a meticulous approach recalls Marcel Proust's detailed descriptions of social occasions. In *The Guermantes Way*, a work in which 525 pages stand for two and a half years, Proust dedicated 110 pages to recount a two- to three-hour dinner (Bacon 1998, 91–92). Visconti's superabundance in *The Leopard* led 20th Century Fox to shred the Italian version on the cutting room floor, bringing Geoffrey Nowell-Smith to quip that the US version of this sequence "is an indefinable mixture of the ball in *The Big Country* [William Wyler, 1958] and a fancy-dress party in a small town in the Mid-West" (Nowell-Smith 2003, 80). The obsessive patterning and excessive length of the sequence accentuates the film's two great themes, one political, the other aesthetic: Italy's political transformism, symbolized through the pairing of Angelica and Tancredi; and the decadent musing on the passage of time and mortality by way of Prince Fabrizio, whose alienation and fading vitality are punctuated by the encounter with Jean-Baptiste Greuze's painting *Le fils puni* (*The Son Punished*, 1778) in one of the ballroom scene's quieter moments. The fanatical ornamentation of the palazzo, Piero Tosi's extraordinary costumes, and the constant, relentless diegetic music seem to move the scene beyond any simple correlation with transformism or the theme of death, although Visconti translates the abundance of patterns that characterizes Lampedusa's original work in a distinctly musical fashion. The ballroom scene is also carefully framed by two carriage rides, and it is significant that Visconti structurally uses these two departing groups to frame the final microsection of the film in a notably Gramscian terminology. The first, just prior to the commencement of the diegetic music, features the departure of Chevalley de Monterzuolo, a representative from the north who comes to offer Fabrizio a role in Italy's new government. Chevalley ventriloquizes the typical tropes of postunification political stability, trying to convert Fabrizio and other wealthy and influential figures to the national cause, but Fabrizio decides not to accept, resigning himself to a passive place. Conversely, once the ballroom scene concludes, Tancredi, Angelica, and Don Calogero are seen departing in their carriage (fig. 5.5) when shots ring out, pointing to the revolutionaries being executed. Unlike the various denizens of the ball (Fabrizio included) whose ancient customs are indicative of their inescapable association with the past, this triumvirate represents the future leaders of Sicily, who will do whatever is necessary in the interest of creating a functioning state—even killing the revolutionaries who helped bring unification about.

At various times, Visconti noted his intent to "marxify" Lampedusa, whose novel's Sicilian perspective Visconti believed to already be consistent with Gramsci's interpretation of the Risorgimento, and he simply needed bring it out in his film (Rondolino 2003, 434). In doing so, he redeemed a progressive historical interpretation latent in Lampedusa, recrafting *The Leopard* to fit his views of Italian unification, which were undercutting the myth of Italy's heroic formation. Commenting on traditional narratives of Italian history, Visconti provides a work that would be common to the historical film genre as studied by Robert Burgoyne, who notes that such a film "critiques the way in which history is conventionally represented" (Burgoyne 2008, 43). *The Leopard* is what Robert Rosenstone would call a "history film"; a "fictional drama that not only devotes itself consciously to constructing a world of the past on screen, but in doing so manages to engage the discourse of history, the

Figure 5.5. Angelica and Tancredi leave the ball in a carriage.

body of data and debates surrounding any historical topic" (Rosenstone 2016, 71–72). Although *The Leopard*'s rewriting of the Risorgimento certainly undermines the conservative narrative of national unity, one must also recognize how *The Leopard*, like *Senso* before it, also features some of the defining characteristics of another, less politically left critical category: the heritage film, a maligned designation not often associated with Italian cinema. As mentioned above, this category is often linked to the Merchant Ivory Productions films *A Room with a View* (1985) and *Maurice* (1987), works directed by James Ivory and produced by Ismail Merchant that spotlighted their status as adaptations of Forster novels. As Andrew Higson notes, this was typical: "In each case, the 'original' text is as much on display as the past it seeks to reproduce. The literary source material, of course, functions as an important selling point, playing on the familiarity and prestige of the particular novel or play, but also invoking the pleasures of other such quality literary adaptations and the status of a national intellectual tradition" (Higson 1993, 115). The same can be said of *The Leopard*, where Visconti and Titanus placed the literary source at the center of the promotion of the film. *The Leopard* contains many of the identifying marks of the heritage film: its basis in a contemporary literary classic of historical fiction, its big-name director and star cast, the suggestion of its "European" artistic quality, a large budget, the use of classical music, and the appearance of an extravagant mise-en-scène that includes detailed period costumes and a meticulously researched decor. All anticipate the surface pleasures of the English heritage films of the of the 1980s and 1990s (Vincendeau 2001, xviii). Although the criticism of (rather than glorification of) Italian history in *Senso* and *The Leopard* might disqualify them as unlikely heritage films, the overall emphasis on style, indulgence in the artifacts of historical reconstruction, and nostalgic overtones are unmistakable (Marlow-Mann 2016, 47–48).

In my view, elements of the heritage film need not deny that Visconti's film engages with the Marxist-inflected discourse. How he did so, however, introduces some of the problems of the historical film genre introduced by other Italian films set in the Risorgimento. The permeability of the Italian historical film by other cinematic genres had already been illustrated by the unification films of 1952, where *Camicie rosse* (*Red Shirts*, Goffredo Alessandrini and Francesco Rosi), *Eran trecento* (*There Were Three Hundred*, Gian Paolo Callegari), and *Il brigante di Tacca del Lupo* (*The Bandit of Tacca del Lupo*, Pietro Germi) recount the unification story through the filter of the film western, resulting in what Paolo Noto refers to as the "western of our nation" (Noto 2011, 93). As Vito Zagarrio observes, *The Leopard* also features sequences that seem borrowed from Hollywood westerns, aided by Lancaster's work in the genre: the carriage trip to Donnafugata is shot like a wagon train scene with Tancredi on horseback like a western hero (Zagarrio 1996b, 66–67) (fig. 5.6).

Viewed from outside of the context of Italian-specific debates over political engagements in literature and film, *The Leopard* reflects the transnational interest in historical films, adaptations, and the combination of the two that was characteristic of the early 1960s, in politics and spectacle-rooted films from around the world. From Hollywood, *Lawrence of Arabia* garnered Best Picture and Best Director (among other awards) at the Academy Awards, and with *Mutiny on the Bounty* (Lewis Millstone and Carol Reed, 1962) popularized Technicolor in the Hollywood historical epic. As Marco Pistoia remarks, notions of high and low are simply part of the broader dialectics that operate in a Visconti film: "Like other opposing couples—beauty and ugliness, youth and old age, rich and poor, order and disorder, splendor and decadence, love and hate—'high' and 'low' are elements—though at varying levels—that are constantly present in the work of Luchino Visconti" (Pistoia 2008, 227). Balancing high and low from *The Leopard* reached a new precariousness in his next adaptation, the Nazi film *The Damned*, where the "low" figurations of kitsch and camp aggressively entered Visconti's filmography in the figure of the queer Nazi.

Figure 5.6. The wagon train to Donnafugata.

6

La caduta degli dei (*Götterdämmerung*) (*The Damned,* 1969)

A Queer Macbeth in Nazi Uniform

> The story you have sent me is, in my opinion, instead, a very gimmicky one which doesn't transfer the grandeur of Shakespeare but only makes a big effort to follow the plot mechanically with characters who are shadows and pale imitations of Shakespeare's ones. In other words, if I can give you an example, it is like a painting inspired by a landscape and another painting which is just a copy of the first one. The murder, which in Macbeth made a great impact, in the present modern story is, in my opinion, forced and silly.
>
> —Letter from Joseph Janni to Luchino Visconti, May 19, 1967

Given that Shakespeare represents the most commonly adapted author in the history of cinema, it comes as no surprise that as notable an adaptor as Visconti would incubate a Shakespearean film for many years. Visconti viewed Shakespeare's *Macbeth* (1606) as a story that was strongly suited to structuring an account of Nazism, what

Figure 6.1. Sophie dead on the couch in *The Damned* (Luchino Visconti, 1969).

he called "a great tragedy, that, like a bloodstain, flowed throughout the entire world" (Visconti 1969, 14). In *The Damned* (1969), a film about a family of German industrialists, Shakespearean themes of prophecy, betrayal, and ambition provided stable footing. *Macbeth* was also part of a problematic film that is, at least among critics, considered to be one of Visconti's most vexing, least appreciated works. As much as it is ignored by scholars today, it was disliked by critics when it was released.

A summary of the film's many characters, convoluted plot, and ties with *Macbeth* is useful for understanding some of the criticism the film received. Baron Joachim von Essenbeck is a modern Duncan who hands control of the family steelworks to his nephew Konstantin, a Nazi Banquo, whose connection to Ernst Röhm and the Sturmabteilung (SA) promises a safeguard for the family business during Hitler's reign. After news arrives that the Reichstag is burning (this occurred on the night between February 27 and 28, 1933), the historical pretext for Hitler's consolidation of power triggers a similar scheme for control in the von Essenbeck family. As in previous Visconti films, history is conveyed through the family unit, here an allegory for historical developments outside of Italy (Baldelli 1982, 261). Herbert, who like Joachim is against National Socialism, plays an unfortunate Macduff who is framed for Joachim's murder and must escape, leaving behind his wife, Elisabeth (Lady Macduff), and two daughters, who are sent to die in the concentration camp at Dachau. The culprits for Joachim's murder are actually Friedrich and Sophie—the ambitious Macbeth and Lady Macbeth—who know that Joachim's demise will elevate Sophie's son, Martin, to Konstantin's position of power. Martin (Malcolm in *Macbeth*) is Joachim's grandson, the child of the baron's only son (who died in World War I). With Martin's rise to head of the steelworks, the nefarious Friedrich and Sophie are convinced that Friedrich's position will be secured. They are mistaken: Martin falls under the thumb of Aschenbach, a demon-like member of the Schutzstaffel (SS) who takes the role of *Macbeth*'s three witches by predicting Friedrich's rise and ultimate demise. When Konstantin is killed during the SS purge of the SA during the beer-fueled orgy of the Night of the Long Knives (June 29 and 30, 1934), Martin and Aschenbach orchestrate a suicide by cyanide from which Friedrich and Sophie will die on their wedding night. In this decadent inversion of the Wagnerian conclusion, heroic Siegfried and Brunnhilde become the degraded Adolf Hitler and Eva Braun: debased rather than glorified symbols of the disintegration of Germany and the von Essenbeck family.

The Damned is a claustrophobic picture that includes representations of mass murder, pedophilia, incest, rape, drug addiction, matricide, patricide, and child suicide, which together with the entangled plot make it one of the more difficult Visconti films to countenance. Italian reviewers like Anna Banti and Pier Paolo Pasolini criticized its excessive violence, while in the United States, *The Damned* was panned for its campy theatrics and poor dubbing (Banti 1969; Pasolini 1969; Crowdus 1970). Critics ultimately agreed that Visconti failed to accurately explore the historical rise of Nazism, allowing the frameworks of history to retreat into the background or, as Guido Aristarco claimed, be converted into an infernal sickness. "Visconti would like to be both poet and critic of decadence at the same time," Aristarco wrote, "but the poet ultimately eliminates the critic; decadence, while denounced, is viewed with extreme grandeur, as a fascinating and beautiful illness" (Aristarco 1969b, 6). Others thought the film revealed more about Visconti's artistic mien than the true causes of the Nazi phenomenon (B.T. 1969/1970). Visconti countered these interpreters in an interview with Stefano Roncoroni from 1969, foregrounding *The Damned* as a critique of fascism in which Nazism was "the final phase of capitalism in the world" (*LV*, 130).

Despite its negative reception among critics, *The Damned* was a popular hit when it was released, marking Visconti's third blockbuster of the decade. It was second only to *Nell'anno del signore* (*The Conspirators*, Luigi Magni) at the Italian box office in 1969–1970, with these two large-scale productions garnering a massive 23.5 percent of all domestic ticket sales that year. *The Damned* was marketed for its "unabashed sensationalism" and "zestful vulgarity," featuring what one reviewer called "one of the most blood-thirsty five minutes ever to be shown on film" (Tarrett 1970, 44). Reflecting a loosening of censorship and a lessening of Catholic influences in Italy after 1968, Italian auteurs in the late 1960s featured an increasingly frank approach to sexuality, nudity, and explicit themes designed for their "shock" effect (Wood 2005, 61). This sexual sensationalism is foregrounded almost immediately in *The Damned* with the introduction of the character Martin (Helmut Berger), seen performing in drag (fig. 6.2). This is no generic display of transvestment but a metacinematic impersonation of Marlene Dietrich, who memorably sang the same song "Kinder, heut' abend, da such' ich mir was aus" ("Children, This Evening I'll Choose Something for Me")—in Josef von Sternberg's *Der blaue Engel* (*The Blue Angel*, 1930).

In that film, Dietrich's performance toys with heterosexual norms in "a playful, ironic imitation of the conventions of femininity and masculinity," embodying the excessive theatricalization, self-reflexivity, and commercial appeal that were foundational components of camp (Mayne 2000, 16). In *The Damned*, Martin's drag performance inaugurated a tour through sexual deviance, ambiguity, nudity, and violence that marked this character throughout the rest of the film and attracted accusations of obscenity.

Visconti suggested *The Damned* was not particularly offensive. When asked about perversion in the film, he replied, "Well, there are a number of scenes in the New American Cinema that make the one between Helmut and Ingrid look tame—like a family matter. What happened in Andy Warhol's *Trash* was a little stronger than incest, wouldn't you say?" (Cardullo 2011, 6). *The Damned*'s connection between Nazism and non-heteronormative sexuality, however, was soon followed by other Italian portrayals of the sexually deviant Nazi, as in Liliana Cavani's psychological thriller *Il portiere di notte* (*The Night Porter*, 1974) and Pasolini's *Salò e le 120 giornate di Sodoma* (*Salò or the 120 Days of Sodom*, 1974). These "high" representations of sexualized Nazis by established Italian auteur filmmakers became fundamental models for the "low" *sadiconazista* (sadistic Nazi) subgenre of Nazi exploitation films that subsequently bloomed into provocatively titled works such as *La bestia in calore* (*Beast in Heat*, Luigi Batzella, 1977), *L'ultima orgia del III Reich* (*The Last Orgy of the Third Reich*, Cesare Canevari, 1977), and *Ilsa: She Wolf of the SS*

Figure 6.2. Spanish film poster of *The Damned* depicting the scene in which Martin performs Dietrich.

(Don Edmonds, 1975). These soft-core, sexploitation B-films, formulaic illustrations of BDSM, were produced in Italy and successfully marketed internationally, where they were promoted for representing sensational acts of sex and violence based on those "real" ones allegedly committed during the Third Reich. Two of *The Damned*'s lead actors, Helmut Berger and Ingrid Thulin, provide a direct link between Visconti's film and one of this genre cycle's most notorious illustrations, *Salon Kitty* (1976), made by the director Tinto Brass, who later filmed another period piece sexploitation picture and international box-office hit, *Caligula* (1979). In *Salon Kitty*, set in 1939, Berger and Thulin reprise their roles as malevolent, sexualized Nazis. Berger play an SS chief tasked with Aryanizing one of Berlin's most frequented brothels, run by the madame played by Thulin. Berger's character converts the brothel into a surveillance post through which he (and we, the spectators) can peep in and observe an array of outrageous sexual acts committed by Nazi officials. Both *The Damned* and *Salon Kitty* depict the internecine tensions in the Nazi rank and file together with Nazi sexual otherness, and *Salon Kitty*'s conclusion represents something of an inversion of *The Damned*, with Thulin's maternal character metaphorically avenging her murder at the end of Visconti's film by framing Berger's character and having him killed.

The Damned was notable not just for its depiction of Nazi deviance but also as an adaptation. Like *Rocco and His Brothers* and *Sandra*, this film is a hybrid work, mixing a constellation of textual borrowings and appropriations. Characters, settings, and themes were appropriated from Thomas Mann's *Buddenbrooks* (1901) and *Death in Venice* (1912), Richard Hughes's *The Fox in the Attic* (1961), Dostoevsky's *The Demons* (1871), and Shakespeare's *Macbeth*. Shades of *Hamlet* (1609) also appear when the "king" is murdered at the beginning of the film (Bellocchio 2006, 18–19). These literary sources were fused with events from German history of the 1930s that Visconti gleaned from the pages of William Shirer's *The Rise and Fall of the Third Reich* (1960), a book that chronicles the Bavarian industrialist family Krupp, who served as real-life models for the von Essenbecks. The film's full title, *La caduta degli dei: Götterdämmerung* (Twilight of the Gods) invokes Richard Wagner's fourth opera of the Ring Cycle, as well as Nietzsche's *Götzen-dämmerung*, in which the philosopher rails against cultural decadence in Germany and elsewhere. These are a few of the great number of textual and cultural reference points for the film, creating a textual landscape some critics found confusing (Bondanella 2004, 204).

Of these literary and cultural references, *Macbeth* is easiest to identify and certainly the most important. I examine how *Macbeth* intertwined with the cinematic representation of the queer Nazi that became popular in Italian cinema at the time. Through Shakespeare's figure of Lady Macbeth, an exemplary queer literary character who defies norms of femininity and motherhood to support her husband's pursuit of power, *Macbeth* offers an approach to otherness and evil that Visconti channeled in *The Damned*. Transferring Lady Macbeth's queer potential to the character Martin, a pedophile who rapes and then kills his mother, Visconti crafts a dark, complex symbol of extreme sexual otherness that explores the boundaries around notions of queer, a term that eschews fixity and unity. Critics of *The Damned* vilified Martin's difference, listing a variety of epithets from "abnormal" to "depraved with disquieting beauty" (Giori 2012, 126–27). Through the character played by Helmut Berger, the director introduces his own status as a gay auteur, whose "gay sensibility" added to the queer (and camp) qualities of the film. (For the problematic interpretations of "low" and "high" camp in the film, see Giori 2012, 138–51.) In its baroque array of literary, autobiographical, and cinematic intertexts, *The Damned* becomes a model of queer adaptation, one that is redeployed in the film that followed it, *Death in Venice* (1971).

Macbeth, Titan of Industry: Visconti and a Modern Shakespeare

The Damned satisfied at least two of Visconti's long-held intentions. The first was to make a film about the rise and fall of an industrialist family that traced history from the nineteenth century to the postwar period. Between 1946 and 1951, he and Antonio Pietrangeli worked on a project about a multigenerational film titled "A Film on the Milanese Bourgeoisie," split into three parts and modeled loosely on Visconti's mother's family. The film was to begin with the industrialization of Lombardy, in which the family transitions their ancestral estate to a modern industrial complex, then it would portray the eventual ruin of the family business, concluding with one youngster's attempt to lift the company from the ashes by reestablishing "contact with reality and men whom his family, enclosed in a dynastic egoism, had disregarded and ignored" (Pietrangeli and Visconti 1976, 75). Tracing this wealthy family's lineage as it crossed the end of the century suggests the works of Thomas Mann; the film becomes a sort of Milanese *Buddenbrooks* with a hopeful ending.

Visconti's second purpose was to adapt a Shakespeare work to film. Shakespeare was part of his reading while he was incarcerated in the San Gregorio prison in 1944, accused by the fascists of clandestine activities with the Roman resistance. Traces of a treatment for a film on *Othello* from that same year evolved into *Otello, Il Moro di Venezia* (*Othello, the Moor of Venice*), written with Antonio Pietrangeli (Bellocchio 2008, 70–71). Theater adaptations of *As You Like It* (1948), panned for its perceived break with neorealism, and *Troilus and Cressida* (1949) demonstrate Visconti's early interest in Shakespeare's works for Italian theater. During preparations for *The Damned*, Visconti was slated to direct a version of *Othello* for the Maggio Musicale Fiorentino Festival of 1968, but it never came to be. Moreover, after filming *The Stranger* (1967), he and D'Amico prepared a treatment for a film called *Macbeth 1967* to be produced by Atlantisfilm that certainly influenced the shape and character of *The Damned. Macbeth 1967* opens with a reunion held by Italy's most important industrialist, Duncan, to announce a new administrator to take the reins of his vast business holdings. There, the protagonist Macbeth encounters a group of beautiful "witches" in a swimming pool who tell him that he will be nominated over the more anticipated selection, Banquo. When their prophecy comes true, Macbeth's bloody ascendance to power is set in motion. He frames the murder of Duncan and Banquo as accidents; he shoots Duncan during a hunting trip, then kills Banquo by loosening the tires of his Mercedes. After urging her husband to take action, Lady Macbeth displays her guilt and symptoms of insanity by washing her hands ("They are dirty, I got them dirty, I'm not sure how. I'll wash them. I'm washing them, see?") and is soon found dead of a barbiturate overdose. The story ends with Macbeth pursued in his car by the marshal Macduff, who has been investigating the strange deaths. After a brief chase, Macbeth shoots himself rather than be captured.

A subsequent 1968 treatment written in preparation of a script for *The Damned* highlights how the Shakespearean elements of *Macbeth 1967* became an integral part of the film's literary and historical apparatus (*FV*, 7, 36, 40). In terms familiar to Visconti's filmography, the director describes the project as "the story of a family's end. A family of gods . . . Money is the instrument of their power, the great factory full of smokestacks is the temple of their cult" (*FV*, 7, 36, document 40, 3). The section titled "Literary and Historical Precedents for Our Film" discusses *Macbeth*'s transferability from epoch to epoch. Shakespeare's tragedy "belongs to every era," it reads, and "across the centuries has conserved the actuality of its material and its psychological mechanism intact." Having considered the basis of the tragedy—Macbeth's ambition, urged on by circumstance, prophecy, and his wife—Visconti pondered how Germany from 1933 to 1934 reenacted it and helped revert civilization from the twentieth century back into "the medieval night:"

> Let us now imagine, for a moment, that the protagonist of our story not only resembles Macbeth, but also Hitler; that the old president of a steelworks not only resembles kind Duncan, but also the decrepit Hindenberg; that the protagonist's rival not only resembles Banquo, the general from the Shakespearean tragedy, but also Röhm, Hitler's friend and brother. Let us also imagine that a young Hitlerian, extravagant and ambiguous, mad and prophetic, cultured and violent, is both he who pushes the protagonist and a synthesis of Shakespeare's three witches: and we will find ourselves in the new climate of tragedy. (*FV*, 7, 36, 40, 10)

Although the document goes on to question why the film will focus on the family (written to resemble the "great Nordic family sagas") and establishes Wagner's *Götterdammerung* as a key intertext ("the most authentically German, closest to the moment in which the events occur"), this fusion of literature and history evokes *Senso* and *The Leopard* and adaptations in historical settings. Yet *The Damned*'s difference from these films is found not only in its location outside of Italy and its historical context of the rise of National Socialism but in its presentation of sexual abnormality.

Mother to Son: *The Damned*'s Queer Inheritance

At the point of intersection between the project on a family of Lombardy industrialists, the script for *Macbeth 1967*, and the 1968 treatment for *The Damned* sits the remarkable figure of the queer heir to the industrialist throne. In the Visconti-Pietrangeli project, the two outlined this character as "a fragile boy, aimlessly impulsive, [with] an over-refined sensibility that leaves him disturbed and unable to support the increasingly heavy weight of the mammoth industry" (Pietrangeli and Visconti 1976, 75). Later on, the youngster is described as possessing the qualities of a potential artist, "a fanatic prodigal son who exhausts himself in impossible dreams and absurd projects: a meteor that passes without leaving anything more than its ephemeral flicker" (75). (This description matches the character Ludwig from the historical biopic *Ludwig* [1972], the story of Bavarian King Ludwig II and his ruinous exploration of aesthetic delight.) This figure of the weak heir, unsuited to the task at hand, found its Shakespearean equivalent in *Macbeth 1967*, where Duncan's son Malcolm is described as "a beautiful lad, clever, mad" who his father suspects may not be his own (D'Amico and Visconti 1976, 56). After Malcolm has been caught up in some unidentified wrongdoing, he fulminates at his father: "I hope he dies! It is what we all want. He's put us all in place to hope he dies as soon as possible" (60). This cruelty of the young heir is paired with a decadent lifestyle in the 1968 treatment for *The Damned*, which describes the Martin/Malcolm character as immature and unpredictable: "He combines a fussy and evil infantilism with a blunt and diabolic senility, something that makes him appear simultaneously foolish and dangerous, fanatical and disenchanted, clever and boring . . . he drinks often and is surrounded by strange friends of questionable social extraction" (*FV*, 7, 36, 40, 19).

When we compare the character in these preparatory texts with Martin von Essenbeck in the film, we realize how Visconti combined industrialist saga with Shakespearean tragedy. Whereas Shakespeare's Malcolm is seen as a reflection of the benevolent Duncan, Visconti presents Martin as his grandfather's opposite. As cited already, Martin's depravity and difference are highlighted at the beginning of the film when the children perform for Joachim's birthday.

While Herbert's daughters recite a poem and Günther plays a song on his cello, Martin appears in drag (fig. 6.3) to perform Dietrich's song, an emblem of sexual otherness. Contrasted against Günther's solemn cello solo, Martin's performance suggests the debased, uncivilized popular culture of the Nazis as opposed to the German high culture of authors such as Goethe or Mann. Later, Günther is identified as an avid student

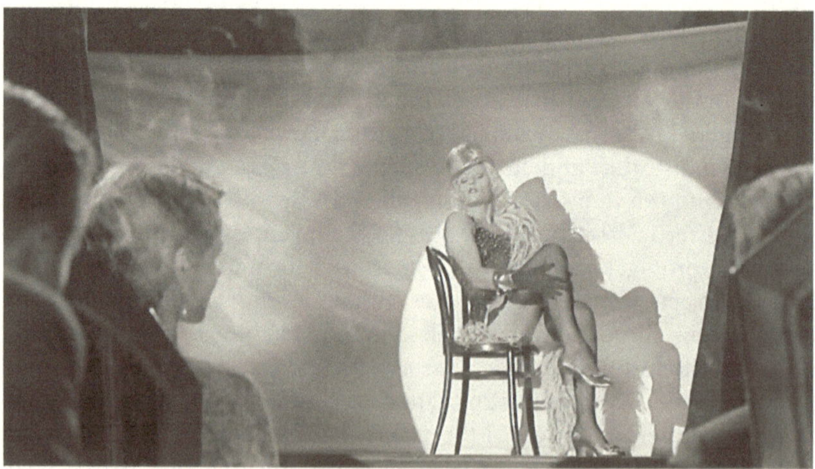

Figure 6.3. Martin's performance in drag at the beginning of *The Damned.*

of literature, who listens with dismay at the list of authors—many of them Visconti's personal favorites—whose books are banned by the Nazis. After his performance in drag, Martin kisses the child Thilde during a game of hide-and-seek, then she is heard screaming off camera. This hint of pedophilia is confirmed when Martin visits a local prostitute in a nearby tenement. There he abuses a young Jewish girl who lives next door and subsequently kills herself. Aschenbach's explanation to Martin that because she is Jewish, he need not worry about consequences, is one of the few references to the Shoah in Visconti's filmography. As Millicent Marcus notes, unlike other Italian films of the era, *The Damned* is similar to the earlier *Sandra* in that it does not take the Holocaust head on, echoing criticisms that Visconti was not focused enough on actual Nazism (Marcus 2007, 42–44).

Although pedophilia is just one of the aspects of Martin's perversity, it is a particularly egregious one and thus might require more scrutiny than it has been previously granted. The fear of pedophiles and the need to protect children from sexual deviancy are some of the most powerful themes in discourses on sexual otherness and can trigger moral panics more than other nonheteronormative sexual practices. In his pederastic dalliance at the prostitute's home, Martin becomes a crossroads for elements of Gayle Rubin's circle of "sexual hierarchy": promiscuity, nonprocreative sex, sex for money, sinfulness, and operating alone (Rubin 1984, 282). Rather than merely signifying another piece in the aggregation of queer behaviors, Martin's implication in the girl's suicide triggers the key turn in the film's plot, in which he becomes allied with Aschenbach and the SS against his mother and Friedrich. It directly leads to the rape and murder of his mother, Sophie, the Lady Macbeth character.

Establishing Sophie–Lady Macbeth as the mother of the deviant Martin-Malcolm (in the play, Malcolm is Duncan's son) underscores the character's difference found in Shakespeare's original text (Alfar 1998). In *Macbeth*, Lady Macbeth comes to exemplify a queering of gender convention. She has been regarded as a paradigmatic representation of female malevolence who undermines basic oppositions of male/female, active/passive, good/evil—binaries explored by Eve Sedgwick—through her unceasing pursuit of power. In two sections of the play, Lady Macbeth outlines her difference from conventional femininity. In act 1, scene 5, she pleads with her husband to take action against Duncan to realize the prophecy of the witches (these "strange sisters," also representing a bending of gender). Lady Macbeth associates Macbeth with breast-milk, accusing him of being "too full o'th'milk of human kindness" (1.5,

16), and thus politically passive and unwilling to take advantage of the opportunity before him (Sperry 2018, 37). Not only does Lady Macbeth feminize her husband, but she invites her own empowerment through the transformation of her breastmilk into poison:

> Lady Macbeth: Come, you spirits
> That tend on mortal thoughts, unsex me here,
> And fill me from the crown to the toe top-full
> Of direst cruelty! make thick my blood;
> Stop up the access and passage to remorse,
> That no compunctious visitings of nature
> Shake my fell purpose, nor keep peace between
> The effect and it! Come to my woman's breasts,
> And take my milk for gall, you murd'ring ministers
>
> 1.5, 39–46

Although short of inviting a sex change, in indicating her desire to be "unsexed," Lady Macbeth suggests that the sacrifice of her procreative capacities will be worthwhile to fulfill her and her husband's ambitions. This renunciation of motherhood is made most gruesome in a following scene, when Shakespeare subverts the figure of the nurturing mother through an infanticidal Lady Macbeth:

> Lady Macbeth: I have given suck, and know
> How tender 'tis to love the babe that milks me:
> I would, while it was smiling in my face,
> Have pluck'd my nipple from his boneless gums,
> And dash'd the brains out, had I so sworn as you
> Have done to this.
>
> 1.7, 54–58

These quotes accentuate Lady Macbeth as both the queerest of characters and cruelest of mothers. Whether appropriating masculine power or claiming a willingness to murder her own suckling child, these lines reveal a woman capable of doing whatever it takes to slake her thirst for power and achieve her political goal. In this way, Lady Macbeth is wrapped up in the fundaments of queerness: antinormative, bodily, subject to desires. Visconti will link these queer attributes of Shakespeare's maternal figure to Martin through his pairing with his mother, Sophie, especially in overdetermining the Oedipal nature of the mother–son relationship. Early in the film, Sophie suggest that she "knows what Martin desires" from the beginning, cradling him like a baby during the scene in which he declares that he will take over the steelworks from Konstantin (fig. 6.4).

He is turned against her by the diabolic Aschenbach, who plies Martin with drugs and convinces him that Sophie and Friedrich aim to marginalize him completely. Just as Shakespeare's Macbeths have wrested power from Duncan and Banquo and Friedrich and Sophie have taken over from Joachim and Konstantin, Martin makes his own grab for the throne of the steelworks at Aschenbach's behest, definitively installing the SS in control of the industry, a turning point in the film. The histrionic sequence that follows, in which Martin confesses his hatred for his mother and jealousy of Friedrich and then attacks her, displays Martin's most fundamental evils (incest, rape, drug use), condensed beneath an expressionistic green and red lighting; high-pitched, nondiegetic music; and melodramatic dialogue ("I will destroy you mother!"). In the film's final scene, Martin makes good on his promise, forcing Sophie and Friedrich to poison themselves after a grotesque marriage ceremony.

Figure 6.4. Sophie cradling her son, Martin.

Casting Helmut Berger in this deviant role considerably exacerbates this queer reading of the film. Berger was Visconti's partner at the time and a virtually unknown actor; his emergence in so large-scale a picture as *The Damned* immediately attracted attention to their romantic connection. It was seen as another signal of an autobiographical phase in Visconti's work, inaugurated with the prince of Salina character in *The Leopard* and continued in *Death in Venice*. Nancy Warfield ties this autobiographicality to the German trilogy: "Berger, together with Bjorn Andresen in *Death in Venice*, created for Visconti an autobiographical fantasy in which the Italian permitted his German alter-ego to enter the fin de siècle world of Mann, Mahler, Wagner, Nietzsche, et al." (Warfield 1981, 8). Berger and Visconti met in Volterra in 1964 during the shooting of *Sandra* and remained together until the time of Visconti's illness while working on *Ludwig*, in which Berger starred as the mad king Ludwig II of Bavaria. In Berger's autobiography, *Ich* (*Me*), he describes their life together as one of man and wife, although only behind closed doors, where even at Visconti's house, the two never shared a bedroom since Visconti feared what his servants might think (Laurenzi 2000, 150). The aristocratic milieu and attention to family dynamics in *The Damned* have been regarded as a direct references to Visconti's upbringing, with Günther, who expresses an affection for the classics of modern European literature and the cello, seen as a stand-in for the director himself. This autobiographical figure becomes more interesting when Günther eventually succumbs to Nazism's seduction at the film's conclusion, perhaps a nod to Visconti's early fascination with Nazism, which he witnessed firsthand on a trip to Munich with Coco Chanel in 1933. There is a blending of the biographical connection between Visconti, Berger, and Nazi deviance, a mixture that rebukes facile interpretation and shrouds this figure, already marked by the cross-dressing performance at the beginning of the film, in another layer of indecipherability that confuses the fictional with autobiographical (Flynn 2004, 178).

Night of the Long Knives

Based on an already queer Lady Macbeth, Martin's queer identity as an incestuous, pederastic rapist in *The Damned* reflects the common association between Nazism, homosexuality, and deviance that can be found elsewhere in Italian film of this period and in some of the most famous theorizing about fascism and sadism. Susan Sontag, for example, describes the relationship among fascism, homosexuality, and sadomasochism as essential to representations of fascist eroticism: "The sadomasochistic fantasies and practices are to be found among heterosexuals as well as homosexuals, although it is among homosexuals that the eroticizing of Nazism is most visible" (Sontag 1980, 97). In his analysis of the Nazi cycle of films within which *The Damned* is located, David Forgacs illuminates the problems with what he calls the pseudo-history of Nazism that many of these films and theorists created by melding fantasy with the historical tragedy of Nazi Germany. Forgacs viewed the popular linkages between Nazism and homosexuality as particularly dangerous, and he criticizes how Sontag (and others) point to a "natural" affinity of Nazis toward homosexuality. As an example, he notes how the sexually ambiguous Martin is attached to the homosexually charged sequence of the "Night of the Long Knives" scene. In correlating the sadistic Martin with the punitive reaction to gay carousing in this sequence, Forgacs sees yet another case of using Nazi history in the interest of box-office returns (Forgacs 1999, 233).

The "Night of the Long Knives" scene runs almost seventeen minutes and depicts the summer get-away of SA troops in the Bavarian resort of Bad Wiessee. In contrast to the dimly lit interiors of the von Essenbeck house, where the majority of the film takes place, this idyllic rural location is first shown in broad daylight, with a cheery group of vacationing soldiers engaged in shooting, boating, and frolicking nude in the lake (fig. 6.5).

Figure 6.5. Soldiers in the lake.

As day turns to night, the soldiers are pictured in an increasing state of inebriation, drinking beer and parading around, dancing and singing. The long, methodical pans from one face to the next match the laconic chorus of German hymns being sung. Visually, there is a link to the performance that begins the film, where an identical shot captures the faces of the von Essenbeck family, entranced by Günther's cello solo. In comparison to the opening scenes depicting the luxurious decor of the von Essenbeck home, the cheapness of the resort represents the debased course of early Nazism that is crucial to the film's trajectory. Henry Bacon notes how these two scenes demonstrate Visconti's overarching strategy of tying this family's decadence to when "The Weimar Republic died and the Assassin State was born . . . a new leading class of criminals, of perverted men, was born" (Bacon 1998, 148). The connections between the drunken soldiers and the von Essenbeck family show the national debasement of Nazism that was developing in all spheres of German society. The political background that will soon enter violently emerges in a brief discussion between two soldiers outside the main hall who express their distaste for Hitler.

While preparing for the film, Visconti wanted to insert actual documentary footage, but he felt it would be too incongruous and changed his mind. This desire to document history returns to the roots of Visconti's first experience as a cinematic documentarian, most famously with his collaboration in the resistance documentary from 1945, *Giorni di Gloria* (*Days of Glory*), discussed in chapter 8. It also emphasizes the importance of nonfiction historical texts in the preparatory phase of the film, particularly Shirer's *The Rise and Fall of the Third Reich*, a book Visconti referred to as his "bible" during preproduction. Shirer outlines the problems facing Hitler in the early part of 1934. The chancellor had become increasingly concerned with the SA, whose thuggish tactics were no longer useful to him once the Nazis were in firm control. One of the most pressing issues was the rumored rearmament of the SA forces under Ernst Röhm, their chief of staff (Shirer 1960, 214). Appropriately, *The Damned* deals with the von Essenbecks' ability to manufacture the arms that will supply the expansion of the army. This is made clear by a previous scene in which Aschenbach, figurehead of the rival SS, declares that no arms will leave the von Essenbeck factory, much to the chagrin of Konstantin, an SA official. In the film, the role of Konstantin invokes the real-life Edmund Heines, an SA leader: "The generals were shocked by the tales, now beginning to receive wide circulation, of the corruption and debauchery of the homosexual clique around the S.A. chief. Dietrich [the Führer's press chief] asserted that the scene of the arrest of Heines, who was caught in bed at Wiessee with a young man, 'defied description,' and Hitler . . . declared that for their corrupt morals alone these men deserved to die" (Shirer 1960, 224–25). It is thus fitting that Visconti would attach "The Night of the Long Knives" scene to the theatrical incipit with Martin's drag performance, with many of the soldiers bedecked with make-up and women's undergarments, all shot beneath a similar multicolored lighting. The atmosphere of the tavern at Bad Wiessee is a tawdry one, with the coarse soldiers engaged in a late-night bacchanal, and although initially some soldiers are shown molesting a waitress, the scene channels a potent homosexual energy. Political-allegorical readings of the "Night of the Long Knives" sequence do not account for the attention that Visconti lavishes on the individual soldiers; the slow movement of the camera matching the singing of the German hymn (fig. 6.6), and the overwhelming sense of cinematic artifice augmented through lighting effects and a complex mise-en-scène.

The scene is overflowing with props: streamers, ribbons, Nazi flags, confetti, and bottles crowd the reoccurring long takes while announcing the presence of the camera. The music, which at first provides support for the cinematic realism, becomes asynchronous and difficult to make out over the din of voices and laughter of soldiers speaking in German. This asynchronicity is reflected in the movement of the camera, which

Figure 6.6. Drunken soldiers singing their hymn.

vacillates between long panning shots of the interiors to a jarring use of zoom to capture the dancing soldiers and identify Konstantin. Rather than a docufictional re-creation of this event in the history of Nazi Germany, the viewer is presented with a completely denatured account of history. As the camera pans up a staircase, it signals a shift. The young men are shown exiting the showers, nude or covered only with towels. One official pushes a soldier into a bedroom, and an open door reveals another man undressing. Below, Konstantin sings Wagner's "Lament of Isotta," which ushers the next narrative phase: the surprise SS attack in which Konstantin and his group of SS revelers are executed in cold blood.

This punishment comes in the form of a bloody action sequence in which SS soldiers invade the lakeside retreat with machine guns and cut down the partiers. The ambush proceeds rapidly, with SS soldiers raining bullets on some unsuspecting men in their bedrooms, while others are taken outside to be executed by firing squad. When Konstantin is similarly dispatched with, we realize the assassins are led by Aschenbach himself. For Pasolini, this was both the film's most sublime moment and its turn for the worse: "Your film falls apart in the second part: from the moment in which from a dark street, suddenly illuminated by a dreadful daybreak, an opaque flashing of a motorcycle headlight (that is a sublime moment, as a man from the *Cahiers* would say a bit fatuously, but which I say in all seriousness). From that moment on, your inspiration dissipated: the massacre is done *cinematographically*, without mystery, with liters of red coloring on the generic bodies" (Pasolini 1969, 224). Visconti thus transferred the event into a form of cinema, preferring visual excess to stark, historical documentary. Although this portrayal of nonheteronormative sexuality is not as explicit as Pasolini's own *Salò*, made some years after *The Damned*, homosexuality is hardly hidden or "delimited" as it was during the neorealist period (Ginsberg 1990, 245). Here, Visconti is most certainly working cinematographically, as Pasolini suggests: he is playing off the cinematic conventions of action and horror film that stage the German past "with history, sexuality, and the body" (Flynn 2004, 201). When viewed in the light of the queer *Macbeth* and Visconti's own public status as a gay auteur, *The Damned* becomes a problematic and contradictory work that cannot be summed up as a simple vilification of nonheteronormative sexuality by its association with Nazi immorality. Instead, it is a work that underscores questions of autobiography, subjectivity, and the erotic that become increasingly prevalent in the adaptations examined in part III.

Part III

The Late Works, Page to Screen

7

Vaghe stelle dell'Orsa (*Sandra,* 1965) and *L'Innocente* (*The Intruder,* 1976)

D'Annunzio, Decadence, and Tragic Masculinity

> How many times have I been called a "decadent." But I have a high opinion of decadence, just like Thomas Mann did, for example. I am steeped in this spirit.
>
> —Visconti on decadence, 1975

Novels by Italian fin-de-siècle author Gabriele D'Annunzio were at the basis of two of Visconti's family tragedies, *Sandra* (1965) and *The Intruder* (1976). *Sandra*, another hybrid adaptation, draws themes, characters, and settings from D'Annunzio's final novel, *Forse che sì forse che no* (*Maybe yes, Maybe no*, 1910), to tell the story of two siblings who return to their ancestral city of Volterra to memorialize their father, killed years before at Auschwitz. In the film, Volterra becomes the site of a sort of archeological dig into the family's history with their eerie

Figures 7.1, 7.2. Cardinale on the bed, Giannini looking jealous in *Sandra* (Luchino Visconti, 1967).

home haunted by clues of a mother's misdeeds and the incestuous bond between brother and sister. *The Intruder*, set in the late nineteenth century, reinterprets D'Annunzio's protagonist Tullio Hermil, who in the novel punishes the wife who betrayed him by murdering the child who was the result of her infidelity. The film takes place in various palatial estates, giving textures to D'Annunzio's novel with ornately decorated interior spaces. Both films spin beauty and death together within the confines of ghostly architecture, claustrophobic buildings casting a shadow that foretells the tragic fate of each family.

Sandra and *The Intruder* share a predominance of weak, flawed men performing in the gilded interiors of Italian palaces. In *Sandra*, male characters succumb to the enchanting beauty of Sandra, who compels her brother, Gianni, to commit suicide and sends her husband, Andrew, into exile. *The Intruder* centers around Tullio, whose suicide is the direct result of his wife's infidelity and his lover's insensitivity. Such portrayals of disempowered men partake of a certain tradition of masculine representation in postwar Italian cinema. Postwar neorealism began a period in which the *inetto* (inept man)—"the cuckhold, the impotent and feminized man"—flourished in Italian films, forwarding a fragile portrait of masculinity that was distant from the prewar portrayal of male dominance and virility under fascism (Connell 1995). Ruth Ben-Ghiat ties Italian cinema of this period to a notion of masculine "crisis" after fascism (Ben-Ghiat 2005), whereas others viewed a similar trend in Hollywood in the same period (Cohan 1997, 34–36). *Sandra* and *The Intruder* might be seen alongside other films of the 1960s and 1970s, a period in which notions of masculinity were undergoing a transformation. The idea that cinema of this era represented masculinity as a predicament—given men's changed place in Italian society after the war and the advancement of feminism in the late 1960s—demonstrates the prevalence of the "crisis discourse" in Italian film criticism, with critics frequently exploring how filmmakers harkened wistfully to a bygone, perhaps mythological age of male empowerment. As Catherine O'Rawe notes, "If Italian masculinity is seen as at risk of feminization, and as constantly vulnerable, the films often employ new strategies for shoring up that masculinity, foregrounding nostalgia and the recuperation of prior models of masculinity" (O'Rawe 2016, 7). As we will see, *The Intruder* in particular might easily be seen as typical of Italian cinema of the 1970s, when "narratives of male crisis generally conjure up the demise of men as the effect of the empowerment of women and the social transformations that accompanied the rise of feminism" (Rigoletto 2014, 20).

That D'Annunzio's works provided essential frameworks for *Sandra* and *The Intruder* suggests that a certain notion of masculinity, one attached to the decadent literature of the nineteenth century, became part Visconti's adaptation process and was interrogated as these books were translated to screen. D'Annunzio was as colorful a literary and intellectual figure as any that Visconti adapted, and his personal exploits garnered him celebrity in turn-of-the-century Italy. Over the years, he became increasingly associated with the most bellicose elements of unified Italy in his popular, nationalistic oratory celebrating war and imperial conquest in the years before Mussolini's rise to power. D'Annunzio anticipated the fascist rhetoric of virility and martial might by several decades, and he became famous for constructing a uniquely Italian-Nietzschean Übermensch or "superman" in the protagonists of his most renowned novels (Frese Witt 2001, 37). Associations with D'Annunzio, the superman, and literary decadence did not bode well for critical reception of *Sandra* or *The Intruder*. Indeed, few words in postwar Italian film criticism provoke as much antipathy as *decadence*, which connotes a favoring of aesthetics over political engagement, decoration over insubordination, and the ornate mediation of life through the eyes of an artist who is more concerned with beauty than reason. Italian film critics applied the term *decadence*, inherited from a long tradition of criticism (discussed further below), to their descriptions of Visconti and contemporaries such as Michelangelo Antonioni, Federico Fellini, and Bernardo Bertolucci, hinting at an unclear marriage between aesthetic and erotic innovation. This decadence was seen as a by-product of artistic alienation and a distancing from the engagement with political reality that distinguished neorealism. For Visconti's critics, decadence was an ideological criticism, a way of contrasting the realist or engaged "Gramscian" Visconti with the political retreat of the "Proustian" Visconti. To them, the films of the "decadent" phase bore all of the hallmarks of nineteenth-century decadent literature: irrationality, moral and erotic ambiguity, and the elevation of the figure of the artist whose overrefined aesthetic sensibility evoked the increasing distance between art and society.

In what follows, I demonstrate how Visconti addresses questions of decadence and D'Annunzio head on in these films, directly countering the depiction of men in the author's novels by adapting them through the idea of crisis masculinity circulating in postwar Italian film and culture. The noticeable transformation of this iconic masculine figure from literature into a relative weakling on film highlighted the process of adaptation, boldly displaying how D'Annunzio's men could be reconfigured cinematically through their placement in atmospheres that are markedly gothic. As in *The Leopard*, Visconti brings the practice and position of adaptation under the microscope with these two films, accentuating the significance of book-to-screen transformations that became increasingly self-conscious over the final half of his career. Even in an article in which he was trying to protect Visconti from the critique of decadentism, Guido Aristarco underscored the late works as suffering from some ailment of alienation:

"After *Rocco and His Brothers*, Visconti fell victim to the moral crisis of the sixties, passing from revolution to disillusionment, to pessimism, and to a retreat into inwardness" (Aristarco 1988, 62). Taking Aristarco at his word, I display how Visconti was both critic (*The Intruder*) and poet (*Sandra*) of D'Annunzian decadence. *The Intruder* displays a textually bound subversion of the D'Annunzian superman through the suicide of the male character, Tullio, weakened by the ghosts of his wife's betrayal and his own unthinkable infanticide. *Sandra* looked outside D'Annunzio's text to cine-literary categories of *giallo* and gothic, presenting an indomінable female protagonist who subdues the male figures who court her.

The Intruder: Decadence Remastered

First, a brief and incomplete history of literary decadence and its relevance for D'Annunzio and Italian culture in the early years of unification. As early as the 1830s, French critic Désiré Nisard critiqued the decadent style of Romantic poets, arguing that their emphasis on detail, fragmentation, and aesthetic excess damaged the fragile balance between a work's parts and its whole. He specifically targeted Victor Hugo, whose literary innovation and excess of imagination, Nisard opined, were to be avoided:

> When we say that [Victor Hugo] has been an innovator, we are not praising him. In France, a country of practical and reasonable literature, a writer who has only imagination, though it be of the rarest sort, cannot be a great writer . . . In him the imagination takes the place of everything; imagination alone conceives and performs: it is a queen who governs unchecked. Reason finds no place in his works. No practical or applicable ideas, nothing or next to nothing of real life; no philosophy, no morals. (Calinescu 1977, 161)

Nisard's contempt for the seductive quality of Hugo's prose returns in Nietzsche's critique of Richard Wagner, whom the philosopher condemned for the arousal of mass audiences. "Victor Hugo and Richard Wagner," Nietzsche wrote, "they signify the same thing: in declining cultures, wherever the decision comes to rest with the masses, authenticity becomes superfluous, disadvantageous, a liability. Only the actor still arouses great enthusiasm" (Calinescu 1977, 161). In France, the decadent poetry of Verlaine and Baudelaire, the prose of Hugo, and the paintings of Delacroix attracted the ire of literary historians and philosophers. The portrait of the artist from J. K. Huysmans's 1884 novel, *À rebours* (*Against the Grain*) has become paradigmatic of the decadent literary protagonist. The book's main character, Des Esseintes, retires from society to investigate the aesthetic intimacies of a solitary life, fueling artistic invention with the dark energy of modernity. "The decadent artist," notes Giorgio Bertellini, "is not concerned with a mimetic representation of the external reality (social, political, or historical), but with his own unexplored and spiritual inner life (Verlain, Rimbaud)" (Bertellini 1997, 12). Under Huysmans's spell, D'Annunzio created his own avatars of decadentism in Italy (Drake 1982, 75). These came in the form of D'Annunzio's novelistic alter egos: Tullio Hermil (*The Intruder*, 1892), Giorgio Aurispa (*Triumph of Death*, 1894), Andrea Sperelli (*The Child of Pleasure*, 1889), or the later Paolo Tarsis (*Maybe Yes, Maybe No*, 1910). These characters voiced Huysmans's decadent dictum that "one must fashion one's own life, as one fashions a work of art." In the essay "On the Character of the Most Recent Literature" from 1907, Benedetto Croce denounced decadentism as a degenerate form of mysticism that was characterized by "the air of insincerity" he found in Italian authors like D'Annunzio, Pascoli, and Fogazzaro. Croce contrasted these with the "good," healthy art of Carducci and realism: "We no longer have the patriot, the realist, the positivist; but the imperialist, the mystic, the aesthete" (Croce 1917, 186). Lukács picks up this discourse in his *Healthy or Sick Art?* to describe the socially abnormal position of such artists, whose works folded inwardly upon themselves and not outwardly to the collectivity. "Such abnormality in the artist's relationship to society is always the product of a decaying class society," he once wrote. "This false attitude of the artist toward society fills him with hate and disgust for it and isolates him from the great social currents pregnant with the future. The isolation of the individual implies a personal psychic and moral degeneration" (Lukács 2005, 105). Gramsci likewise linked sickness directly to the decadent D'Annunzio, noting how the writer constituted "the final paroxysm of sickness in the Italian people" (Gramsci 2014, 1738).

Besides *Death in Venice*, discussed in chapter 9, such tones of decadence, decline, and illness all surfaced with particular force in discussions of Visconti's film *Ludwig* (1972). After a stroke on July 27, 1972, the director suffered partial paralysis to the left side of his body and damage to the right side of his brain, injuries that were seen to influence his following aesthetic choices. One study suggests that Visconti's use of the close-up in his final two films, *Conversation Piece* and *The Intruder*, signals a change in "cognitive style" (Blanke and Pasqualini 2012). In *Ludwig*, the main character is King Ludwig II (Helmut Berger), who takes an Des Esseintes–esque retreat into the aesthetic dream to the grandest of scale, ruinously spending on his castles and palaces until he is declared insane. Such parallels between physical decline and thematic decadence dominated *The Intruder*, Visconti's final film, released after his death on March 17, 1976. *The Intruder* opens with a close-up of Visconti's functioning right hand turning the pages of D'Annunzio's novel, the liver-spotted fingers shadowing the film with the director's disability and oncoming death. This image is a poignant symbol of a life in adaptation, lived through the books and the films they became. In his comments on the film, Visconti claimed that the age of the superman was definitively over, contextualizing this film as a portrait of a prefascist Italy: "Tullio and Giuliana are part of the great Italian bourgeoisie, that is responsible for the advent of Fascism. *The Intruder* is not only the story of one family's decadence, but of a certain society and a certain Italy" (Scütte 2008b, 270). *The Intruder* was also inspired by other works by D'Annunzio, such as *Il piacere* (*The Child of Pleasure*, 1889), which according to Suso Cecchi D'Amico, was the first D'Annunzio text the screenwriting crew consulted before turning to *The Intruder* (D'Amico 1996, 64). What results is an adaptation that demonstrated a "close reading" of a literary precursor without the constrained fidelity of a project like *The Stranger*, discussed in the next chapter. In *The Intruder*, Tullio's transformation from book to film demonstrates how adaptation re-creates literary figures to fit in the modern world (Rondolino 2003, 525). Like other D'Annunzian supermen, Tullio is a semi-autobiographical model of intellectual and physical superiority, whose personal force and virility ignores the boundaries of conventional moral judgment.

In the book, D'Annunzio establishes that owing to Tullio's superior intelligence (he also alludes to his own "genius"), he is free to commit adultery as he sees fit, and even in his confessions that dot the novel, he bolsters his position above judgment (Spackman 1989, 144). After the pseudo-confession at its incipit, D'Annunzio begins *The Intruder* with Tullio's admission that he has been unfaithful to his sickly wife, Giuliana, with his beautiful mistress, Teresa Raffo. Over the course of the novel, the author strikes a balance between Tullio's successful love affairs and the fruitful consummation of his marriage. On the side of his extramarital affairs, Tullio notes that "I had been the lover to two of her close friends. I had spent a few weeks in Florence with Teresa Raffo" (D'Annunzio 1996, 3). Alongside these infidelities, Tullio has managed to sire two daughters with his wife, pointing to the fecund bond that once existed in his marriage and providing evidence of the superman's reproductive powers. After reconciling with Giuliana, it comes to Tullio's knowledge that in his absence, his wife gave in to the advances of Filippo Arborio, a writer who becomes Tullio's seductive alter ego. A child, Raimondo, was conceived from this union, sending Tullio into a spiral of jealousy, anger, and contempt for Arborio, who subsequently dies, leaving only the child as confirmation of his wife's infidelity. To extinguish any living sign of Giuliana's betrayal, Tullio murders the child by exposing its fragile body to the cold night air, and the novel ends with a burial scene where a guiltless Tullio explains his innocence in all its D'Annunzian "denegations and displacements" (Spackman 1989, 147). For all of the illness and death the novel contains, the story concludes with a happy ending as far as Tullio is concerned. With his competitor dead and the last vestige of his wife's disloyalty buried, Tullio is free to proceed guiltless, much as he did at the beginning of the novel, reestablishing his position high above the conventional strictures of civil society. Tullio's aggression against Raimondo is acceptable in a world where the risk of being labeled as a feminized cuckhold, dispossessed of his privileged female property, and thus inept in his dealings with women, is objectionable to respectable men of society.

It is from this latter perspective—that of masculinity—that Visconti's alterations to D'Annunzio's hero must be regarded. Visconti reverses Tullio's fortune, subverting the all-powerful superman by introducing in him a fatal self-consciousness. The imperiousness of the D'Annunzian man, Visconti claimed in an interview from 1975, was no longer possible: "I'll do just as in the book, even though I took the liberty to offer suicide to Tullio: the age of the 'supermen,' that for D'Annunzio was acceptable, is now finished for good" (*LV*, 152). To do so, Visconti made textual changes the character of Tullio (Giancarlo Giannini) and to the female characters and amplifies the haunting aspects of the interior spaces. In the novel, Teresa exists solely as a symbol of Tullio's infidelity and the indulgence of extramarital sex. She is replaced by the cinematic Teresa (Jennifer O'Neill), portrayed as conniving, ambitious, and sexually aggressive. Her dialogue is characterized by bold condescension: she continually chides Tullio for his boyishness in being at her beck and call and later for exhibiting an unmanly oversensitivity when dealing with his wife. Teresa also becomes Tullio's unsupportive confessor at the end of the film, rejecting his advances and solidifying his position as the weaker one in their relationship and his failure to forge an emotional bond with others. Visconti further chips away at the literary character's omnipotence by removing the doting daughters who inhabit the beginning of the novel. Their erasure exacerbates Tullio's torment at Raimondo's conception. Instead of the pale, ailing Giuliana of the book, Visconti's Giuliana (Laura Antonelli) recovers from an initial frailty to appear vital and voluptuous, her naked body displayed on the bed in one brightly lit sequence as a sensual paragon of good health. The film's Giuliana contains nothing of D'Annunzio's "sisterly" Giuliana, and her affair with Arborio is shown as one of reciprocal desire rather than primarily a result of Arborio's attraction, as D'Annunzio depicts it in the book. Giuliana's final admission in the film that she was in love with Arborio is a final twist of the knife that leads to the infanticide (fig. 7.3).

This representation of a man brought down by the women who surround him would seem to echo a crisis of masculinity that allegedly reigned in postwar Italian cinema, especially during the 1970s, when men were supposedly emasculated by a radicalized post-1968 feminism (O'Rawe 2016, 4). *The Intruder* does not offer up such a clear-cut example of female dominance as it might appear, however. Arborio, who barely appears in the novel, is reconfigured in the film to emphasize his position as Tullio's mirror image, arriving to care for Giuliana after Tullio abandons her for Teresa. This Tullio-Arborio doubling is foregrounded in the film's first shot of men fencing, the masked duelers engaged in a sport laden with symbolic potential for male potency. Fencing returns in a second scene, when Tullio faces off against Arborio. The sequence is notable for the encounter that follows, set in the men's dressing room, where Tullio stares intently at Arborio showering. The camera tilts up

Figure 7.3. Tullio with the child in *The Intruder* (Luchino Visconti, 1975).

in a shot-countershot that captures his envious, angered frontal view of the naked Arborio, who shows his uncovered penis as he reaches for a towel (fig. 7.4).

The third and final representation of fencing begins with Tullio mistaking his brother Federico, who arrives in fencing gear, for Arborio. In the conversation that follows, Tullio cautions his brother against hoping that Giuliana's pregnancy will produce a healthy child, mentioning the failure of a previous pregnancy earlier in their marriage. This suggestion of weakness, that his seed was not powerful enough to take hold, develops further when he fails to convince Giuliana to have an abortion. These textual differences between the Tullio of the film and the Tullio of the novel were further underscored by the performance of Giancarlo Giannini, who conveys a contemplative, sympathetic Tullio who is a far cry from D'Annunzio's intractable superman. Nowell-Smith writes: "Visconti and his scriptwriters (Suso Cecchi D'Amico and Enrico Medioli) worked hard on the screenplay to remove from the character of Tullio the strident quality that D'Annunzio gives to his 'superman' heroes. Aided by a really excellent performance from Giannini they situate Tullio so that he comes over as perfectly believable, in a way sympathetic—and morally quite abhorrent" (Nowell-Smith 2003, 203). Giannini's anguished visage, particularly at the end of the film after Giuliana's admission of being in love with Arborio, underscores a characterization far different from D'Annunzio's. By far the most striking notes of the film as a critique of the novel is in its conclusion, where Visconti does away completely with the solemn burial of the unfortunate child. In its place, Tullio gives a long confession of his deeds to Teresa, then puts a pistol to his chest

Figure 7.4. Frontal view of Arborio.

and commits suicide. The film closes with Teresa hurriedly leaving the scene. In this final sequence, Visconti turns the novel's opening ("The justice of men does not touch me. No tribunal on earth could judge me") on its head, bringing the untouchable Nietzschean superman to Earth. Rather than the presumptuous, infanticidal Tullio calmly observing as the victim of his revenge is put to rest, the film Tullio exits in the overwrought light of a Shakespearean tragedy, a monster rejected by wife and mistress. Giannini's theatrical departure from the main room into the sunlit foyer, the gunshot, and the cut to a long shot of Tullio's wretched corpse splayed across the carpet provides a ghastly image that concludes the film. Killing off Tullio in such a fashion was a final blow against the superman and its nationalistic and imperialistic resonances in twentieth-century Italian literature, politics, and culture. By destroying Tullio, Visconti denies the possibility of an exceptional being, immune to the tragic vagaries of nature and himself. Yet it is not just the physical expiration of the superman that is central to Visconti's final film. It is the death of that D'Annunzian "genius," a shadow from under which Visconti, in the final chapter of his career as a literary filmmaker, ultimately sought to escape.

Volterra: From D'Annunzio to the Gothic *Giallo*

Unlike *The Intruder*, *Sandra*, drawing from D'Annunzio's novel *Maybe Yes, Maybe No*, centers on an empowered female protagonist, Sandra (Claudia Cardinale), whose astounding beauty is the source of peril for the male characters surrounding her. Her actions and motivations drive the plot: she returns to her native Volterra with her American husband, Andrew (Michael Craig), to attend a memorial service to honor her father, Jewish scientist Emmanuele Luzzatti, who was captured and sent to Auschwitz. She suspects her mother, Corinna (Marie Bell), and her mother's lover, Gilardini (Renzo Ricci), of secretly orchestrating her father's capture; while her suspicions of betrayal are unsubstantiated, the inquiry into the family's past reveals the truth of another crime: the incestuous relationship between Sandra and her brother, Gianni (Jean Sorel). Having learned of their improper bond, her husband returns to the United States, but Sandra decides to follow him and leave Volterra behind for good. Gianni, who hoped she would stay with him, poisons himself in the elaborate conclusion of the film, in which the paroxysms of his suicide are cross-cut with the memorial service for Emmanuele in the palace garden.

Sandra is built on a variety of contrasts: reality versus illusion, memory versus dream, past versus present. Yet there is no more significant juxtaposition in the film than that of female versus male, with Sandra as the object of every male character's unfulfilled erotic desire. As a woman whose limitless power overwhelms her male counterparts, Sandra exudes the sort of innate capacities for seduction that was typical of the D'Annunzian superman, indicating how the literary superman could be upended cinematically, this time in the form of a superwoman. In this film, the superman against which Sandra's character was built is aviator Paolo Tarsis from D'Annunzio's final novel, *Maybe Yes, Maybe No*, who is himself the crux of the intersecting passions of the novel's five main characters. Masculine figures are central in *Maybe Yes, Maybe No*. Tarsis mourns his friend, Giulio Cambiaso, in the novel, establishing an "all-male culture of mourning and commemoration" (Boylan 2011, 4) that continues throughout. Tarsis is an advanced, technologized iteration on the superman, his passion linked to the desire for speed permitted by modern vehicles, not to the artistic or moral experimentation of Stellio Effrena in *The Flame* (1900) or Tullio in *The Intruder*. In the film, this passionate individual is replaced by an ensemble of enfeebled men—Andrew, Gianni, Dr. Fornari—who are subordinated by the female character.

Maybe Yes, Maybe No was one of a complex set of literary sources circulating in *Sandra*, making the film akin to other hybrid adaptations (*Rocco and His Brothers*, *The Damned*) discussed in chapters 4 and 6. Still, *Maybe Yes, Maybe No* was a fundamental source for the film's characters, themes, and setting. Palazzo Inghirami and Volterra, where the film is set, were both in D'Annunzio's novel, and *Sandra*'s concluding shots of the garden, where the camera pans past a large tree encircled by a wall (fig. 7.5), echoes D'Annunzio's text, where the character Lunella sits "on the round wall that circles the trunk of the patriarchal oak" (D'Annunzio 1910, 164).

In place of Paolo, Sandra is both the narrative and erotic fulcrum on which the film balances. *Maybe Yes, Maybe No* is built on its own system of doubling: Aldo and his rival Paolo (together with Paolo's alter ego, Guilio Cambiaso), Isabella and Vana (and with them, Lunella). In the film, Sandra's counterparts also proliferate in a complex series of doubling. This mirroring begins with Sandra's dead father, whose presence is felt throughout the film, then is reflected in Gianni, Andrew, and her former lover, Dr. Fornari. In the book, only after Paolo escapes from Isabella's clutches does he achieve real triumph, as the empowering marriage of

Figure 7.5. The tree on the family plot from book to film.

man and machine on his flight to Sardegna transforms what appears to be an attempted suicide into a successful solo flight across the sea. In *Sandra*, Visconti erases this heroic male, and unlike the demonized Isabella—a Calypso to Paolo's Ulysses—Sandra disengages from the cloying Gianni. The film's themes of suicide, incest, and complex love triangles are also transported from D'Annunzio's book, where Aldo has an incestuous sexual relationship with Isabella, and then Vana, who is in love with Paolo, ultimately kills herself. In his comments published in 1965, Visconti highlighted his interest in exploring the literary theme of incest taken from *Maybe Yes, Maybe No* in his adaptation: "The last sexual taboo to remain intact is incest: society can be corrupt, but the structure of the family must still be defended. Incest is thus the only impossible, cursed, dramatic love: therefore, I chose to represent it, had I lived before I would have represented *Tristan and Isolde*, *Paolo and Francesca*, or even *Madame Bovary*" (*LV*, 109). The importance of *Maybe Yes, Maybe No* is heralded from the beginning of the film, when Visconti photographs Sandra and Andrew's automobile tour from Geneva to Volterra. Their journey echoes that of Paolo and Isabella, who open the book careening down the road in a red speedster: "The fury swelled the man's chest against the wheel of the rushing red car that ran along the ancient roman road with a warlike rumble similar to the roll of a massive metallic drum" (D'Annunzio 1910, 2). The opening titles of the film are accompanied by a similarly precipitous journey in the car, the dynamic movement of the auto together with the shots of the landscapes rushing the transition from the modern Swiss location toward an ancient, fantastic, dreamlike Volterra (Parigi 2000, 221). (The couple's voyage is also in dialogue with Rossellini's *Voyage to Italy* (1954), a film that was at the basis of Jean-Luc Godard's *Contempt*) (Liandrat-Guigues 2000, 28). The modernity of Europe's modern highways, its rest stops and signage, filmed from the perspective of this luxury vehicle (Visconti's white BMW 507 Spider convertible), introduce a touristic Italy seen from the viewpoint of foreigners who encounter the new and marvelous landscape of a distant land. This perspective is underscored in the ensuing shots from the rear of the car that capture the vehicle's approach to the ancient Volterra as the passengers exclaim, "See the cliffs!" and "Look, the Etruscan walls." In a letter to Emilio Treves dated October 30, 1909, D'Annunzio described Volterra as "constructed from that Etruscan stone that imprisoned the sun, above an infernal chasm that seemed excavated from an angry dantesque fantasy" (D'Annunzio 1999). In one pan, the car passes the massive ramparts in the background, fixing the fundamental contrast between modern and ancient life that will continue when they reach Sandra's home, the actual Palazzo Inghirami in Volterra's city center. Here, the film enters the museum-like interiors of the palazzo, cluttered with items that come from a personal rather than public collection (Frosali 1965).

As in D'Annunzio's novel, Volterra is a city condemned to sickness, the walls of its ancient past concealing a dark and deadly secret. With images of the decaying old abbey, threatened by the eroding cliffs, the family's semi-abandoned palazzo at the city center, and the nighttime shots of the neglected church of San Giusto, Visconti presents a disinhabited Volterra much like the one in the book. In his reading of Volterra's place in D'Annunzio's oeuvre, Luigi Pescetti noted: "In *Maybe Yes, Maybe No*, the characters . . . live in an ambiguous mode, where here and there names of cities and villages resound, but usually it is an uninhabited land, filled only with the passions of the characters who create a desert around themselves, everywhere in which they appear" (Pescetti 1943,

24). Before *Maybe Yes, Maybe No*, Volterra had appeared in D'Annunzio's *The Child of Pleasure* when the book's protagonist, Andrea Sperelli, is described perusing wares and antiquities in a market in Rome's Via Sistina. There he notices "an embossed silver helmet by Antonio del Pollajuolo presented by the City of Florence to the Count of Urbino in 1472 for services rendered during the taking of Volterra" (D'Annunzio 2006, 31). Federico da Montefeltro's helmet becomes a metonym for the massacre of civilians that occurred during "the capture" of Volterra, a massacre that shadows the city's history. Volterra's morbid historical background aided Visconti and his collaborators in transporting the ancient family tragedy into the modern age (Bianchi 1965, 22). In the film, the city's history is voiced by Gianni while he and Andrew stand precariously on the precipitous cliffs overlooking the abandoned ruins of an ancient abbey. Gianni explains: "Volterra is the only city that I am aware of that is inexorably condemned to die of sickness. Like the majority of human beings." D'Annunzio describes this vista, including the church where they walk next, as "the steep cliffs of the Balze . . . on the edge of the naked bulk of San Giusto, similar to a cast iron colossus" (D'Annunzio 1910, 316).

Other texts besides *Maybe Yes, Maybe No* coalesce in *Sandra*, beginning with the Electra myths by Aeschylus, Sophocles, and Euripides. Modern renditions of this myth, in particular Eugene O'Neill's *Mourning Becomes Electra* and Richard Strauss's opera *Elektra*, are also present. Sandra (Electra) and Gianni (Orestes) attempt to avenge the death of their father, Emmanuele (Agamemnon), who was allegedly betrayed by his wife, Corinna (Clymenestra), conspiring with her lover, Gilardini (Aegisthus), to send him to the concentration camp. Another literary source for the film is signaled in its Italian title, *Vaghe stelle dell'Orsa*, a reference to the first poem in romantic poet Leopardi's *Le ricordanze* (*Memories*), which is recited by Gianni in the film. Leopardi's poem is situated in a familial garden: "Glimmering Stars of the Great Bear / I never thought I'd return to see you / Shining down on my father's garden / Nor talk to you ever again from the windows / Of this house where I spent my childhood." Although the palazzo in the film is also a repository of the family's secrets, the "father's garden" from the poem is depicted as a graveyard. It is first seen at night, when the commemorative bust of Emmanuele (fig. 7.6) is shown at its most funereal, its shroud blowing in the wind. Finally, John Ford's play *'Tis a Pity She's a Whore* (1630) has been recognized as an important early source, along with notes of Proust and Bassani rounding out a complicated group of literary forebears (Giori 2011b).

Figure 7.6. Emmanuele's shrouded bust.

Visconti described the project as a *giallo* (yellow), a term that has both literary and cinematic resonances in the Italian tradition: "this film is an unusual 'giallo.' It has been discussed as a 'modern Electra,' but to explain what I mean by 'giallo,' I'll cite another classic tragedy: 'Oedipus Rex,' one of the first 'gialli' ever written, in which the guilty party is the character one might least expect (at the beginning of the tragedy, Oedipus defines himself as 'the only outsider')" (Giori 2011b, 90). He went on to describe the film as "a *giallo* in which everything is clear at the beginning and obscure at the end," mentioning the term that was used to describe Italian crime and mystery novels published in pulp form with distinct yellow covers. It was in these exact years when *Sandra* was made that the Italian cinematic *giallo* was quickly developing, with films by Mario Bava (*La ragazza che sapeva troppo*, *The Girl Who Knew Too Much*, 1963; *Sei donne per l'assassino*, *Blood and Black Lace*, 1964) providing stylish innovations on the crime film that set the stage for the great Italian *gialli* to come (Bianchi 1965, 32). The *giallo* reached the arthouse cinema as well, with films like Antonioni's *Blow-Up* (1966) and *Professione: Reporter* (*The Passenger*, 1975), Bertolucci's *La commare secca* (*The Grim Reaper*, 1962) and

La strategia del ragno (*The Spider's Strategem*, 1970), and Giulio Questi's *La morte ha fatto l'uovo* (*Death Laid an Egg*, 1968) exemplifying more artsy takes on the *giallo* form (Koven 2014, 205). One obvious point of contact between *Sandra* and the *giallo* is its emphasis on amateur investigators tasked with uncovering evidence of a crime. Sandra's husband, Andrew, reports how the two met while documenting the experiences of Holocaust victims who provided evidence that would presumably serve to implicate guilty parties. This investigation, one that also underscores Sandra's father's victimhood at the hands of the Nazis, continues when the characters arrive in Volterra. Photographic documentation is portrayed metacinematically through Andrew, who is seen recording home movies throughout the first part of the film on a hand-held camera. Through his eyes (literally displayed in the scene in which the spectator views Sandra through his camera's viewfinder), the inquiry progresses from a mother's murder to a sister's incest. On Andrew's viewpoint, Visconti once wrote: "This character is closest to the spectator's conscience. He would like a logical explanation to everything, and instead he encounters a world dominated by the most profound, contradictory, and unexplainable passions" (Bianchi 1965, 32). As Pierre Bourdieu once noted, such amateur photography intimates the limits of documentation and with it, realism, questioning photography's capacity to accurately capture family histories and etch them in celluloid (Bourdieu 1990, 19).

Significantly, the moribund state of D'Annunzio's literary city is contrasted against the cinematic woman Sandra, portrayed as a force of natural vitality and beauty. Visconti intended the film to be a vehicle for actress Claudia Cardinale, with whom he had recently finished working in *The Leopard*: "The Sandra character . . . was written for her and not only for that which is enigmatic hidden behind the apparent simplicity of this actress, but also for the somatic adherence of her figure (her head, specifically) to that of the Etruscan women whom she conveyed" (Bianchi 1965, 34). This reference to the Etruscan origins is suggestive of the racial quality of Sandra's character, whose Jewish identity was to be established through her father, Emmanuele. As in *The Damned* a few years later, here Visconti fails to develop any meaningful reflection on the Holocaust, leaving the Shoah as a minor piece of the film's palimpsestic puzzle. Millicent Marcus describes how Visconti locates the Shoah as one of the various historical and personal pasts referenced in the film: "[Emmanuele] Luzzatti remains a cipher, just as the Shoah itself remains outside of representation in Visconti's film" (Marcus 2007, 44). Visconti admitted that the Holocaust was never supposed to be central to the film (Rusconi 1965, 11). Rather than a profile of Jewishness, Sandra's Etruscan physiognomy is designed to connect her to Volterra, providing a physical conduit from its ancient past to modern times that, as we will see, reflects D'Annunzio's perspective on the city. Describing his decision to cast Cardinale, Visconti indicated the potentially dangerous, almost inhuman aspects of her persona, referring to her as "an animal, a phenomenon, a physical presence" whose erotic magnetism could be capable of threatening the men around her (De Franceschi 1999, 136). Years later, Cardinale remarked how the director spoke of her in similarly animalesque terms: "Claudia seems like a cat who lets herself be pet on a couch in the parlor. But be careful, this cat can transform into a tiger, and tear its tamer to pieces" (Cardinale 2006, 101). To my knowledge, the only other performer Visconti referred to in such animalesque terms was Maria Callas, whom he once described as "half a man, a strange temperament; a tigress and wild animal are stupid terms to apply, but she is a savage" (Biagi 1973, 3). Introducing a monster-like female protagonist, Visconti here gestures toward a complementary generic category—the gothic—and like other Italian directors of this era, fuses it with his cinematic *giallo* (Marlow-Mann 2011, 156). Like many gothic heroines, Sandra is a new bride who will inhabit an abandoned "castle" (the cavernous Palazzo Inghirami), haunted by the spirit from the past: her dead father manifested in the ghostly commemorative bust, first seen covered in a white shroud. The palazzo will come to represent all of the contradictions of female domestic life that was typical of eighteenth-century fiction. As Kate Ferguson Ellis notes in terms that are relevant to the erotic dimensions of the palazzo in *Sandra*, "The Gothic novel of the eighteenth century foregrounded the home as fortress, while at the same time exposing its contradictions. Displacing their stories into an imaginary past its early practitioners appealed to their readers not by providing 'escape' but by encoding in the language of aristocratic villains, haunted castles, and beleaguered heroines, a struggle to purge the home of license and lust and to establish it as a type of heaven on earth" (Ferguson Ellis 1989, xi–xii). Volterra is the quintessential gothic setting, portrayed as a premodern necropolis filled with crumbling churches and hollowed-out town squares. Such settings are frequently found in prototypical gothic novels, such as Horace Walpole's *The Castle of Oltranto* (1764) and Anne Radcliffe's *The Romance of the Forest* (1791), or gothic films such as Hitchcock's *Rebecca* (1940) and Robert Siodmak's *The Spiral Staircase* (1946), where the haunted castle and the newlywed bride were also stock features. *Sandra* is on the decidedly realist end of the gothic spectrum, like Radcliffe's books, where phenomena thought to be of otherworldly provenance are eventually revealed to have material origins. This realism was part of Radcliffe's rumination on the actuality of womanhood in the nineteenth century (Moers 1963). The interior shots of the palazzo include a cluttered mise-en-scène: an antiquarium of objects and poorly lit frames (windows, doorways, mirrors) that exacerbate themes of memory and family conflict. These clearly predict the approach to interiors in *The Intruder*, designed to mirror the cold materialism and lack of spiritual fiber in the main character and his horrific deed. Home to the ancient Etruscan civilization seen in the stagey museum scene, where the funerary urns are a backdrop to Andrew's conversations with Gilardini, this Volterra features a Roman cistern with a spiral staircase (fig. 7.7), one of the more common architectural signifiers of the gothic in film and literature (Huckvale 2010).

Gothic is not only defined by its setting, characters, and atmospheres but also by its emphasis on the encounter between old and new, history and modernity. In *Sandra*, this encounter is signaled musically, with memories of the family past, linked to the mother and the family home,

Figure 7.7. Sandra descending the spiral staircase into the Roman cistern.

triggered by the leitmotif of the César Franck's prelude. Music likewise indicates the historical present in Italy of the mid-1960s. In the scene in which Sandra and Andrew are first seen dining in the family palazzo, the radio plays Mina's "E se domani" ("And If Tomorrow"), a song that had been performed by Fausto Cigliano at the Festival di San Remo in 1964 and was released by Mina as a single together with "Un anno d'amore" ("A Year of Love") later that year. The use of contemporary pop music gives the necropolis a living element in the present, voiced in Le tigri's "Let's go and if you don't want" that accompanies Gianni's arrival at the house, then by "Una rotonda sul mare" ("A Roundabout on the Sea"), performed by Fred Bongusto and heard in the local bar. To this musical signification, a textual one, common in the gothic, can be added. Throughout the film, there is an emphasis on subterfuge in writing: the secret notes that Sandra finds hidden around the house; Gianni's tell-all book, *Memories of My Youth*, which reveals the incestuous relationship (uncoincidentally, the manuscript is dramatically cast into the burning fireplace); the voiceover of the letter's contents in the film's conclusion. Other gothic themes, such as the imprisoned woman (the mother's institutional imprisonment), madness, suicide, and "abnormal" family (at one point Corinna calls her children "two monsters"), round out the film's gothic identity.

Breaking from *Maybe Yes, Maybe No* by inserting the female protagonist in the dominant role, *Sandra* demonstrates a woman's strength and resolution to deposit her past in history, leaving the ancient and cursed Volterra forever. As a hybrid adaptation in which literary texts are combined with cinematic forms, *Sandra* demonstrates a continuation of the cine-literary project that defined Visconti's adaptations of the 1960s. In its metacinematic and metaliterary apparatus, however, the film reveals the kind of self-conscious adaptation that prevailed in the director's late works, where questions of subjectivity and intermediality were brought further toward the center of his artistic concerns. Employing *Maybe Yes, Maybe No* as a primary but not isolated source text, *Sandra* represents Visconti's capacity to harness a multitude of sources to create a single film. The creative manipulation of a literary source was a far cry from the pedantic adaptation that followed. In the next chapter, I discuss *The Stranger* (1967), a film that was condemned for reproducing Camus's literary text on screen in an overly literal fashion.

8

Lo straniero (*The Stranger*, 1967)

Crime and Punishment in a "Failed" Adaptation

> The moviemaker's art is not all that different from the lawyer's—especially the courtroom advocate's. Both must capture, in a very short space, a slice of human existence, and make the audience see a story from their particular perspective. Both have to know which facts to include and which ones to leave out; when to appeal to emotion and when to reason.
>
> —Judge Alex Kozinski on courtroom movies (Bergman and Asimow 1996, xi)

Many consider Visconti's 1967 adaptation of Camus's *L'étranger* (*The Stranger*) to be the low point of his filmography. Some of the film's problems result from what some regarded as an overdetermined literariness in the adaptation. As various critics noted, the sluggish pace, laconic long shots lingering on surface details, and stilted voiceover and dialogue taken directly from the pages of Camus's novel all pointed to an excessive—and uncinematic—bookishness. To his

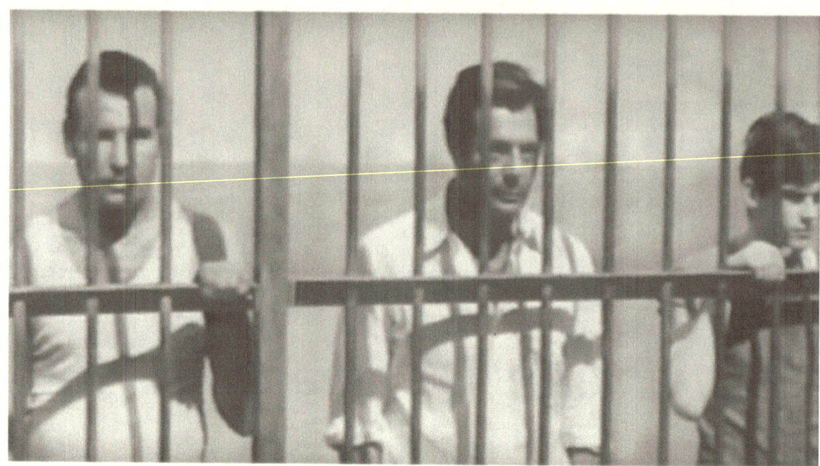

Figure 8.1. Meursault behind bars in *The Stranger* (Luchino Visconti, 1967).

critics, Visconti had remained too faithful to his literary source, creating an illustration rather than an interpretation. Rather than counter these accusations, Visconti reinforced his absolute fidelity to Camus's book. In an interview from 1965, he noted, "I see exactly how Camus wrote it. I don't want to even write a screenplay. My idea is to follow the book . . . I want to take the book in my hands and film what is written . . . Yes, I want exactly what is on the page: in and between the lines . . . I don't want to superimpose Visconti over Camus" (De Franceschi 1999, 21). His extreme fidelity to a literary original evokes the schema commonly referred to as "the fidelity discourse," which suggests that films based on books are held to an unreachable standard of literature and that audiences or theoreticians are compelled to view adaptations of any kind as unfaithful. In his seminal article, "Beyond Fidelity: The Dialogics of Adaptation," Robert Stam remarks, "The notion of 'fidelity' is essentialist in relation to both media involved . . . it assumes that a novel 'contains' an extractable 'essence' hidden 'underneath' the surface details of style" (Stam 2000, 57). Stam's article is a key text in the wave of adaptation study that sought to subvert the primacy of fidelity, viewing adaptations as films in a lateral rather than subordinate (in Mikhail Bakhtin's terminology, dialogic) relationship with literature. Thomas Leitch regards fidelity's continued relevance in studies of adaptation to be institutional, as an "appeal to anteriority, the primacy of classic over modern texts" (Leitch 2003, 162) in which critics evaluate films as inferior to their literary touchstones, whereas Kamilla Elliot sees cinema as a combination of multiple media that destabilizes film-literature, verbal-visual dichotomies (Elliot 2003). Stam, Leitch, and Elliot all prefigured the movement away from a "fidelity discourse" and toward more intertextual and intermedial approaches that characterize the field of adaptation studies today.

More literal translations of books on film are not necessarily less creative adaptive approaches, however. Francesco Casetti, for example, calls films that remain excessively faithful to their literary sources "dis-adaptations": a creative avenue of adaptation that forges a new direction toward (rather than away from) a literary source (Casetti 1999, 17–26). For Visconti, the strange case of overfidelity to Camus's *The Stranger* contrasts with the director's reputation for reading against the grain of his literary sources, where textual betrayal was celebrated as a key characteristic of his subversive nature. Renowned for using words in the service of his own images was part of a larger portrayal of Visconti as a European auteur whose aesthetic intransigence and political radicalism reduced literature to mere frameworks. A concept based in Romantic literature, cinematic auteurism was based on evaluating a film as the individual expression of its director, whose personal style and vision were on full display. Following Alexandre Astruc's argument that the filmmaker wielded the camera as a writer did a pen, the development of auteurism in France during the 1950s and 1960s consistently referred to literary authorship. "The 'camera-pen formula,'" Stam remarks, "valorised the *act* of filmmaking; the director was no longer merely the servant of a pre-existing text (novel, screenplay) but a creative artist in his/her own right" (Stam 2000, 83). In his 1954 essay, "A Certain Tendency of the French Cinema," François Truffaut critiqued the respectful adaptations of France's "tradition of quality" that he saw as too beholden to the canonical literature they reproduced (Truffaut 2008). This was not a criticism of adaptation tout court but of unoriginal or uninspired filmmaking that Truffaut associated with commercial cinema in France. For Truffaut and his fellow New Wave critics and practitioners, "good" adaptations required the guiding hand of the auteur director whose own artistic sensibilities were sufficient to transform the source text into the new medium of cinema.

By the mid- to late 1960s, British auteur-structuralists like Peter Wollen and Geoffrey Nowell-Smith transformed this romantic figure of the elite filmmaker into a critical construct. Influenced by Claude Lévi-Strauss and his work on myth, they analyzed patterns across a filmmaker's oeuvre that might help to distill deeper meanings behind their works. In the introduction to Nowell-Smith's 1967 monograph, *Luchino Visconti*, the author outlines the auteur-structuralist viewpoint that he used to analyze Visconti's oeuvre. The project, Nowell-Smith remarks, is

> To consider the work as a whole, as the product of a single intelligence, and to seek out the connections between each film at whatever level they are to be found. In Visconti's case the connections are multifarious, and can be traced in his choice of actors, his use of decors, his concern with certain historical questions, and so on. . . . But there are further links within his work which exist at a deeper level, less easily discernible, and which are perhaps even more important. It is these hidden structural connections which bind his works together and which combine to form a picture of the author and his work which is far more complex and interesting, as well as more coherent, than is generally imagined. (Nowell-Smith 2003, 9–10)

Nowell-Smith eventually expressed reservations about the auteur-structuralist program that he helped found. Indeed, 1967—the year in which Nowell-Smith's study was published and when Visconti's *The Stranger* debuted—was a moment in which this unified author of a creative work was about to be felled by semiotics and structuralism, then put to rest (temporarily) by poststructuralism. In cinema, Christian Metz's "imaginary signifier" pulled attention away from the director or "speaker" to evaluate the usage of signs in the act of communication. The study of film was also influenced by other attacks on authorship by Roland Barthes's "The Death of the Author" (1968) and Michel Foucault's "What Is an Author?" (1969), Julia Kristeva's influential championing of intertextuality, and Jacques Derrida's questioning of the relationship between original and copy. These thinkers asserted the importance of ideological, historical, and cultural forces rather than the vision of one individual. With poststructuralism's contestation of unified subject and text, the figure of the unitary director from Truffaut and the pages of the *Cahiers*, functioning as the film's creative mainspring, quickly became outdated. In the third edition of *Luchino Visconti* (Nowell-Smith 2003) the author notes how " 'auteurist' has become a term of abuse among some practitioners of film studies to whom it seems positively indecent that an individual should be thought of as the inspirational power behind a work of art. Homing in on the director as author is seen as a dangerous shortcut that stops critics from giving proper attention to other factors which make a film what it is" (221). He outlines how the presence of Marxist (especially Lukácsian) interpretations of Visconti's work during the 1960s created critical blind spots, such as Visconti's identity as a gay director that remained mostly unexplored. Mostly, Nowell-Smith acknowledged the limitations of reducing so collective an art form as cinema to the expression of a single individual.

The twenty-first century has seen a renewed interest in authorship in film and literary studies that, although not necessarily redeeming the auteur-structuralist position, allows for some reconstitution of the auteur director. Already at the close of the 1980s, James Naremore observed that "Auteurism is surely dead, but so are the debates over the death of the author" (Naremore 1990, 20). As Jack Boozer inquires,

> Must we forget that in the end, it is always certain individuals who write a novel or a screenplay and who direct actors and films? And while the majority of their decisions may be recognized as resulting from larger historical and cultural contexts, and from certain guiding perspectives adapted from the source, that the primary talent in a given film adaptation can also serve as very specific individual antennae of interpretation that may be more than the sum of those larger influences? Whatever remains of the creative subject and individual inspiration and effort implies a particular voice, and not necessarily only a culturally mimetic one. (Boozer 2008, 22)

In what follows, I return to reconsider the subconscious readings of the auteur-structuralist school in an interpretation of adaptation in *The Stranger*. Commonplaces that Visconti was too literal in his transposition of Camus's book distract critical attention from two significant motifs, crime and punishment, seen elsewhere in his cinema that make their way into *The Stranger*. The trial, the courtroom, justice, and jurisprudence are all on display from the opening shot of the film, in which Arthur Meursault (Marcello Mastroianni) is being led through the courthouse and states: "My case is so simple." Images of Meursault in handcuffs introduce themes of crime, guilt, and judgment that reoccur throughout Visconti's filmography, making *The Stranger* just one of many approaches to the apparatus of justice throughout the director's career. This is an undervalued thread running through Visconti's filmography that deserves further attention. This chapter is not an attempt to resurrect *The Stranger* as a forgotten masterpiece, unfairly treated by critics and forgotten by film historians. Instead, it suggests how the various court trials represented in Visconti's cinematic oeuvre suggest a career-long meditation on law and order and a more nuanced reading of Camus's book than those who dismissed the film acknowledged. "Film adaptation has traditionally been about fidelity only in that it is about authority," remarks Timothy Corrigan, indicating how the fidelity discourse frequently shed light on questions of both literary and cinematic authorship (Corrigan 2002, 160). With *The Stranger*, Visconti makes Camus's text his own, creating an existentialist legal drama and successfully reclaiming a classic piece of literature for his auteurist cinema.

The Reception of *The Stranger*, the Film that Illustrated the Novel

Histories of *The Stranger* tend to exculpate Visconti for the film's remarkable failure, placing the blame directly at the feet of Francine Camus, Albert Camus's widow and the executor of his literary estate, who allegedly constrained Visconti's vision for the adaptation. Accounts of the screenwriting and filming phases tell a story that is more complex, however. Following Albert's death in 1960, producer Dino De Laurentiis obtained the rights to the novel from Francine under the condition that she maintain full control over the screenplay and could choose her preferred director. When she picked Visconti (Mauro Bolognini, Joseph Losey, and Richard Brooks were also considered), she also hired Emmanuel Roblès and then Georges Conchon to work out the script, decisions that foreshadowed the limited control exercised by Visconti and Suso Cecchi D'Amico (De Fransceschi 1999, 18). This arrangement was a necessary bargaining chip to access a literary work that had rapidly become a European classic. After it was published in 1942, *The Stranger* helped spread existentialism in popular and high culture of the immediate postwar period, becoming a major French cultural export. Simone de Beauvoir made this connection when she noted that with the *succès de scandale* of existentialism, "France was exalting her most characteristic national products with an eye on the export market: *haute couture* and *littérature*" (Judaken 2012, 99).

In its cumbersome and submissive relationship to a source (in this case a written rather than historical one), *The Stranger* can be disparagingly compared to director Gillo Pontecorvo's realist drama, *La battaglia di Algeri* (*The Battle of Algiers*, 1966), also set in Algeria and a project that Visconti had been considered for. A direct, unvarnished look at the Algerian revolution, *The Battle of Algiers* takes the perspective of the Algerian revolutionaries, who in the tradition of neorealism were played by nonprofessional actors and shot on location, in what Pontecorvo called the anti-authoritarian, postcolonial portrayal of "the dictatorship of truth" (Bignardi 2000, 16). Pontecorvo acknowledged his debt to neorealism, noting a special affinity with Roberto Rossellini's *Paisà* (1946) (O'Leary and Srivastava 2009, 252). Leonardo De Franceschi traces how Visconti's interest in adapting Camus in the context of this anticolonialist struggle was thwarted. De Franceschi notes that in the project's infancy, the director intended to situate Camus's story against the backdrop of the Algerian war for independence, fought between 1954 and 1962, and ending in Algeria's successful secession from French colonial rule (De Franceschi 1999). Visconti had planned to transport the book from its setting in 1938 to the mid-1960s: "Shooting the film in 1967, I felt obligated to underline, to bring this silent and obsessive silence of the Arab that Camus had touched on only limitedly, into the foreground. I cannot forget one fact: that the film is presented to a public who knows exactly what happened afterwards and how the story got to where it is" (Baldelli 1982, 257). In 1963, Visconti had expressed his interest in this struggle when he spoke of staging a version of Shakespeare's *Troilus and Cressida* set in contemporary Algiers (De Franceschi 1999, 20). He believed the Franco-Algerian conflict to be relevant to Italy, especially to the historical perspective on Italian unification that he had crafted in *The Leopard* (De Franceschi 1999, 19). Over the course of a collaborative screenwriting process that included Roblès, Conchon, and De Laurentiis (in a script written together with Vittorio Bonicelli), the resulting script did away with any of this historical or political intertext, locating the film in Algeria of the 1930s and making no reference to the nation's anticolonial battle. The resulting adaptation was what Adelio Ferrero criticized as an "illustration" that lacked the political verve and ideological impulses that had underpinned Visconti's previous films (Ferrero 1967). Some critics took issue with things as simple as Visconti's use of color, seen as excessive and unrelated to the existential themes of the book (Baldelli 1982, 260). Others observed that the film had a commercial look, even borrowing from Hollywood cinema. Tomasino notes that the cinematographer's colors are like those in a Hollywood adventure film (Tomasino 1967, 428–29).

Figure 8.2. Meursault and Marie swimming.

In retrospect, part of the problem lay in Visconti's attempt to translate the book not only into film but into his own "decadent" terms (Micciché 1975, 265). The few good reviews the film received were outnumbered by a significant margin (for positive reviews, see Alpert 1968; Durgnat 1968). Although the script was actually a collaborative effort, Visconti continued to be criticized for appearing to retreat from rather than embracing political engagement with the Algerian struggle, putting him at odds with the position laid out by existentialism's main proponents. Jean-Paul Sartre and De Beauvoir put great importance on existentialism's commitment to political realities. This commitment, established in Sartre's essay "Qu'est-ce que la littérature," published in 1948, was influential in the Italian notions of *impegno*, or political engagement (Jansen 2001; Antonello and Mussgnug 2009). Visconti was seen as an aged director withdrawing from politics, an auteur out of touch with the more militant generation of the 1960s (Castellani 1967, 587–88; on the failure to touch on experiments in subjective cinema of that period, see Bernardini 1969).

Circumstances surrounding the filming were fraught with practical challenges. First, as during the filming of *The Earth Trembles*, there was unexpected weather. Actress Anna Karina noted, "We had gone to Algiers to find that hot sun described by Camus, but it was December and terribly cold, Marcello shivered in his bathing suit from the thirties" (De Franceschi 1999, 148). But the next mistake was in the choice of who should play Meursault. De Laurentiis preferred Marcello Mastroianni to Visconti's choice, Alain Delon, and after a falling out between Delon and De Laurentiis, Visconti had no other option but to cast Mastroianni, an actor he esteemed highly but thought (quite correctly) to be unsuitable for the role. D'Amico described the issue with the casting decision: "In the book, Meursault is not a character, but a philosophy, a mode of existence, and a refusal to participate in life. Marcello, on the other hand, brought with him a friendly, careless approach to life, not the detachment described by Camus" (De Franceschi 1999, 147). For D'Amico, Mastroianni was too old and had established himself as too jovial a figure in Italian and European cinema (Reich 2004). Others preferred a more French-looking actor to channel Meursault's signature lack of affect, icy worldview, and unrepentant nature. Visconti offered up Laurent Terzieff or Jean-Paul Belmondo as French options, although De Laurentiis's choice of Mastroianni ultimately won out (De Franceschi 1999, 22). Similar issues had emerged with the casting of American Burt Lancaster in the role of the Sicilian Prince Fabrizio a few years before, and with Delon's casting in the role of Rocco before that.

The casting issue aside, there is a broader question of how interesting an existentialist character like Meursault could be in a film by any director. Although Meursault's dalliance with Marie, murder of the Arab man, and trial might lend themselves to cinematic drama, the character is mostly defined by his introversion and failure to play-act socially, and thus narrates *The Stranger* in a detached voice of a nonparticipant. "I never understood," Pietro Notarianni once stated, "why Visconti wanted to make a film out of [*The Stranger*]; if it were up to me, I would have chosen *The Plague*" (De Franceschi 1999, 143). Meursault lacks the affect of characters like Maddalena from *Bellissima* or Rocco from *Rocco and His Brothers*, the passion of Livia from *Senso* or Ludwig II from *Ludwig*, or even the sense of Sartrean revulsion expressed by characters like Aschenbach in *Death in Venice*. In the place of the melodramatic peaks and valleys more often associated with Visconti's cinema, Meursault's attitude—consistent with existentialist philosophy—was one of a quiet resignation to the lack of meaning in the world. That Visconti wanted to employ a multiperspectival approach, one that he thought might mirror *Rashomon* (Akira Kurosawa, 1950) to highlight Meursault's subjectivity, simply did not suffice in embodying this iconic existentialist on screen.

At the Courthouse: Visconti, Existentialism, and the Transmuted Legal Drama

Condemnation is a central metaphor for the condition of humankind in existentialism and a means for expounding on the tenets of existentialist thought. In "Existentialism Is Humanism," a lucid (if not exhaustive) commentary on Camus's early existentialism, Sartre noted the symbolic weight of the condemned individual, claiming that the existentialist "thinks that every man, without any support or help whatever, is condemned at every instant to invent man" (Sartre 2007). The existentialist idea of man as condemned to be free is manifested in literary form in Sartre's short story "The Wall." Set in Spain, "The Wall" is the story of Paolo Ibbieta, a member of an international brigade fighting against Franco to preserve the republic from fascism. He and two others, Tom and Juan, have been captured and are interrogated about the whereabouts of an anarchist, Ramon Gris. In the hopes of being spared from death, Ibbieta provides false information about Gris. Although the information turns out to be true and leads directly to Gris's death, the dilemma Ibbieta faces is not one of a guilty conscience. The exercise of the option to inform, not the consequences of providing that information, is the key point for Sartre. In Ibbieta's decision, the prisoner shows he is not bound by some predetermined essence, instead defining himself through his actions and words. Thus, Ibbieta becomes a powerful symbol of existentialism's dictum "existence precedes essence"—that humans exist first and choose to create themselves later. Enacting his potential for self-determination and individuality, Ibbieta takes the path toward living the authentic life of a sovereign being. For Kierkegaard, the first existentialist, the individual is proven through making decisions and then living by them, separating themselves from the "numeric masses" that do not. The anxiety felt by Ibbieta and his fellow prisoners at the beginning of "The Wall" echoes with society's hostility toward the emergence of such selfhood. The dread that accompanies condemnation serves as a placard of realization: realization that the authenticity of life can be seen only from the perspective of one standing on the precipice of death. From Kierkegaard to Heidegger, Jaspers to Camus, existentialist thinkers and writers repeated such themes of alienation, absurdity, and empowerment, choosing prison cells like Ibbieta's as a metaphor for the human ability to rebel against dreadful mediocrity.

There is a debatable convention that suggests existentialism never took root in Italy as it did in France and elsewhere. If perhaps less prevalent in Italian philosophy, existentialism's undeniable significance in postwar Italian cinema was recognized early on (Pacifici 1955). Italian filmmakers offset the lack of an existentialist "school" in Italian literature by offering films with a clear relationship to existentialist themes and tropes. It is no coincidence that many did so through adaptation. In his book on existentialism in cinema, William C. Pamerleau argues for cinema's suitability for existentialist themes: "film, precisely because of its concrete depictions, can convey insights that inform even the abstract ideas of theoretical philosophy. Generally speaking, there are two ways in which it does so: through its ability to deliver realistic narratives and through the expressive nature of visual imagery" (Pamerleau 2009, 85). Problems of alienation in Antonioni's *Le amiche* (*The Friends*, 1955) and perception in *Blow-Up* (1966), imprisonment in De Sica's *I sequestrati di Altona* (*The Condemned of Altona*, 1962) (an adaptation of Sartre's play) or the obsession with adhering to societal strictures in Bertolucci's *Il conformista* (*The Conformist*, 1970), based on the work of Moravia, all express Italian existential concerns at the time. In Visconti criticism, existentialism was first mentioned relative to *White Nights*, a film rife with themes of loneliness and marginalization taken directly from the proto-existentialist Dostoevsky, whose story was being adapted. These themes had appeared in Visconti's work in theater as well. He directed Sartre's *Huis clos* (*No Exit*) in 1945 during his most fervent period of theatrical production. There is archival evidence showing that Visconti was also in talks to direct *Les Mouches* (*The Flies*) in the summer and fall of 1946, then *Morts sans sepulture* (*Men without Shadows*) in 1947 (*FV*, 1, 1, 119; *FV*, 5, 15, 1).

Still, something more than the director's interest in French existentialism is at play in *The Stranger*. Visconti's interest in crime, adjudication, and condemnation was apparent in one of his earliest experiences in filmmaking: the collective resistance documentary, *Days of Glory* (1945). In this film, Visconti was charged with filming the trial and execution of Roman Police Chief Pietro Caruso. Visconti had himself been a prisoner in a fascist jail during the war, punished for his active antifascist work: "After the armistice, although he had not been admitted into the antifascist lines, under the name Alfredo Guidi, he organized clandestine political activities; at his house on Via Salaria there were meetings and he hid arms and men" (D'Amico de Carvalho and Favino 2003, 10). He was arrested on April 15, 1944, and transported to the infamous Pensione Jaccarino, then the prison at San Gregorio, where he was incarcerated until June 4, when Rome was liberated. His imprisonment by Pietro Koch and his Roman group led to the semi-autobiographical screenplay *Pensione Oltremare*, written with Mario Chiari, Franco Ferri, and Ronaldo Ricci. The story is of a young man who becomes politically aware while incarcerated with a group of partisans in the SS prison (Chiari 1959, 146–56). Documentary footage shot by unknown Anglo-American cinematographers and Visconti's own footage were spliced together by Mario Serandrei. The scenes of *Days of Glory* that Visconti was responsible for are key precursors to the approach he takes in *The Stranger.* His section of *Days of Glory* begins with a chilling cinéma vérité scene of bloodlust that took place outside of the trial. A high-angle shot from above observes one defendant, Donato Carretta, attempting to free himself from the clawing hands of the angry crowd. The dramatic effect was augmented by the use of eight cameras placed strategically throughout the building that allowed Visconti to alternate between the high-angle shots of the crowd with medium close-ups of individuals reacting to the attack (Musumeci 2000, 59). Much of the footage of Carretta's lynching was suppressed, as the filmmakers were conscious of the potential power to incite violence the film might have during this sensitive period immediately after the war. The subsequent trial and executions achieve an entirely different tone from that of the preceding chaos. Visconti establishes a measured pace that complements the adherence to justice that Italy's high court is about to exercise, with the restoration of order occurring on aesthetic and thematic levels. The members of the court are visually introduced with a pan that displays the opulent seats they occupy, and the slow camera movement matches the ordered bureaucratic preparations performed by an array of functionaries. Visconti frames the lawyers from both the prosecution and defense symmetrically, illustrating how they receive equal attention from members of the judiciary who busily take notes, ask questions, and examine evidence. The same order is applied to the executions that follow, with high-angle shots of the condemned in their final moments.

The objectivity of the trial sequence in *Days of Glory*, in which a balance is struck between witnesses and testimony, sentencing and punishment, can be contrasted with the subjective filter through which Visconti represents Meursault's trial in *The Stranger*. The second half of *The Stranger* adapts the second part of Camus's novel, which is about Meursault's incarceration and trial. Visconti uses the visual and sonic

Figure 8.3. Commissioner Mario Berlinguer in the courtroom.

fields to underscore two physical sensations—dizziness and heat—that are repeatedly described in the book. The subjective register of Meursault's discomfort can be observed in the sequence in which he is pictured in a mass holding cell with a group of Arab prisoners. When one of his fellow prisoners asks Meursault what crime he committed, he responds, "I killed an Arab." A low-angle shot from the seated position of the Arab men seated on the dirt floor appears, then transitions to Meursault's point of view, with the men staring up at him and into the camera. The camera pans left and cuts to the corresponding movements of Meursault's head, then back to the fellow prisoners staring up at him, eerie flute music playing in the background. Once moved to his own cell, Meursault's point of view appears again as he looks out at the port through the barred windows. The cramped space in the cell is expressed through a mid-shot of Meursault's face, partially hidden behind a small shelf and its shadows. It continues when Marie (Anna Karina) visits him, a scene described in the novel as "The room was divided into three sections by two large grates that ran the length of the room. Between the two grates was a space of eight to ten meters which separated the visitors from the prisoners" (Camus 1989, 73). In the film, this tripartite expanse is framed by a soundtrack that captures the shouting voices of other prisoners and their family members. These overwhelm Marie, who entreats Meursault to maintain hope, but he responds with indifference. Visconti mixes a pseudo-subjective perspective in which Meursault's point of view organizes the sequence; the shot-countershot between him and Marie is supplemented by pans of prisoner and visitor sides. Camus describes Meursault as slightly disoriented by "the sound of the voices echoing" and "the harsh light pouring out of the sky," inducing "a kind of dizziness." Visconti shows Meursault's state of distraction through another point-of-view shot in which the camera first rests on his face (fig. 8.4), peering through the bars, then pans right to survey the long group of visitors, cutting to mid-shots of others, then back to Meursault, leaning against the bars as if exhausted.

To exteriorize Meursault's choppy interior monologue from the novel, Visconti films a series of one-sided bits of dialogue, allowing other characters (Meursault's lawyer, the prosecutor, Marie) to explain the danger he is facing if he does not express more "human" emotions. This is reinforced in the next sequence of Meursault looking out the window of the prison cell, followed by a subjective shot of the city and ocean from behind bars. That Meursault is to be both the viewer and the viewed is teased with the shots of him looking at his reflection in a steel dish in his cell, where he raises up his blanket to cover his face like a shroud or headdress worn by his fellow Arab prisoners, another reference to the man he killed.

Figure 8.4. Meursault regards Marie, who visits him in prison.

This interpolation of the main character's gaze returns in the courtroom sequence will take up the bulk of the film's second half. It is a section dominated by a languorous camera capturing the interactions between witnesses, judge, and jury, much of it achieved with the use of the zoom. The scene begins somewhat conventionally, highlighting Meursault's face but also that of the other characters, especially the prosecutor, his lawyer, the ruling magistrate, and a shot-countershot of witness and their interrogators. In the book, Meursault continues to describe his discomfort: "I was feeling a little dizzy too, with all those people in that stuffy room" (Camus 1989, 83). Visconti visually shapes Camus's almost stream-of-consciousness narration, forwarding the book's distanced narrator whose thoughts are interspersed with his observations. After he describes the heat and light of the courtroom, Meursault proceeds to detail the crowd, outlining the sensation of being looked at. "They were looking at me: I realized that they were the jury," then, "I think that at first I hadn't realized that all those people were crowding in to see me" (83), feeling as if he was "the odd man out, a kind of intruder" (84). Meursault focuses his attention on the clothing worn by the magistrates, then the reporters ("One of them . . . wearing gray flannels and a blue tie, had left his pen lying in front of him and was looking at me"; 85). From this "shapeless mass of spectators," Meursault identifies individuals who are familiar to him, then the way the spectators were fanning themselves from the heat: "I was getting hotter, and I could see the people in the courtroom fanning themselves with newspapers, which made a continuous low rustling sound" (85–86). In the film, witnesses gaze directly into the camera, a rarity in a Visconti film. These aspects point to the greater emphasis on interior states that emerge in the second part, which, like the book, occurs while Meursault is imprisoned.

Where Camus's text is made most theatrical is in the concluding sequence, one that in many ways sums up the problems with the literal adaptation unfolding. As Meursault is in his cell awaiting his execution and refusing to see the prison chaplain, the voiceover reads directly from the novel (part 2, chapter 5): "They always come at dawn, I knew that" (113). The scene follows Camus's description of Meursault's anticipation almost verbatim, moving from his thoughts expressed through the voiceover interior monologue to his conversation with the chaplain, where he outlines his atheism and rejection of the chaplain's pleas that he pray for his own soul. If any dramatic crescendo exists in this final sequence, it is in the dialogue that leads up to Meursault's angry reaction to the priest, which is supplemented by the musical score. In the book, Meursault says, "I started yelling at the top of my lungs, and I insulted him and told him not to waste his prayers on me," then he enunciates the basic existentialist argument that the imprisoned man is actually freer than the priest: "He seemed so certain about everything, didn't he? And yet none of his certainties was worth one hair of a woman's head. He wasn't even sure he was alive, because he was living like a dead man" (120). The film concludes with a close-up of Meursault's face; the voiceover ("Once he'd gone I felt at peace again") simultaneously works through the final pages of *The Stranger* in which Meursault thinks of his mother during her final days, departing from the text for only a moment when the guard enters to bind his hands behind him, ending with the final lines of the book: "for me to feel less alone, I had only to wish that there be a large crowd of spectators the day of my execution and that they greet me with cries of hate" (123).

Genuflecting at the Altar of Literature: Worshiping a Novel

In the director's public statements before and following *The Stranger*'s release, his admiration for Camus was seemingly limitless. In 1962, he emphasized his desire to adapt the original with utmost respect: "I will not betray this little, important book. I want to respect its entire essence and humbly subjugate myself to the text" (Rondolino 2003, 460). In this way, Visconti rhetorically pays homage to the author whose masterpiece he has humbly adapted, introducing a trope of fidelity that filmmakers often use in presenting cinematic versions of classic modernist works (Geraghty 2008, 47). In these statements, Visconti seemed to be suppressing adaptation's transformative capabilities demonstrated in his other films, asserting that he would illustrate rather than transform the novel. Or was the book itself resistant to adaptation? One might view *The Stranger* as a "difficult" modernist text presenting formal and philosophical obstacles that thwarted attempts to adapt. Part of its difficulty can be found in the connection between *The Stranger* and the philosophical treatise *The Myth of Sisyphus*; critics have regarded the novel as a fictional counterpart for Camus's doctrine of existentialism in that work. The novel's minimalist prose is a challenge for any adaptor to a visual medium (Camus, on the contrary, seemed convinced of existentialism's status as an imagistic outlet for philosophy, famously noting that "a novel is never anything but a philosophy put into images" (Camus 1968, 199). Existentialism, at least the existentialism of the French exponents (Sartre, Camus, De Beauvoir, Marcel), was almost always identified with literary rather than philosophical writing and, therefore, a philosophy that was artistically expressible. Nonetheless, critics of Visconti's *The Stranger* tended to underscore the essential untranslatability of Camus's text, identifying the novel as a textual impediment that would have to be overcome in realizing a film. But Henry Bacon notes, the difficulty was perhaps less about anything inherently untranslatable in *The Stranger* and more about the misguided attempt to adapt the text to screen in a literal way: "It was obviously naive to assume that the excellence of the novel could be translated to another medium by adhering faithfully to its 'characters, locations, costumes, actions, and strings of narrative.' Visconti could not help but lose the elusive essence of the original because he was unable to explore cinematic equivalents that would have had the same effects as the literary devices used by Camus" (Bacon 1998, 206). Hemmed in by the strictures of a literal translation, Visconti's film perhaps demonstrates the tyranny of fidelity and its suffocating effect on the process of adaptation, not necessarily cinema's inability to render philosophically rich texts (Camus 1968, 145).

This stated, suggestions of *The Stranger*'s untranslatability fortified the belief that "one may perhaps make a good film out of a bad novel, but never out of a good one" that was still widespread when the film was made (Balász 1970, 259). Visconti addressed the adaptation in terms of difficulty, first noting how laborious the screenwriting process had been and then explaining the challenges of unearthing the "secret" meaning in the author's work:

> Utilizing a work as a trampoline, deforming it by making changes is a confession of impotence. To read a book is already a creative act. Fidelity does not mean a lack of creative power. Each thing that we do is attached to some myth or story that has already been told. What is more important than a new way of seeing? However, when I choose a precise literary work, it is to give it a new dimension, or rather a dimension that it already implicitly contains, but that only an "other" look can give it. That look is exactly what reclaims the creator and his status as creator. My ambition is to go in the most difficult direction that the author would have chosen, towards the secret meaning that he desired to be found by his most attentive

> readers. I believe that this is also a work by an author. (De Franceschi 1999, 25)

Visconti underscores the crossroads he faced when adapting Camus's work and emphasized the openness of the literary text that was susceptible to the creative act of reading (Lake 2014, 409).

Equating adaptation with impossibility allied *The Stranger* with Visconti's legendary failure to eventually adapt Proust's *In Search of Lost Time* that forever shadowed his legacy of adaptation. Fundamental to ideas on both film and literary modernism is that artistic struggle increases with the level of radical aesthetic innovation (Kira'ly 2013). As one interpreter remarked, "Having lost two of the motivations for making *The Outsider* [another English title for Camus's novel]—one being Delon, the other his own adaptation—there remained a beautiful but impossible novel to translate on to the screen" (Servadio 1983, 188). As Christine Geraghty notes, this was a typical comment on adaptations of modernist novels, thought to be "beyond the capacity of a shared, popular culture" (Geraghty 2008, 48). Either way, *The Stranger* becomes a prime example of what Stam calls the "undesireability" of literal fidelity (Stam 2000). As we have seen elsewhere, adaptation relies on the freedom to make the literary cinematic, for additions and subtractions, elisions. Beneath the surface of claims to overfidelity and impossibility lies the dogma that the literary was above or beyond the capacities of cinema. In the next chapter, I conclude with a discussion of *Death in Venice* to examine how questions of fidelity and betrayal were set aside in the adaptation of Thomas Mann's modernist classic. The film not only problematizes issues of fidelity and authorship that were prevalent in the criticism of *The Stranger*, it sheds light on the question of adaptation itself as the central feature of Visconti's cinematic poetics. With *Death in Venice*, Visconti both abandons and embraces the notion that a film should transmit a literary original, moving from the restrictive precincts of Camus's prison cell to the visual and aural horizon of Venice in Mann's novella.

9

Morte a Venezia (*Death in Venice*, 1971)

Ode to the Elegant Art of Adaptation

> Naturally, one might turn to the definition given to aestheticism, decadentism, but I seriously think that one must apply the Greek definition to the artist and, in practice, say that the realization of a complete and perfect equilibrium must be the goal of all artists.
>
> —Visconti in a radio interview with Henri Chapier, September 1971

DEATH IN VENICE (1971) IS structured around a series of carefully organized shots that view the main character, Gustav von Aschenbach, gazing at a boy, Tadzio. In associating the image of the boy with infection and mortality, the camera adopts the lethal visuality of Thomas Mann's novella, *Der Tod en Venedig* (*Death in Venice*), on which the film is based. Mann's work is famous for the danse macabre of Beauty and Death, summarized in a verse from "Tristan" by August Von Platen, quoted in Mann's 1930 essay "Platen": "He who once his eye hath bent on Beauty, He to death already is devoted" (Mann 1948, 260). Despite frequent evocations of myth and the philosophical discussion of beauty in

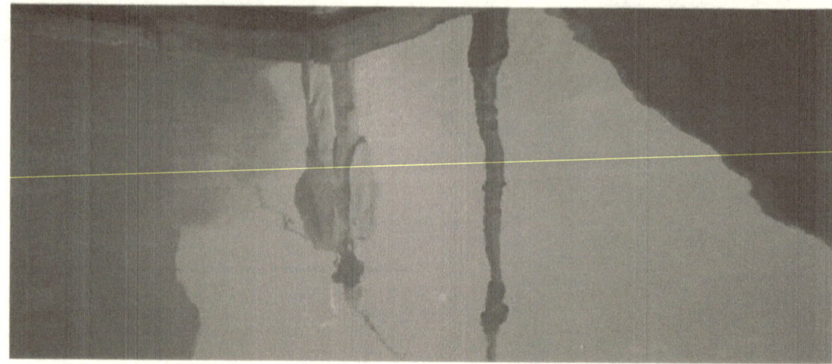

Figure 9.1. Aschenbach and his image in the water, *Death in Venice* (Luchino Visconti, 1971).

the abstract, Mann ultimately describes the boy as a stimulating object, viewed by a man whose interests are at least as erotic as they are intellectual. In his adaptation, Visconti intensifies this eroticism, compulsively cinematizing visual exchanges through a complex use of the zoom. He eroticizes Venetian locations: the city's watery surfaces, reflecting with pictures of splendor and desire. These spring from the novella, where the sea is the source of attraction and wonder: "His love of the ocean had profound sources: the hardworking artist's longing for rest . . . and another yearning, opposed to his art and perhaps for that very reason a lure, for the unorganized, the immeasurable, the eternal—in short, for nothingness" (Mann 1954, 31). This sublime sensuality of the seascape appears in *Death in Venice*'s first shots, in which a ship cruises across the glassy surface of the Adriatic Sea at dawn. The lagoon's waters soon eddy with cinema's reflective and reflexive capacities, with the Lido beach and the Venetian canals mirroring the aging Aschenbach slowly succumbing to physical and mental illness. Visconti matches this liquid mirror with sound. In the opening sequence, the adagietto from Gustav Mahler's Fifth Symphony—an aural signature that frames the whole film—is heard. The composition will return. The film's melodic complexion is so prevalent as to prompt Franco Mannino, conductor of the film's score, to suggest that music constitutes a veritable "third protagonist" along with Aschenbach and Tadzio (Visconti 1971, 141).

The coupling of mirror with music evokes the myth of Narcissus and Echo, in which image and sound combine with grievous results. Ovid's story, like Mann's novella and Visconti's film, hinges on questions of vision and misrecognition. When Liriope asks Tiresias whether her son Narcissus will live into old age, the oracle replies, "If he never know himself," presaging Narcissus's iconic inability to identify his own reflection, with which he becomes enamored. "He desires himself without knowing it himself, Praises himself, and is himself what is praised, Is sought while he seeks, kindles and burns with love" (Ovid, Book III, ll. 461–66, 78). Mirroring is rendered acoustic by Echo, who sees the beautiful boy, falls in love, and tries in vain to communicate her burning desire. Only able to repeat back the words that he utters (a reflection in sound), Echo fails, leaving only the disembodied tones of her voice. As prophesized, when Narcissus finally recognizes his error (and himself), he wastes away into the form of an aquatic flower. The same dilemma of misrecognizing the image of the self for another is at the center of *Death in Venice*, the novella and the film. Mann and Visconti present an Aschenbach who, like Narcissus, is confronted by an image of a boy that is difficult to decipher, where the act of watching has deadly consequences for the beholder.

Misrecognition of this type is a fitting metaphor for cinematic adaptations of literature. Since the birth of cinema, scholars of adaptation have strived to provide a clearer definition of what films based on books ought to be, premising their research on exploring a shared set of questions. Are adaptations more like literature or film? What do films owe to their literary predecessors? Are films extricable from the books they adapt? In what follows, I analyze *Death in Venice* as a celebration of the misrecognition that is fundamental to the myth of Narcissus and the mystery of film adaptation. From the outset of the film, Visconti highlights his adaptation's polytextual, polyartistic nature. Multiple literary and nonliterary texts, subjective and autobiographical echoes of literary and cinematic authors, unclear viewpoints on Self and Other, Eros and Thanatos, all combine to underscore that the art of adaptation is essentially an art of ambiguity. *Death in Venice* celebrates adaptation's artistic hybridity as no other Visconti film does, underscoring its essential polyvalence and almost limitless capacity for intertextual play. In doing so, it points to the broader approach to adaptation that has been reviewed heretofore. Thus, *Death in Venice* becomes a manifesto on the enigma of adaptation's aesthetic potential of shifting borders between different art forms.

Versions of *Death in Venice*

Death in Venice is the central chapter in Visconti's "German trilogy," which began with *The Damned* and ended with *Ludwig*. By putting these films in reverse chronological order (*Ludwig—Death in Venice—The Damned*), one can clarify a certain linear progression that begins in the late nineteenth century and stretches into the first part of the twentieth. *Ludwig* tells the story of the "mad" king of Bavaria from the time of his coronation in 1864 until his death in 1886. The film unfolds like a biography, with the events from Ludwig's life narrated in a series of chapters introduced by members of his court, who provide eyewitness testimony directly to the camera. *Death in Venice* is set in the period after Ludwig's death and before the Great War, with Venice's Grand Hôtel Des Bains hosting the German Aschenbach and his bourgeois class on the cusp of decline in 1911. As the final installment, *The Damned* takes the trilogy's scope on European history up to the rise of Nazism, depicting the degradation of a German industrialist family of the 1930s. Contextualized as such, *Death in Venice* inherited the theme of aristocracy in decline that characterized all three films, serving as the linking *caput medio* of the trilogy. "In the years between '11 and '18," Visconti remarked in a 1971 interview with Lino Micciché, "not just for Mann, but for the entire European bourgeois culture . . . every problem was reproduced beneath a new light and the war swept away all of the old solutions and ancient illusions" (*LV*, 139). Visconti's vision of Italy's fraught transition to modernity, seen in films from *The Earth Trembles* through *The Leopard*, here took an extended German turn. There are other, less world-historical accounts that underpin the film *Death in Venice*, however. Mann once recounted how the novella was based on a trip he took to Venice with his wife in 1911, and as we will see, Visconti asserted that his own family visits to Venice when he was child were foundational for his film (Mann 1960, 44, 46). Both Mann's and Visconti's *Death in Venice* partly drew from autobiography. As we will see, Visconti had no intention of overshadowing this personal perspective with a more broadly historical one, once opining that adapting Aschenbach from novella to film might result in an overdetermined historical context or didacticism. For example, he refused to appease his communist brethren to include a "positive" character as an ideological voice box (*LV*, 142).

In the novella, Mann introduces Aschenbach as an acclaimed Bavarian author who decides to flee Munich for points south, hoping to escape a creeping sense of creative stagnation. Aschenbach eventually journeys to Venice and becomes a guest in the Grand Hôtel Des Bains on the Lido, where he encounters a beautiful and captivating Polish boy, Tadzio. The inclement weather flusters Aschenbach, who decides abruptly to travel home to Munich, only to end up back at the hotel after a mishap with his luggage. The return, at first felicitous, becomes fatal. After initially feeling restored by Tadzio's reappearance, Aschenbach visits the city, where he contracts Asiatic cholera and then dies on the beach. The simplicity of the story and its paucity of characters and action, as well as Mann's lengthy ruminations on the meaning of beauty and decline, combine to make a story that might appear to be as difficult to transpose to screen as *The Stranger* was. The rights to *Death in Venice* had been acquired from actor José Ferrer and producer Joseph Besch, who bought it from the Mann estate in 1963 for $18,000. According to English actor Dirk Bogarde, Ferrer wanted to play the role of Aschenbach himself before selling the rights to Visconti (Coldstream 2005, 352). To some, Visconti's choice to adapt *Death in Venice* was a doomed venture from the outset, and questions materialized early on as to the novella's adaptability. For Vincent Canby, "Luchino Visconti, now in his mid-sixties, is neither a stupid nor frivolous filmmaker, but his special talent for a kind of (and I mean this in praise) epic vulgarity, which allowed him to transcend melodramatic excesses in movies like 'Rocco and his Brothers' and 'The Damned,' has led him to make a series of wrong decisions with 'Death in Venice,' including his initial decision to attempt the movie in the first place" (Canby 1971, 11). Yet Visconti's version was the first of many adaptations across the arts that would breathe life into Mann's novella. Indeed, its proliferation in literature and film around the world would seem proof of its essential adaptability. *Death in Venice* came to the stage in Benjamin Britten's opera in 1973, a work with an enduring legacy of its own (the opera was also adapted to screen by Tony Palmer in 1981). In literature, authors of varying nationality and skill have taken up Mann's text, with *Death in Venice* being parodied by the sex- and cocaine-filled visits of *Jeff in Venice, Death in Varanesi* (Geoff Dyer, 2015), as well as in the figure of Professor Pinenut of *Pinocchio in Venice* (Robert Coover, 1991). Other authors have transformed Aschenbach's solitary trip to Venice into the stories of soul-searching couples, with Ian McEwan's *The Comfort of Strangers* (1981), Daphne du Maurier's story "Don't Look Now" (1971), and Gilbert Adair's *Love and Death on Long Island* (1990) all sourcing *Death in Venice* in multiform ways. These books were subsequently adapted to the screen, extending the novella's lifeline through its distant cinematic ancestors, and this reveals the surprising and essential adaptability of Mann's source text (Shookman 2003, 224–25). Visconti's film has itself been the source of an adaption, with Singaporean artist Ming Wong's 2009 video installation *Life and Death in Venice* created for the fifty-third Venice Biennale. These are just a few in a long line of international rewritings of Mann's novella that span a variety of artistic forms. James Wilper, for example, includes *Le malheur au Lido* (1987) by Louis-René des Foret, *The Folding Star* (1994) by Alan Hollinghurst, *By Nightfall* (2010) by Michael Cunningham, *The Art of Fielding* (2011) by Chad Harbach, and *Death in Venice, CA* (2014) by Vinton Rafe McCabe (Wilper 2014, 3). This points to the Darwinian resonances of adaptation in general, which through mutation, helps the source text "survive" (Von Der Lippe 1999; for the discussion of this metaphor for adaptation see Stam and Raengo 2005).

Although *Death in Venice* has since proven its adaptability, Visconti's version was not well received by many critics when it was released in 1971. Most took special aim at the sexualized portrayal of Tadzio, which they deemed excessive and out of line with Mann's novella. The actor who played Tadzio, Björn Andrésen, himself voiced opposition to the representation of a man's attraction to an adolescent boy (fig. 9.2) (Seaton 2003), and the cinematic Aschenbach was compared unfavorably to Humbert Humbert from Nabakov's *Lolita*, adapted to screen by Stanley Kubrick in 1962 (Mellen 1971).

"Since *Death in Venice*," Dirk Bogarde once remarked, "I am only asked ever to do senile old sex-perverts or school teachers in love with their nymphettes" (Coldstream 2005, 371). Visconti denied that he had eroticized Tadzio: "The love in my film is not homosexual," he stated, "it is love without eroticism, without sexuality" (Cardullo 2011, 5). Yet the images in his film suggests otherwise, and *Death in Venice* has since become a key referent in the history of gay cinema. In a reading that repeats the anticorporeality stance taken by so many critics of adaptation, who reject the embodiment of imagined literary characters, Phillip Reed found that what in Mann was filtered through the protagonist, in Vis-

Figure 9.2. Aschenbach leering at Tadzio.

conti "appear[s] much too explicit, almost consciously seductive" (P. Reed 1987, 183). Reed was just one of the critics to direct a critique against Visconti—a gay man—for homosexualizing Aschenbach. *Time* magazine, for example, found this seduction to be absent in the novella: "Mann's 'Death in Venice' is, in fact, no more about homosexuality than Kafka's 'Metamorphosis' is about entomology. The film is worse than mediocre; it is corrupt and distorted . . . it is irredeemably, unforgivably gay" (Aitken 2011, 19). Themes of art and death, senescence and creativity, typical of Visconti's late period and the German trilogy, were seen as preferable to those of homosexuality, which some rejected outright (Cosulich 1971). Peter Bondanella notes: "Aschenbach's infatuation with Tadzio is meant to represent more than an old man's flirtation with homosexuality; it becomes a graphic image for the composer's confrontation with intellectual sterility and old age. And Visconti, a product of the same 'decadent' world he depicts in the film, seems to have identified Aschenbach's dilemma with his own" (Bondanella 2004, 207). Although Visconti's own homosexuality would certainly be inscribed on the adaptation, the gay eroticism most certainly originated with Mann's novella, making for a certain fidelity in this cinematic version. In a letter from July 18, 1911, Mann described his novella as "a really strange thing that I brought from Venice, a novella, serious and pure in tone, concerning a case of pederasty in an aging artist" (Aitken 2011, 96). As Mann's diaries later proved, the author's representation of homosexual desires in his literary works were not mere figures of fiction but a projection of his own interests (Aitken 2011, 110). Although the film was released prior to the publication of diaries that contained evidence of the writer's homosexuality, Mann's position in a gay literary canon was already well established around the time of Visconti's film. In this light, various scholars have argued convincingly that Visconti's film recovers the homosexual theme in *Death in Venice* in a way that "lays claim to the novella for the gay literary canon" (Wilper 2014, 2). Rather than deviate from it, Visconti was simply augmenting a theme that was already prevalent in a text that is now seen as pioneering in gay literature (Webber 2002).

Indeed, one might consider how Mann carefully balances expectations, reality, and appearances to be one enchanting aspect of his work that Visconti sought to bring to his film. As the primary mediator of the novella, Aschenbach proves unreliable, his observations interspersed with uncertainty and narrated with philosophical tangents and digressions. Unlike the more straightforward opening of the book set in Munich ("Gustav Aschenbach was born at L—, a country town in the province of Silesia"), Aschenbach's approach to Venice is marked by an increasingly murky perspective: "Aschenbach was driven to seek the open and look at the sky—perhaps it would lighten presently above Venice. He had not dreamed it could be otherwise, for the city had ever given him a brilliant welcome. But sky and sea remained leaden, with spurts of fine, mist like rain; he reconciled himself to the idea of seeing a different Venice from that he had always approached on the landward side" (Mann 2008, 18–19). Here and elsewhere, Mann narrates Aschenbach's perceptions with phrasings such as *es schien* (it seemed) and *ihm war als ob* (to him it was as if), omnipresent throughout *Death in Venice*, accentuating the character's struggles to come to clear interpretations. His view of Tadzio's gestures at the conclusion, for example, are indefinite, and whether Tadzio is waving, pointing, or indicating something specific is uncertain (Shookman 2003, 126).

Beyond Aschenbach's uncertain purchase on the narrative world of *Death in Venice*, there is also the question of doubt visible in the use of free indirect discourse. While direct discourse reports words as they are actually used (Aschenbach saw Tadzio and wondered, "Do I love him?") and indirect discourse indirectly reports words without quotation marks (Aschenbach saw Tadzio and wondered if he loved him), free indirect discourse melds the voice of the narrator with the voice of the character, reporting words without an introductory clause or quotation marks (Aschenbach saw Tadzio, did he love him?). In *Death in Venice*, filmmaker and character fuse together in the spirit of literature's free indirect style. Like its literary predecessors, especially authors of modernist fiction, free indirect discourse in film functions to express an interiority divided by characters and their creators. Pier Paolo Pasolini viewed the cinematic technique as one of "immersion" in which filmmaker and character's mind made up for cinema's nonexistent "faculty of interiorization and abstraction" and, as Deleuze developed later, the cinematic free indirect offers a perspective that is neither objective nor subjective, but essentially "semi-subjective" (Pasolini 1976; Deleuze 2003). It was likewise a way the filmmaker might achieve "internal focalization" that Bordwell sees as typical of the art film in which the spectator "knows only that there exists a mixture of internally focalized and narrated descriptions" but cannot differentiate between them (Bordwell 1997, 168).

Various studies of *Death in Venice* emphasize how Visconti uses the zoom to embody the free indirect discourse from Mann's work. Michael Wilson argues that the zoom performs a correlative function to the free indirect by alternating between sympathy and irony, while also contributing to the film's characteristic "musical motion": "On one level it represents the free indirect narration of Mann's novel which allows an alternately sympathetic and ironic view of the protagonist. The aesthetics of the zoom, moreover, from its isolating depth of field to its constant, musical motion, reflect aspects of Aschenbach's character—even when they undermine his own professed beliefs" (Wilson 1998, 156). Augusto Sainati sees the free indirect as one ways Visconti uses the zoom, and most often it represents Aschenbach's struggle between intellectual and erotic impulses (Sainati 2000, 272). When asked about the use of the zoom, Visconti was coy in his response, understating its significance:

> You thought [the zoom] was used often? Too often? [He laughs]. When you have a means that helps you express yourself, there's no reason to use it too seldom. I don't think I overdid it, or it does not seem so. Generally, my technique is not too noticeable, I try to avoid having someone notice the process first and the story only after. With many films I have the impression that they are solely technical works. I want the work to remain in the background, almost unrecognizable. Maybe in a story like *Death in Venice* that consists almost solely of looks, the zoom helped me to give the impression that those looks approach an essence, a person. (Visconti 1986, 150)

Overall, the zoom is one of the multiple ways the director highlights the camera and its visual operation over the course of *Death in Venice*. The initial zoom introduces Aschenbach, dozing on the ship's prow as he approaches Venice, then is used to equate this character with others, as in the case of the drunken dandy whom Aschenbach meets as he is exiting the boat. The dandy is shown with a quick zoom as he begins to speak, then the identical method is used to show Aschenbach's reaction. In another early scene, when the gondolier ferries Aschenbach to the Lido, Visconti signals the camera's presence with an unusual shot-countershot of Aschenbach in the hull of the gondola. The low angle of the menacing gondolier juxtaposed against the high angle of Aschenbach's back seems a textbook case of visual empowerment/disempowerment, giving visual emphasis to the composer's meek attempt to demand the boatman turn around at once. This classical technique is subtly disrupted, however. While the high angle looking down rather oddly on Aschenbach's shoulders is unquestionably that of the boatman, the corresponding low angle is that of the spectator, not Aschenbach; his orientation in the boat, facing forward and addressing the boatman over his shoulder, dislocates the shot-countershot of two people in conversation. By inserting the spectator's view into what one would assume to be that of the character, Visconti signals that the film will progressively challenge orthodox expectations about point of view.

Perspective is in fact the dominant creative problem the film explores. This is most evident in the long scene when Aschenbach visits the hotel lobby and encounters Tadzio for the first time. It opens with a long take, the camera panning to follow Aschenbach as he walks in and around the lobby, searching for a place to sit. In a time when Visconti's films took a decidedly loquacious turn (the interminable dialogue of *The Stranger* and *The Damned*, the long conversations featured in *Ludwig* and *The Intruder*, and what must be the most voluble of all Visconti films, *Gruppo di famiglia in un interno* (*Conversation Piece*, 1974), the dialogue in *Death in Venice* occupies a surprisingly tertiary position after image and music. Instead of serving a narrative or descriptive function, dialogue soundtracks the atmosphere for Aschenbach's roaming eyes. Layers of ambient noise, voices, diegetic music, and so on, append a crowded visual clutter, with the camera and character navigating a space obstructed by animate and inanimate objects that reverberate with sound. When Aschenbach looks up from his newspaper and peers intently into the distance, the spectator assumes the following shot offers his perspective. The camera pans from left to right, moving from one character to the next: Tadzio's sisters, then their French governess, and finally to Tadzio. The cut returns us to Aschenbach, who looks down for a moment, then looks up again. Once again correlating with Aschenbach's surveillance of the area, the next cut shows Tadzio as he was previously, but then pans away, slowly moving the camera through the crowd. When we next see Aschenbach looking intently in Tadzio's direction, the camera suggests his gaze at the boy, only to zoom out and capture Aschenbach in the same shot, seated. Significantly, the next character zoomed in on with Aschenbach looking on is Tadzio's mother, who also seems to capture his attention. This is also the first instance in which Tadzio (unlike in the novella) returns Aschenbach's gaze. While looking at Tadzio in the following scene, the voiceover of the flashback chimes in without a corresponding image. "Artists are like hunters aiming in the dark," to which the other voice—that of Aschenbach's interlocutor, Alfred—replies, "Beauty belongs to the senses."

Visconti breaks from the unidirectional perspective of a mixed Mann-Aschenbach by jettisoning Aschenbach's one-sided objectification of Tadzio, allowing the boy to reciprocate the old man's gaze and adding another layer to film's perspectival landscape. The cold, distant, inexpressive boy of Mann's novella is gone, replaced by a photogenic, prepossessed Tadzio who regards the leering old man with the intent and knowledge of someone much older (fig. 9.3). This is another means of signaling the

Figure 9.3. Tadzio smiles at Aschenbach.

presence of the camera. Irving Singer notes, "The rhythmic zooming shots establish an ebb and tide that invests us with a moving image of affective consciousness. They implicate the camera as an erotic go-between, a messenger, an obliging servant as in so many courtly and romantic love stories" (Singer 2000, 106). This polyphony of viewpoints also draws the spectator into the web of perspectives; a web that is further complicated by sources that are extratextual to *Death in Venice*.

Mahler and Mann, Visconti and His Mother

As stated already, the film's soundtrack is often devoid of dialogue, the lack of words highlighting the music in general and the repetition of Mahler's adagietto in particular. Composer Franco Mannino noted that the orchestral pieces "were not considered by Visconti as 'musical commentaries' and I directed them having never seen the film. Visconti wanted me to arrange my rendition without any inhibitions and he later adapted the visuals to this sound 'character' " (Visconti 1971, 141). The decision to transform Aschenbach from an author in Mann's novella to a composer in the film is also consistent with Visconti's overall approach to adapting Mann's text, with music achieving a profound degree of prominence. In another statement that must be admired for its reductive quality, Visconti pointed to the medium of cinema as a reason for making this switch in the protagonist's occupation, claiming that a musician is far easier to depict than an author: "The basic point of departure is that, in cinema, a musician is more 'representable' than a novelist, seeing as how while a musician can always make his music heard, a novelist is constrained to resort to aggravating and inexpressive expedients such as the voice off" (Visconti 1971, 114). Visconti's *Death in Venice* is perhaps most famous for its musicality and use of tonic expressivity in the narration, with Aschenbach's decline articulated through the music of the Bohemian Mahler, whose adagietto becomes the film's dominant musical motif. Mahler's theme is one of many musical sources that appear in the film, with various orchestras providing music from the film's diegesis. We see an infantry band from the ship in early shots of Aschenbach's approach to Venice, then Visconti presents a dance orchestra, a popular band of musicians who visit the hotel late in the film. The film features the sound of church singing, a Russian lullaby, and finally, piano pieces played by Tadzio and Alfred (Venturini 2006).

With this musicality in mind, transforming Aschenbach into a composer adds two significant overlays to Mann's novella. The first is the biographical figure of Gustav Mahler, who as Visconti noted was also Mann's model for his Aschenbach (P. Reed 1987, 180). In an interview in 1970, Visconti claimed that "Only a fake nose is necessary to make Bogarde a perfect Mahler: as always, I seek to remain faithful to the real model" (*LV*, 136). The soundtrack contains multiple Mahler pieces: beyond the reoccurring adagietto (the fourth movement of the Fifth Symphony), there is another diegetic instance played by Alfred on the piano during a flashback, then the fourth movement of Mahler's Third Symphony, heard when Aschenbach is seen composing on the beach (Carocci 2014, 153). As the flashback attests, Mahler's presence was not solely musical but textual as well. Biographical episodes from the composer's life gird the film's flashbacks: the loss of Mahler's daughter to scarlet fever, his own suffering from a heart condition, and finally his unpleasant relationship with functionaries at the Vienna State Opera all supplied a backstory for Aschenbach in the film (Bacon 1998, 163). Adding to the Mahlerian reference point, Visconti created an interlocutor for Aschenbach, Alfred, thought to be based on Arnold Schoenberg, a friend and colleague with whom Mahler was known to debate. Aschenbach's conversations with Alfred make up the majority of the flashbacks and conceive some of Aschenbach's philosophical musings from Mann's *Death in Venice*. Through these exchanges with Alfred, Visconti sketches out Aschenbach's belief that beauty is the product of labor, not the senses. Their conversations underscore how Aschenbach's Apollonian balance is upset by the spontaneity of beauty manifested in the ephebe Tadzio.

The transformation from author to composer nods to a second significant intertext for Visconti's Aschenbach: Mann's novel *Doctor Faustus*

(1947) and its composer hero Adrian Leverkühn (for an early discussion of *Faustus* in *Death in Venice*, see the screenwriter's comments in Badalucco 1970, 92). The presence of *Doctor Faustus* is immediately established in the film's first image, when, through the illuminating darkness, a boat arrives in the distance with the word *Esmeralda* emblazoned on its hull. This is the name of the demonic prostitute in *Doctor Faustus* whom Leverkühn meets when he is misdirected to a brothel (fig. 9.4). At first disgusted, Leverkühn later returns to Esmeralda and knowingly contracts syphilis. In doing so, he unlocks his creative potential as a musician. This episode was believed to have derived from the biography of Nietzsche, who describes being misled to a brothel where he was comforted by the presence of a piano that aided in his exit (Singer 2000, 113). Because syphilis is frequently thought to have caused Nietzsche's dementia, the composer's fateful return to the brothel mirrors the philosopher's. Thus, opening the film with Aschenbach being ferried to the virulent Venice on a ship bearing the prostitute's name introduces Leverkühn's lethal, satanic bargain. The diabolical figure of the prostitute makes an appearance during a flashback in which Aschenbach is pictured visiting a brothel, a scene that uses *Doctor Faustus* to foreshadow the noxious potential of the encounter with Tadzio. The danger of infection from the prostitute is tied aurally to Tadzio with the song "Für Elise," which Tadzio plays on the piano in the hotel lobby, and which is played in the next scene by the prostitute in a flashback. When asked if this link intentionally conflated Tadzio with the prostitute ("made Tadzio a bit prostitute and the prostitute a bit Tadzio"), Visconti demurred, replying that, "the girl from the bordello recalls Tadzio somewhat because she has the pure face

Figure 9.4. The prostitute Esmerelda from *Doctor Faustus*.

of a child, and also recalls *Doctor Faustus*, at least for those who have read it, and, more precisely, the allusion to the biography of Nietzsche contained in *Faustus*" (*LV*, 141).

Moreover, *Doctor Faustus* contains reference to Mann's homosexuality, with Mann's relationship with the painter Paul Ehrenberg in 1901 inspiring both the adolescent remembrances of *Tonio Kröger* and the episode between Leverkühn and Rudi Schwerdtfeger, the novel's violinist (T. J. Reed 1987, 165). These are just two indicators of *Doctor Faustus* in the film, another equally important being the presence of the hourglass (Hutchinson 1974). Splicing Mann's *Death in Venice* with *Doctor Faustus* introduces yet another form of hybridity to Visconti's adaptation, even one that openly purports to be based on a single text.

Visconti added himself to this group of real and fictional authors and artists. Gian Piero Brunetta saw Aschenbach as a cinematic alter ego for Visconti, consistent with his tendency to create such alter egos beginning with *The Leopard* (Brunetta 2006, 263). In that film, Burt Lancaster's prince of Salina was supposedly an elegant avatar for the aristocrat Visconti, embodying the director's preferred late-career themes of decay, the battle with intellectual and political resignation, and erotic flagging. The aristocrat's dispassionate perspective on history, observing from above without soiling himself with the soot of modernity's threshold, continued in other Visconti films to follow, most notably in *Death in Venice* and *Conversation Piece*, where male protagonists became proxies for Visconti, forwarding his personal preoccupations with advancing age, death, and beauty.

In *Conversation Piece*, Visconti reintroduces this director-protagonist by casting Burt Lancaster again, this time in the role of an American academic, called "The Professor," existing hermetically in a Roman apartment he inherited from his mother. The tranquility of his life, spent in the solitary study of "conversation pieces," is disrupted by a family of American children and their Italian mother, as well as by a German radical by the name of Konrad, played by Helmut Berger. The apartment, filmed at first as an architectural correlative to the Professor's intellectual quest for beautiful objects, becomes layered with the complexities of this family unit. Next to the apartment's library exists a hidden room where the Professor's mother once concealed members of the Italian resistance, and where Konrad seeks refuge from his persecutors. Roberto De Gaetano notes how this clandestine alcove stages the budding relationship between the Professor as "father" and his "son" Konrad, safe from any outside influences (De Gaetano 2000, 296). In emphasizing the impassioned gazes between the older and the younger man, Visconti suggests a continuation of the Aschenbach-Tadzio pairing that structures *Death in Venice*. Yet this pairing also contains another seed of autobiography: Visconti's relationship with Berger. *Conversation Piece* presents the theme of paternal sentiment that is present in Mann's *Death in Venice*, in which Mann conceals some of the homoeroticism with insinuations that Tadzio provokes a tenderness in Aschenbach that is more fatherly than sexual. Fatherhood, an organizing absence in many of Visconti's films, is rendered explicit in the conclusion of *Conversation Piece*, when the Professor notes that "the only love story that would suit a man of my age is King Lear's: a father's love for his children," to which Lietta (Claudia Marsani) recommends he adopt Konrad. The concern of the late Visconti with the theme of lacking an heir shows up in the dead daughter of Aschenbach's past in *Death in Venice* and Tullio's bastard child in *The Intruder*.

Mothers, not fathers, were more centrally positioned in Visconti's prior works, and that is also true of the late films. Early mothers, like the tragic pregnancy of Giovanna in *Obsession*, or Magnani's brilliant Maddalena in *Bellissima*, might be contrasted with Sophie in *The Damned* or the cold queen mother in *Ludwig*, who introduce themes of incest and matricide. As Visconti once stated, "Life is a hive: everyone lives and works in their own little cell. Then everyone comes together, in a central nucleus with the queen bee. And the drama explodes" (Baldelli 1982, 340). Once again, mothers will prevail in *Death in Venice* and the later *Conversation Piece*, where flashbacks function as Proustian shifts into the memory world of the protagonists. In *Conversation Piece*, two flashbacks feature the Professor's mother, played by actress Dominique Sanda. In an arresting moment, Sanda gazes directly into the camera as she addresses the Professor as a child; the mother's eyes stare directly at the spectator to indicate a leap into the past, as well as cinema's capacity for representing distant recollections of childhood affection. The mother–son connection is highlighted through the other mother figure in the film, played by Silvana Mangano, whose brash manners and selfish romance with Konrad present a manipulative maternal figure. The casting of Mangano as this loud, undevoted mother in *Conversation Piece* is in contrast to her role as Tadzio's mother in *Death in Venice*, where she plays a rather quieter figure. Though she is virtually silent in *Death in Venice*, Mangano is highlighted visually throughout and so omnipresent as to constitute another protagonist (Naglia 2013, 30). In Mann's *Death in Venice*, the mother is almost completely marginal. Indeed, the mother character in the film was not modeled after the one in Mann's novella at all, but after Visconti's own mother, Carla Erba. Visconti, after all, was also re-creating the world of his childhood. "I myself am from that epoch. I was born in 1906 and the world that surrounded me, the artistic, literary, musical world is that one there . . . I also probably have visual and figurative memories, a type of involuntary memory that helps me reconstruct the atmosphere of that epoch" (Fumagalli 1988, 14). Thus, the Venetian setting was not simply transferred from novella to film but was refracted through the additional prism of Visconti's life (Bacon 1998, 162). For Phillip Reed, this constituted another connection with Mann's *Death in Venice*: "An analogy can be drawn between Visconti's own mother, Donna Carla Visconti, and Mann's Polish mother; the well-disciplined Polish children, and particularly Tadzio, are analogous to the severely brought-up Visconti brood" (P. Reed 1987, 182). Piero Tosi confirmed that Visconti's mother was the model for Mangano's character in an interview in 2004, stating that Visconti was working as much from memory as he was from Mann's novella: "Especially when Silvana Mangano is standing on the beach with those enormous veils around her, that is an exact childhood memory of his. He told me, 'I have forgotten so much, but now things from my childhood and my adolescence are so clear, they have returned so precisely, even smells' " (Blom 2017a, 93).

The costuming in *Death in Venice* was in some cases clearly modeled on clothes worn by Carla Erba (D'Amico de Carvalho 1978). Mangano herself attested to Visconti's intent to have her play his mother (*Per Luchino Visconti*, episode 4, 1987). In 1971, Alberto Moravia and Lino Micciché positively reviewed *Morte a Venezia*, with Moravia remarking that despite its multiple literary and musical references, the film was a work about Visconti (Moravia 1971, 23). Whereas others (such as Ugo Casiraghi) found the equation of director with protagonist to be a misstep, Micciché celebrated this inference, noting that the film was a "Concerted poem of decadence, with which Visconti could finally identify himself with completely, enjoying and suffering to the point of masochism" (Casarighi 1971, 10).

Conclusion: Adaptations of Life and Literature

When Visconti went to pitch *Death in Venice* to Warner Bros. Studios, he summarized his work in rather droll terms: "It's about this aging and not very attractive German who goes to Venice where he falls in love with a pretty pubescent boy. We'll make it virtually a silent film, to emphasize his isolation, and its pace will be very, very slow, with the same unbearably sad music played over and over and over. Did I mention that the old guy dies at the end?" (Aitken 2011, 113). His description suggests he suspected that *Death in Venice* might not be received with great excitement by large audiences. Nevertheless, no longer captivated by the blockbuster form, Visconti asserted his interest in an older, silent age of cinema. At the same time, real innovation took place in *Death in Venice*. For Carlo Testa, the film signaled a "harbinger" of a new era in Italy: "The 1970s in Italy were characterized by an acute public awareness that the personal or emotional aspect can never be separated out of any political issue, and vice versa. In that decade, the personal dimension of life came to be perceived by definition as an already political one ("the personal is political," *il privato è politico*); and Visconti's film opened new paths for this awareness" (Testa 2002b, 57). As we have seen, this personal, interior aspect of Visconti's work consistently emerged during the adaptation process throughout his career in cinema. Absent from his works is the Catholic searching in Fellini or, in a different vein, the premodern Christianity of Pasolini. There is also no interest in representing the ineffable as in Rossellini, the desire for grace as in Bresson, or the existential crises in Bergman, where individuals express their inner emotions through their search for God. In *Death in Venice* as in other Visconti works, spiritual longing is wrapped tightly in the aesthetic and erotic craving for beauty, one that looked to entirely different, secular traditions of literature as its scripture.

Like other Visconti adaptations that used one or more texts to structure individual characters or whole films, *Death in Venice* uses Mann's novella to give shape to the film and to stabilize Visconti's image of cinema as one reinforced by a kaleidoscopic array of historical, interartistic, and personal pixels. Bound together as such makes this image no less cinematic or more literary. Instead, it is exemplary of the art of adaptation, a form and a process defined by its resistance to discriminating between film and the other arts. Indeed, one might take up one of *Death in Venice*'s final shots as symbolic of this refusal to either separate from or completely indulge in the literary text on which the film is based. The film concludes on the beach when Aschenbach dies while looking out to the sea at Tadzio (fig. 9.5), who is slowly wading into the water. Aschenbach's view of Tadzio is obstructed by the sun that shines so brightly as to overwhelm the viewer.

Figure 9.5. Aschenbach's final viewpoint of Tadzio on the beach with a camera in the foreground.

Mann underscores Aschenbach's confusion at the object before him and the struggle to interpret the meaning behind the boy's gesture: "It seemed to him the pale and lovely Summoner out there smiled at him and beckoned; as though, with the hand he lifted from his hip, he pointed outward as he hovered on before into an immensity of richest expectation" (Mann 1954, 75). In the film, a camera—an object literally taken from this sequence of Mann's novella—is seen perched on a tripod, signaling how the cinematic apparatus and the filmic operation under way can derive from a literary source. The novella reads: "A camera on a tripod stood at the edge of the water, apparently abandoned; its black cloth snapped in the freshening wind" (73). The author then describes Tadzio's movements and gestures in the distance: "one hand resting on his hip and looked over his shoulder at the shore" (74). Visconti presents the boy shrouded in the bright light reflecting off the surface of the sea, elongating his arm to the familiar notes of Mahler's adagietto. Here Visconti's adaptation returns to the thoughts and feelings outlined in his essay "Tradition and Invention," relying on "the power and suggestiveness to rely completely on its *intimate and musical rhythm*" (*LV*, 19) that he once sought to reveal from Verga's *The House by the Medlar Tree* a few decades before. *Death in Venice* concludes with a melding of music and image, text and film, foregrounded together and inseparable. Pictured in tandem, cinema and literature combine to "assemble the magic of that rhythm, of that vague yearning for the unknown, of that knowledge that people are not well off, or could be better, which makes up the poetic substance of a play of destinies, which cross without ever touching each other" (*LV*, 20).

Bibliography

Abbreviations

FV (Fondo Visconti): Luchino Visconti Collection, Fondazione Gramsci Onlus, Rome.

LV: *Leggere Visconti*, edited by Giuliana Callegari and Nuccio Lodato. Pavia: Amministrazione Provinciale, 1976.

Adair, Gilbert. *Love and Death on Long Island*. London: Vintage, 1990.

Aitken, Will. *Death in Venice: A Queer Film Classic*. Vancouver: Arsenal, 2011.

Alfar, Cristina Leòn. "'Blood Will Have Blood': Power, Performance, and Lady Macbeth's Gender Trouble." *Journal x* 2, no. 2 (1998): 179–207.

Alicata, Mario, and Giuseppe De Santis. "Verità e poesia: Verga e il cinema italiano." *Cinema* 127 (October 10, 1941a): 216–17.

———. "Ancora di Verga e del cinema italiano." *Cinema* 130 (November 25, 1941b): 314–15.

Alpert, Hollis. "The Stranger." *Filmfacts* 10, no. 24 (January 15, 1968).

Andrew, Dudley. *Concepts in Film Theory*. Oxford: Oxford University Press, 1984.

Anile, Alberto, and Maria Gabriella Giannice. "27 marzo 1963, cinema Barberini." In *Operazione Gattopardo: come Visconti trasformò un romanzo di 'destra' in un successo di 'sinistra,'* edited by Alberto Anile and Maria Gabriella Giannice, 225–44. Genoa: Le mani, 2013a.

———. "Tagli strategici a Cannes." In *Operazione Gattopardo: come Visconti trasformò un romanzo di 'destra' in un successo di 'sinistra,'* edited by Alberto Anile and Maria Gabriella Giannice, 245–68. Genoa: Le mani, 2013b.

Antonello, Pierpaolo. "Di crisi in meglio. Realismo, impegno postmoderno e cinema politico nell'Italia degli anni zero: da Nanni Moretti a Paolo Sorrentino." *Italian Studies* 67, no. 2 (July 2012): 169–87.

Antonello, Pierpaolo, and Florian Mussgnug. "Introduction." In *Postmodern Impegno: Ethics and Commitment in Contemporary Italian Culture*, edited by Pierpaolo Antonello and Florian Mussgnug, 1–29. Bern: Peter Lang, 2009.

Argentieri, Mino. "Visconti e Togliatti, due sensibilità che collimavano: Conversazione con Mino Argentieri." In *Operazione Gattopardo: come Visconti trasformò un romanzo di 'destra' in un successo di 'sinistra,'* edited by Alberto Anile and Maria Gabriella Giannice, 359–66. Genoa: Le mani, 2013.

Aristarco, Guido. "Luchino Visconti: Critic or Poet of Decadence?" Translated by Luciana Bohn. *Film Criticism* 12, no. 3 (Spring 1988): 58–63.

———, ed. *Antologia del Cinema Nuovo 1952–1958: Dalla critica cinematografica alla dialettica culturale*. Rimini-Florence: Guaraldi, 1975.

———. "L'opera di Visconti nella storia del cinema e della cultura italiana." In *L'opera di Visconti, atti del convegno di studi Fiesole 27–29 giugno, 1966*, edited by Mario Sperenzi, 7–39. Florence: Tip. A Lipari, 1969a.

———. "L'ultimo Visconti tra Wagner e Mann." *La stampa* (Turin), December 9, 1969b.

———. "Luchino Visconti e il romanzo." *La stampa* (Turin), November 22, 1960.

Asor Rosa, Alberto. "Il primo e l'ultimo uomo del mondo. Indagine sulle strutture narrative e sociologiche in 'Vita dei campi.'" In *Il caso Verga*, edited by Alberto Asor Rosa, 11–85. Palermo: Palumbo, 1973.

Bacon, Henry. *Visconti: Explorations of Beauty and Decay*. Cambridge: Cambridge University Press, 1998.

Badalucco, Nicola. "Dal 'Doctor Faustus' una guida per 'Morte a Venezia.'" *Il dramma*, no. 8 (August 1970).

Balász, Béla. *Theory of the Film: Character and Growth of a New Art*. Translated by Edith Bone. New York: Dover, 1970.

Baldelli, Pio. *Luchino Visconti*, 2nd ed. Milan: Mazzotta, 1982.

———. *Luchino Visconti*. Milan: Mazzotta, 1973.

———. *I film di Luchino Visconti*. Manduria: Lacaita, 1965.

Banti, Anna. "La caduta degli dei." *L'approdo letterario* 15, no. 48 (1969): 160–61.

Barbaro, Umberto. "Realismo e moralità." In *Neorealismo e realismo*, vol. 2, *Cinema e teatro*, edited by Gian Piero Brunetta, 505–9. Rome: Editori Riuniti, 1976.

Barnouw, Erik. *Documentary: A History of the Non-Fiction Film*, 2nd ed. New York: Oxford University Press, 1993.

Bayman, Louis. *The Operatic and the Everyday: Post-war Italian Film Melodrama*. Edinburgh: Edinburgh University Press, 2014.

Bazin, André. "A Saint Becomes a Saint Only after the Fact: 'Heaven over the Marshes.'" In *Bazin at Work: Major Essays and Reviews from the Forties and Fifties*, edited by Bert Cardullo, 89–93. New York: Routledge, 1997a.

———. "Adaptation, or Cinema as Digest." In *Bazin at Work: Major Essays and Reviews from the Forties and Fifties*, edited by Bert Cardullo, 41–51. New York: Routledge, 1997b.

———. "Theater and Cinema." In *What is Cinema? Volume 1*, translated by Hugh Gray, 76–95. Berkeley: University of California Press, 1967.

Bellocchio, Letizia. 2008. "*Otello* di Visconti." In *La macchina e le muse*, edited by Federica Mazzocchi, 69–92. Bari: Edizioni di Pagina, 2008.

———. "Il Medioevo nei Macbeth cinematografici (Welles, Kurosawa, Polanski, Visconti)." *Doctor Virtualis* (December 2006): 9–22.

Ben-Ghiat, Ruth. "Unmaking the Fascist Man: Masculinity, Film, and the Transition from Dictatorship." *Journal of Modern Italian Studies* 10, no. 3 (2005): 336–65.

Bergman, Paul, and Michael Asimow. *Reel Justice: The Courtroom Goes to the Movies.* Kansas City, MO: Andrews and McMeel, 1996.

Bernardini, Aldo. "Cinema e letteratura, immagini e parola." *Cineforum* 7, no. 69 (November 1969): 727–43.

Bertellini, Giorgio. "A Battle 'd'Arrière-Garde': Notes on Decadence in Luchino Visconti's 'Death in Venice.' " *Film Quarterly* 50, no. 4 (Summer 1997): 11–19.

Biagi, Enzo. "Dicono di Lei Visconti." *La stampa*, May 20, 1973.

———. "Mentre si discute la morale di 'Rocco' un'enorme folle si precipita a vederlo." *La Stampa*, October 19, 1960.

Bianchi, Pietro. "Un romantico dei nostri tempi." In *Vaghe Stelle dell'Orsa*, edited by Pietro Bianchi, 11–28. Bologna: Cappelli, 1965.

Bignardi, Irene. "The Making of *The Battle of Algiers*." *Cineaste* 25, no. 2 (2000): 14–22.

Billington, Michael. "Jude Law Channels Macbeth in Tale of Passion and Murder." *The Guardian*, April 25, 2017. https://www.theguardian.com/stage/2017/apr/26/obsession-review-well-executed-remake-but-power-and-atmosphere-are-lacking.

Blanke, Olaf, and Isabella Pasqualini. "The Riddle of Style Changes in the Visual Arts after Interference with the Right Brain." *Frontiers in Human Neuroscience* 5 (January 2012): 1–10.

Blom, Ivo. *Reframing Luchino Visconti: Film and Art.* Leiden: Sidestone Press, 2017a.

———. "Unaffectedness and Rare Eurythmics: Carl Koch, Jean Renoir, Luchino Visconti and the Production of *Tosca* (1939/1941)." *The Italianist* 37, no. 2 (2017b): 149–75.

Boito, Camillo. *Il maestro di setticlavio.* Edited by Giorgio Bassani. Rome: Colombo, 1945.

———. *Senso.* Milan: Treves, 1883.

Bolongaro, Eugenio. "Representing the (Un)representable: Homosexuality in Luchino Visconti's *Rocco and His Brothers*." *Studies in European Cinema* 7, no. 3 (2014): 221–34.

Bondanella, Peter. *Italian Cinema: From Neorealism to the Present.* New York: Continuum, 2004.

Boozer, Jack. "Introduction: The Screenplay and Authorship in Adaptation." In *Authorship in Film Adaptation*, edited by Jack Boozer, 1–30. Austin: University of Texas Press, 2008.

Bordwell, David. *Narration in the Fiction Film.* London: Routledge, 1997.

———. "The Art Cinema as a Mode of Film Practice." *Film Criticism* 4, no. 1 (Fall 1979): 56–64.

Bourdieu, Pierre. *Photography: A Middle-Brow Art.* Translated by Shaun Whiteside. Stanford, CA: Stanford University Press, 1990.

Boylan, Amy. "Masculinity and Commemoration of the Great War: Gabriele D'Annunzio's *La beffa dei buccari* and Eugenio Baroni's *Monumento al Fante*." *Italian Culture* 29, no. 1 (2011): 3–17.

Bragaglia, Cristina. *Il piacere del racconto: Narrativa italiana e cinema, 1895–1990.* Florence: La Nuova Italia, 1993.

Braudy, Leo. *The World in a Frame: What We See in Films.* Chicago: University of Chicago Press, 1984.

Brooks, Peter. *The Melodramatic Imagination: Balzac, Henry James, Melodrama and the Mode of Excess.* New Haven, CT: Yale University Press, 1995.

Brunetta, Gian Piero. *Attrazione fatale: letterati italiani e letteratura dalla pagina allo schermo.* Milan: Mimesis, 2017.

———. *Il cinema italiano di regime: Da "La canzone dell'amore" a "Ossessione."* Rome: Laterza, 2009.

———. "Cinema e letteratura italiana del '900." In *Sinergie narrative. Cinema e letteratura nell'Italia contemporanea*, edited by Guido Bonsaver, Martin McLaughlin, and Franca Pellegrini, 25–40. Florence: Cesati, 2008.

———. *Cent'anni di cinema italiano, 2: Dal 1945 ai giorni nostril*, 2nd ed. Rome-Bari: Laterza, 2006.

———. "Identità e radici culturali." In *Storia del cinema mondiale, vol. 1*, edited by Gian Piero Brunetta, 3–50. Turin: Einaudi, 1999.

———. "La lunga marcia del cinema americano in Italia tra fascismo e guerra fredda." In *Hollywood in Europa: Industria, Politica, Pubblico del Cinema, 1945–1960*, edited by Gian Piero Brunetta and David W. Ellwood, 75–87. Florence: Casa Usher, 1991.

Bruni, David. "La fortuna critica del film." In *La terra trema: Analasi di un capolavoro*, edited by Lino Micciché, 165–95. Turin: Lindau, 1996.

B.T. "Il crepuscolo del realismo." *Cinema 60* 10, nos. 73/74 (December 1969/ February1970): 93–94.

Buccheri, Vincenzo. "L'immagine al presente." In *Il cinema di Luchino Visconti*, edited by Veronica Pravadelli, 187–98. Venice: Marsilio, 2000.

Burgoyne, Robert. *The Hollywood Historical Film.* Oxford: Blackwell, 2008.

Cain, James M. *The Postman Always Rings Twice.* New York: First Vintage Crime, 1992.

Calinescu, Mattei. *Faces of Modernity: Avant-garde, Decadence, Kitsch.* Bloomington: Indiana University Press, 1977.

Callegari, Giuliana, and Nuccio Lodato, eds. *Leggere Visconti.* Pavia: Amministrazione Provinciale, 1976. (*LV*)

Calvino, Italo. *Saggi 1945–1985.* Edited by M. Barenghi. Milan: Mondadori, 1995.

Caminati, Luca. "The Role of Documentary Film in the Formation of the Neorealist Cinema." In *Global Neorealism: The Transnational History of a Film Style*, edited by Saverio Giovacchini and Robert Sklar. Jackson: University Press of Mississippi, 2012.

Caminati, Luca, and Mauro Sassi. "Notes on the History of Italian Non-Fiction Film." In *A Companion to Italian Cinema*, edited by Frank Burke, 361–73. Oxford: Wiley Blackwell, 2017.

Camus, Albert. *The Stranger.* Translated by Matthew Ward. New York: Vintage Books, 1989.

———. *Lyrical and Critical Essays*. Edited by Philip Thody. New York: Vintage Books, 1968.

Canby, Vincent. "Oh to Be Rich and Sexy in Venice." *New York Times*, June 27, 1971.

Canova, Gianni. "Rocco e i suoi fratelli: Visconti e le aporie anestetiche della modernità." In *Il cinema di Luchino Visconti*, edited by Veronica Pravadelli, 175–86. Venice: Marsilio, 2000.

Canudo, Ricciotto. "The Triumph of the Cinema." In *Early Film Theories in Italy, 1896–1922*, edited by Francesco Casetti, Silvio Alovisio, and Luca Mazzei, 66–74. Amsterdam: Amsterdam University Press, 2017.

———. "Manifesto of the Seven Arts." Translated by Steven Phillip Kramer. *Literature/Film Quarterly* 3, no. 3 (Summer 1975): 252–54.

Cappabianca, Andrea. *Boxare con l'ombra*. Recco (Genoa): Le mani, 2004.

Caputo, Rino. "Un tema di politica culturale degli anni '60: *Il Gattopardo*." *Studi Novecenteschi* 4, no. 10 (March 1975): 35–55.

Carancini, Gaetano. *Rocco e i suoi fratelli: storia di un capolavoro*. Rome: minimum fax, 2010.

Cardinale, Claudia. *Io, Claudia, Tu, Claudia*. Milan: Frassinelli, 2006.

Cardone, Lucia. *Il melodramma*. Milan: Il Castoro, 2012.

Cardullo, Bert. "Reality, Romanticism, Eroticism . . . and the Cinema: An Interview with Luchino Visconti." In *World Directors in Dialogue*, edited by Bert Cardullo, 3–19. Lanham, MD: Scarecrow Press, 2011.

Cardwell, Sarah. "Pause, Rewind, Replay: Adaptation, Intertextuality, and (Re)defining Adaptation Studies." In *The Routledge Companion to Adaptation Studies*, edited by Dennis Cutchins, Katja Krebs, and Eckarts Voigts, 7–17. New York: Routledge, 2018.

Carocci, Antonio. "Un singolare rapporto a tre: Mann, Mahler e Visconti." In *Morte a Venezia Thomas Mann / Luchino Visconti: Un confronto*, edited by Francesco Bono, Luigi Cimmino, and Giorgio Pangaro, 149–70. Soveria Mannelli: Rubbetino, 2014.

Casadio, Gianfranco. *La guerra al cinema: I film di Guerra nel cinema italiano dal 1944 al 1996, Vol. 1, Dal Risorgimento alla seconda guerra mondiale*. Ravenna: Longo Editore, 1997.

Casetti, Francesco. "Lo sguardo novecentesco." In *Storie dislocate*, edited by Sandro Bernardi, 17–26. Pisa: ETS, 1999.

Casiraghi, Ugo. "La caduta di un artista." *L'unità*, March 6, 1971.

Castellani, Leandro. "I film dei vent'anni dopo." *Rivista del cinematografo* 40, no. 10 (October 1967): 587–88.

Castello, Giulio Cesare. "Realismo, romanticismo e senso dello spettacolo nei film italiani sul Risorgimento a partire dal 1930." In *Il film storico italiano e la sua influenza sugli altri paesi*, 94–100. Rome: Edizioni di bianco e nero, 1963.

Chatman, Seymour. "What Novels Can Do That Films Can't (and Vice Versa)." *Critical Inquiry* 7, no. 1 (Autumn 1980): 121–40.

Chiari, Mario, Franco Ferri, Rinaldo Ricci, and Luchino Visconti. "Pensione oltremare." In *Cinema e resistenza*, edited by Massimo Mida and Giovanni Vento, 146–56. Florence: Luciano Landi, 1959.

Chiarini, Luigi. "Tradisce il neorealismo." In *Antologia del Cinema Nuovo 1952–1958: Dalla critica cinematografica alla dialettica culturale*, edited by Guido Aristarco, 882–87. Rimini-Florence: Guaraldi, 1975.

Clapp, Sussanah. "Jude Law Is Stranded in Treacle-Slow Adaptation." *The Guardian*, April 30, 2017. https://www.theguardian.com/stage/2017/apr/30/obsession-review-ivo-van-hove-barbican-jude-law.

Cohan, Steve. *Masked Men: Masculinity and the Movies in the Fifties*. Bloomington: Indiana University Press, 1997.

Coldstream, John. *Dirk Bogarde: The Authorised Biography*. London: Phoenix, 2005.

Collins, Jim. *Bring on the Books for Everybody*. Durham, NC: Duke University Press, 2010.

Connell, Raewyn. *Masculinities*. Cambridge: Polity Press, 1995.

Coover, Robert. *Pinocchio in Venice*. New York: Linden Press/Simon and Schuster, 1991.

Corrigan, Timothy. "Which Shakespeare to Love? Film, Fidelity, and the Performance of Literature." In *High-Pop: Making Culture into Popular Entertainment*, edited by Jim Collins, 155–81. Oxford: Blackwell, 2002.

Corsi, Barbara. *Con qualche dollaro in meno: storia economica del cinema italiano*. Florence: Le Lettere, 2012.

Costa, Antonio. "Tra autarchia ed ecclettismo: invenzione del paesaggio italiano." In *Storia del cinema italiano, 6: 1940–1944*, edited by Ernesto G. Laura, 137–52. Venice: Marsilio, 2010.

Cosulich, Callisto. "Un abito fatto su misura." *ABC*, March 12, 1971.

Croce, Benedetto. "Di un carattere della più recente letteratura italiana." In *Letteratura della nuova italia*, vol. 4, 179–96. Bari: Laterza, 1915.

Crowdus, Gary. "Götterdämmerung / The Damned." *Film Society Review* 5, no. 6 (February (1970): 32–35.

D'Amico, Suso Cecchi. *Storie di cinema (e d'altro)*. Milan: Garzanti, 1996.

D'Amico, Suso Cecchi, and Luchino Visconti. "Macbeth 1967." In *Controversia Visconti*, edited by Fernaldo di Giammatteo, 54–72. Rome: Edizioni dell'Ataneo e Bizzari, 1976.

D'Amico de Carvalho, Caterina. *Album Visconti*. Milan: Sonzogno, 1978.

D'Amico de Carvalho, Caterina, and Alessandra Favino. "Nota biográfica." In *Il Fondo Luchino Visconti: Guida alla consultazione*, edited by Caterina D'Amico de Carvalho and Alessandra Favino, 9–16. Rome: Fondazione Istituto Gramsci onlus, 2003a.

D'Amico de Carvalho, Caterina, and Alessandra Favino. "Fondo Archivistico." In *Il Fondo Luchino Visconti: Guida alla consultazione*, edited by Caterina D'Amico de Carvalho and Alessandra Favino, 27–34. Rome: Fondazione Istituto Gramsci onlus, 2003b.

D'Annunzio, Gabriele. *The Child of Pleasure*. Translated by Georgina Harding and Arthur Symons. Project Gutenberg, 2006.

———. *Lettere ai Treves*. Milan: Garzanti, 1999.

———. *L'Innocente*. Milan: Mondadori Editore, 1996.

———. *Forse che sì forse che no*. Milan: Treves, 1910.

Darbellay, Laurent. *Luchino Visconti et la peinture: Les effets picturaux de l'image cinématographique*. Geneva: Métis Presses, 2011.

De Franceschi, Leonardo. *Il film Lo straniero di Luchino Visconti: dalla pagina allo schermo*. Rome: Scuola Fondazione Nazionale di Cinema, 1999.

De Gaetano, Roberto. "Gruppo di famiglia in un interno: Le cornici del tempo." In *Il cinema di Luchino Visconti*, edited by Veronica Pravadelli, 295–306. Venice: Marsilio, 2000.

De Santis, Giuseppe. "Visconti's Interpretation of Cain's Setting in *Ossessione*." Translated by Luciana Bohne. *Film Criticism* 9, no. 3 (Spring 1985): 23–32.

———. "Per un paesaggio italiano." *Cinema* 116 (April 25, 1941): 262–63.

Deleuze, Gilles. *Cinema 1: The Movement-Image*. Translated by Hugh Tomlinson and Barbara Habberjam. Minneapolis: University of Minnesota Press, 2003.

Doane, Mary Ann. "The Voice in the Cinema: The Articulation of Body and Space." *Yale French Studies*, no. 60 (1980): 33–50.

Dostoevsky, Fyodor. *Dostoyevsky: Notes from the Underground, White Nights, The Dream of a Ridiculous Man, and Selections from The House of the Dead*. Translated by Andrew R. MacAndrew. New York: Signet Press, 1961.

Drake, Richard. "Decadence, Decadentism and Decadent Romanticism in Italy: Toward a Theory of Décadence." *Journal of Contemporary History* 17, no. 1 (January 1982): 69–92.

Drake, Sylvie. "Acting Is Just Like 'Old Times' for Pinter." *Los Angeles Times*, October 29, 1985.

Du Maurier, Daphne. *Not After Midnight, and Other Stories*. London: Gollancz, 1971.

Duncan, Derek. "*Ossessione*." In *European Cinema: An Introduction*, edited by Jill Forbes and Sarah Street, 94–106. New York: Palgrave, 2000.

Durgnat, Raymond. "The Stranger (L'étranger, Luchino Visconti)." *Films and Filming* 15, no. 2 (November 1968): 38–39.

Dyer, Geoff. *Jeff in Venice, Death in Varanasi*. Edinburgh: London Canongate, 2015.

Eisenstein, Sergei. "Dickens, Griffith, and the Film Today." In *Film Form: Essays in Film Theory*, edited and translated by Jay Leyda, 195–255. London: Dobson, 1963.

Ellestrøm, Lars. "Adaptation within the Field of Media Transformations." In *Adaptation Studies: New Challenges, New Directions*, edited by Jorgen Bruhn, Anne Gjelsvik, and Eirik Frisvold Hanssen, 113–32. New York: Bloomsbury, 2013.

Elliot, Kamilla. *Rethinking the Novel/Film Debate*. Cambridge: Cambridge University Press, 2003.

Fabbri, Lorenzo. "Queer Neorealism: Luchino Visconti's *Ossessione* and the *Cinema* Conspiracy against Fascism." *Screen* 60, no. 1 (Spring 2019): 1–24.

Falcinella, Nicola. *Alida Valli: Gli occhi, il grido*. Recco-Genoa: Le Mani, 2011.

Ferguson Ellis, Kate. *The Contested Castle: Gothic Novels and the Subversion of Domestic Ideology*. Urbana: University of Illinois Press, 1989.

Ferrero, Adelio. "Una bella di giorno e pochi sovversivi operanti." *Cinema Nuovo* 16, no. 189 (September/October 1967): 339–49.

Flynn, Caryl. *The New German Cinema: Music, History, and the Matter of Style*. Berkeley: University of California Press, 2004.

Fofi, Goffredo. "Prefazione." In *Operazione Gattopardo: come Visconti trasformò un romanzo di 'destra' in un successo di 'sinistra,'* edited by Alberto Anile and Maria Gabriella Giannice, 5–10. Genoa: Le mani, 2013.

Foose, Thomas. "Authorized Cain: *Postman* Done by French, Pirated by Visconti's *Ossessione*." *Variety*, November 10, 1976.

Foot, John. "La gente e il buon costume: Luchino Visconti's *Rocco e i suoi fratelli*. Censorship and the Left in Italy, 1960–1961." In *Reflexivity: Critical Themes in the Italian Cultural Tradition*, edited by Prue Shaw and John Took, 9–36. Ravenna: Longo Editore, 2000.

———. "Cinema and the City: Milan and Visconti's *Rocco and His Brothers*." *Journal of Modern Italian Studies* 4, no. 2 (1999): 209–35.

Forgacs, David. "The Prince and His Critics: The Reception of *Il Gattopardo*." In *Il Gattopardo at Fifty*, edited by Davide Messina, 17–43. Ravenna: Longo Editore, 2010.

———. "Days of Sodom: The Fascism-Perversion Equation in Films of the 1960s and 1970s." In *Italian Fascism: History, Memory, and Representation*, edited by R. J. B. Bosworth and Patrizia Doglianai, 216–36. Basingstoke: Macmillan, 1999.

———. "Cultural Consumption, 1940s to 1990s." In *Italian Cultural Studies: An Introduction*, edited by David Forgacs and Robert Lumley, 273–90. Oxford: Oxford University Press, 1996.

Frese Witt, Mary Ann. *The Search for Modern Tragedy: Aesthetic Fascism in Italy and France*. Ithaca, NY: Cornell University Press, 2001.

Frosali, Sergio. "Il Visconti più discusso." *La Nazione*, September 24, 1965.

Fumagalli, Paolo. *Il Gattopardo: Dal Romanzo al Film*. Florence: Firenze Libri, 1988.

Galt, Rosalind. "Italy's Landscapes of Loss: Historical Mourning and the Dialectical Image in Cinema Paradiso, Mediterraneo and Il Postino." *Screen* 43, no. 2 (2002): 158–73.

Genette, Gérard. *Paratext: Thresholds of Interpretation*. Translated by Jane E. Lewin. Cambridge: Cambridge University Press, 1997.

Genina, Augusto. "Qualche santo." In *L'avventurosa storia del cinema italiano raccontata dai suoi protagonisti, 1939–1959*, edited by Franca Faldini and Goffredo Fofi, 197–98. Milan: Feltrinelli, 1979.

Geraghty, Christine. *Now a Major Motion Picture: Film Adaptations of Literature and Drama*. Lanham, MD: Rowman and Littlefield, 2008.

Ginsberg, Terri. "Nazis and Drifters: The Containment of Radical (Sexual) Knowledge in Two Italian Neorealist Films." *Journal of the History of Sexuality* 1, no. 2 (October 1990): 241–61.

Giori, Mauro. *Poetica e prassi della trasgressione in Luchino Visconti*, 2nd ed. Milan: Libraccio, 2018.

———. *Homosexuality and Italian Cinema: From the Fall of Fascism to the Years of Lead.* London: Palgrave, 2017.

———. *Scandalo e banalità: Rappresentazioni dell'eros in Luchino Visconti, 1963–1976.* Milan: LED, 2012.

———. *Luchino Visconti: Rocco e i suoi fratelli.* Turin: Lindau, 2011a.

———. "Oresti di paglia ed Elettre sepolte." *LANX* 9 (2011b): 86–109.

Giori, Mauro, and Tomaso Subini. "Questioni aperte su *La terra trema:* Ipotesi preliminari intorno ad alcuni nuovi documenti." *Cabiria*, no. 176 (January–April 2014): 4–37.

Gledhill, Christine. "Rethinking Genre." In *Reinventing Film Studies*, edited by Christine Gledhill and Linda Williams, 221–43. London: Arnold, 2000.

Gorfinkel, Elena, and John David Rhodes. "Introduction: The Matter of Places." *Taking Place: Location and the Moving Image*, edited by Elena Gorfinkel and John David Rhodes, i–xxix. Minneapolis: University of Minnesota Press, 2011.

Gramsci, Antonio. *Quaderni del carcere*. Edited by Valentino Gerratana. Toronto: Einaudi, 2014.

Granger, Farley, with Robert Calhoun. *Include Me Out: My Life from Goldwyn to Broadway*. New York: St. Martin's Press, 2007.

Grazzini, Giovanni. "Il Gattopardo di Luchino Visconti non ha (troppo) tradito il romanziere." *Il Corriere della Sera*, March 28, 1963.

Greenberg, Clement. *Art and Culture; Critical Essays*. Boston: Beacon Press, 1961.

Gremigni, Elena. *Pubblico e popolarità: il ruolo del cinema nella società italiana, 1956–1967*. Florence: Lettere, 2009.

Grindon, Leger. "The Boxing Film and Genre Theory." *Quarterly Review of Film and Video* 24, no. 5 (2007): 403–10.

Guerriero, Stefano. "La fortuna critica." In *La lunga corsa del Gattopardo: Storia di un grande romanzo dal rifiuto al successo*. Turin: Aragno, 2008.

Guidorizzi, Mario. "Filmografia." In *Cinema e letteratura del neorealismo*, edited by Giorgio Tinazzi and Marina Zancan, 167–90. Venice: Marsilio, 1983.

Gundle, Stephen. "Alida Valli in Hollywood: From Star of Fascist Cinema to 'Selznick Siren.'" *Historical Journal of Film, Radio and Television* 32, no. 4 (2012): 559–87.

———. *Bellissima: Feminine Beauty and the Idea of Italy*. New Haven, CT: Yale University Press, 2007.

———. *Between Hollywood and Moscow: The Italian Communists and the Challenge of Mass Culture*. Durham, NC: Duke University Press, 2000.

Hennessey, Brendan. "Patterns of Pugilism: *Rocco e i suoi fratelli* (1960) and the Boxing Film." *The Italianist* 36, no. 2 (2016): 214–42.

———. "Theatrical Spaces in Luchino Visconti's *Le notti bianche* (1957)." *Modern Language Notes* 126, no. 1 (January 2011): 157–78.

Higson, Andrew. "Re-Presenting the National Past: Nostalgia and Pastiche in the Heritage Film." In *Fires Were Started: British Cinema and Thatcherism*, edited by Lester Friedman, 109–29. Minneapolis: University of Minnesota Press, 1993.

Hipkins, Danielle. "'I Don't Want to Die': Prostitution and Narrative Disruption in Visconti's *Rocco e i suoi fratelli*." In *Women in Italy: 1945–1960*, edited by Penelope Morris, 193–210. New York: Palgrave, 2006.

Hochkofler, Matilde. *Anna Magnani: la biografia*. Milan: Bompiani, 2013.

Holden, Stephen. "The Movies that Inspired Martin Scorsese." *New York Times*, May 21, 1993.

Hom, Stephanie Malia. *Beautiful Italy: Tourism and the Impossible State of Destination Italy*. Toronto: University of Toronto Press, 2015.

Huckvale, David. *Touchstones of Gothic Horror: A Film Geneology of Eleven Motifs and Images*. Jefferson, NC: McFarland, 2010.

Hutcheon, Linda. *A Theory of Adaptation*. New York: Routledge, 2006.

Hutchinson, Alexander. "Luchino Visconti's Death in Venice." *Literature/Film Quarterly* (Winter 1974): 31–43.

Ishaghpour, Youssef. "L'arte e la vita: L'unità dell'opera e l'impuro." In *Studi viscontiani*, edited by David Bruni and Veronica Pravadelli, 183–94. Venice: Marsilio, 1997.

Jansen, Monica. *Fragments of Impegno: Interpretations of Commitment in Contemporary Italian Narrative, 1980–2000*. Leeds: Northern Universities Press, 2001.

Judaken, Jonathan. "Sysyphus's Progeny: Existentialism in France." In *Situating Existentialism: Key Texts in Context*, edited by Jonathan Judaken and Robert Bernasconi, 89–122. New York: Columbia University Press, 2012.

Kaes, Anton, and David J. Levin. "The Debate about Cinema: Charting a Controversy 1909–1929." *New German Critique*, no. 40 (Winter 1987): 7–33.

Kira'ly, Hajnal. "The Medium Strikes Back—'Impossible Adaptation' Revisited." In *Adaptation Studies: New Challenges, New Directions*, edited by Jorgen Bruhn, Anne Gjelsvik, and Erik Frisvold Hanssen, 179–202. New York: Bloomsbury, 2013.

Kovács, András. *Screening Modernism: European Art Cinema, 1950–1980*. Chicago: University of Chicago Press, 2007.

Koven, Mikel J. "The *Giallo* and the Spaghetti Nightmare Film." In *The Italian Cinema Book*, edited by Peter Bondanella, 203–10. London: Palgrave Macmillan, 2014.

Lake, Diane. "Adapting the Unadaptable." In *A Companion to Literature, Film, and Adaptation*, edited by Deborah Cartmell, 408–15. Malden, MA: Wiley-Blackwell, 2014.

Lagny, Michèle. "Visconti e la 'cultura popolare.'" In *Studi viscontiani*, edited by David Bruni and Veronica Pravadelli, 241–50. Venice: Marsilio, 1997.

Landy, Marcia. *Stardom Italian Style: Screen Performance and Personality in Italian Cinema*. Bloomington: Indiana University Press, 2008.

———. *The Folklore of Consensus*. Albany: State University of New York Press, 1998.

———. *Cinematic Uses of the Past*. Minneapolis: University of Minnesota Press, 1996.

Lasi, Giovanni, and Giorgio Sangiori. "Indice tematico dei film. 1905–2010." In *Il risorgimento nel cinema italiano: filmografia a soggetto risorgimentale, 1905–2010*, edited by Giovanni Lasi and Giorgio Sangiori, 175–78. Faenza: Edit Faenza, 2011.

Laurenzi, Laura. *Amori e furori*. Milan: Rizzoli, 2000.

Leavitt, Charles L. IV. *Italian Neorealism: A Cultural History*. Toronto: University of Toronto Press, 2020.

———. "Cronaca, Narrativa, and the Unstable Foundation of the Institution of Neorealism." *Italian Culture* 31, no. 1 (March 2013): 28–46.

Leitch, Thomas. "Adaptation Studies at a Crossroads." *Adaptation* 1, no. 1 (2008a): 63–77.

———. "Adaptation, the Genre." *Adaptation* 1, no. 2 (2008b): 106–20.

———. "Twelve Fallacies in Contemporary Adaptation Theory." *Criticism* 45, no. 2 (Spring 2003): 149–71.

Lerner, Giovanna Faleschini. "Visconti's *Senso*: The Art of History." *Forum Italicum* 41, no. 2 (September 2007): 342–58.

Liandrat-Guigues, Suzanne. "Aria di tomba." In *Visconti a Volterra: La genesi di Vaghe Stelle dell'Orsa*, edited by Veronica Pravadelli, 27–52. Turin: Lindau, 2000.

Liehm, Mira. *Passion and Defiance: Italian Film from 1942 to the Present*. Berkeley: California University Press, 1986.

Liguori, Guido. *Gramsci conteso*. Rome: Editori Riuniti, 1996.

Lizzani, Carlo. "Eravamo eclettici." In *Cinema e letteratura del neorealismo*, edited by Giorgio Tinazzi and Marina Zancan, 103–10. Venice: Marsilio, 1983.

Lucente, Gregory. "Scrivere o fare . . . o altro: Social Commitment and Ideologies of Representation in the Debates over Lampedusa's *Il Gattopardo* and Morante's *La Storia*." *Italica* 61, no. 3 (Autumn 1984): 220–51.

———. "Lampedusa's Il Gattopardo: Figure and Temporality in an Historical Novel." *MLN* 93, no. 1 (January 1978): 82–108.

Luchino Visconti Collection. Fondazione Gramsci Onlus, Rome. (*FV*)

Luciani, Sebastiano Arturo. "The Poetics of Cinema." In *Early Film Theories in Italy, 1896–1922*, edited by Francesco Casetti, Silvio Alovisio, and Luca Mazzei, 329–32. Amsterdam: Amsterdam University Press, 2017.

Lukács, György. *Writer and Critic: And Other Essays*. Edited by Arthur David Kahn. Lincoln, NE: IUniverse, 2005.

MacCabe, Colin. "Bazinian Adaptation: 'The Butcher Boy' as Example." In *True to the Spirit: Film Adaptation and the Question of Fidelity*, edited by Colin MacCabe, Kathleen Murray, Rick Warner, and Fredric Jameson, 3–26. Oxford: Oxford University Press, 2011.

MacEwan, Ian. *The Comfort of Strangers*. New York: Simon and Schuster, 1981.

Mancini, Michele, and Fiametta Sciacca. *La città-set: La terra trema di L. Visconti; reperti per una archeologia del cinema*. Rome: Theorema, 1981.

Mann, Thomas. *A Sketch of My Life*. Translated by H. T. Lowe-Porter. New York: Knopf, 1960.

———. *Death and Venice and Seven Other Stories*. Translated by H. T. Lowe-Porter. New York: Vintage Books, 1954.

———. "Platen." In *Essays of Three Decades*, translated by H. T. Lowe-Porter, 259–69. New York: Knopf, 1948.

Marcus, Millicent. *Italian Film in the Shadow of Auschwitz*. Toronto: University of Toronto Press, 2007.

———. *After Fellini: National Cinema in the Postmodern Age*. Baltimore: Johns Hopkins University Press, 2002.

———. "Visconti's *Senso:* The Risorgimento According to Gramsci or Historical Revisionism Meets Cinematic Innovation." In *Making and Remaking Italy: The Cultivation of National Identity around the Risorgimento*, edited by Albert Russell Ascoli and Krystyna Clara Von Henneberg, 277–98. Oxford: Berg, 2001.

———. *Filmmaking by the Book: Italian Cinema and Literary Adaptation*. Baltimore: Johns Hopkins University Press, 1993.

———. *Italian Film in the Light of Neorealism*. Princeton, NJ: Princeton University Press, 1986.

Margulies, Ivone. "Exemplary Bodies: Reenactment in *Love in the City*, *Sons*, and *Close-up*." In *Rites of Realism: Essays on Corporeal Cinema*, edited by Ivone Margulies, 217–43. Durham, NC: Duke University Press, 2002.

Marinetti, Filippo Tommaso. "Primo manifesto per la cinematografia futurista." In *Letteratura e cinema*, edited by Gian Piero Brunetta, 10–14. Bologna: Zanichelli, 1976.

Marlow-Mann, Alex. "Whose Heritage?: *Noi Credevamo* (We Believed) and the National, Regional and Transnational Dynamics of the Risorgimento Film." In *Screening European Heritage: Creating and Consuming History on Film*, edited by Paul Cooke and Rob Stone, 45–60. London: Palgrave, 2016.

———. "Gothic Horror." In *Directory of World Cinema: Italy*, edited by Louis Bayman, 155–56. Bristol: Intellect, 2011.

Martini, Andrea, ed. *La bella forma: Poggioli, i calligrafici, e dintorni*. Venice: Marsilio, 1992.

Materassi, Mario. "'L'ordine, il disordine': il paradigma della circolarità ne *Il Gattopardo*." *Lingua e Stile* 7, no. 3 (1972): 545–60.

Mayne, Judith. *Framed: Lesbians, Feminists, and Media Culture*. Minneapolis: University of Minnesota Press, 2000.

Megale, Teresa. "Alla ricerca di Rocco e dei suoi fratelli: La Basilicata di Luchino Visconti." In *Visconti e la Basilicata*, edited by Teresa Megale, 13–30. Venice: Marsilio, 2003.

Mellen, Joan. "Death in Venice by Luchino Visconti." *Film Quarterly* 25, no. 1 (Fall 1971): 41–47.

Micciché, Lino. *Visconti e il neorealismo*, 3rd ed. Venice: Marsilio, 2006.

———. *Visconti: un profilo critico*. Venice: Marsilio, 2002.

———. "Verso 'La terra trema.' " In *La terra trema: Analasi di un capolavoro*, edited by Lino Micciché, 33–59. Turin: Lindau, 1996a.

———. "Il principe e il conte." *Italica* 73, no. 2 (Summer 1996b): 188–93.

———. "Per una rilettura di *Ossessione*." In *Visconti: il cinema*, edited by Adelio Ferrero, 147–52. Modena: Comune di Modena, 1977.

———. *Il cinema italiano degli anni '60*. Venice: Marsilio, 1975.

Minghelli, Giuliana. *Landscape and Memory in Post-Fascist Italian Film: Cinema Year Zero*. New York: Routledge, 2013.

———. "Storie, paesaggi e cantastorie: la visione documentaristica dal neorealismo al postmoderno." In *Sinergie narrative: cinema e lettertura nell'Italia contemporanea*, edited by Guido Bonsaver, Martin McLaughlin, and Franca Pellegrini, 41–72. Florence: Franco Cesati Editore, 2008.

Moers, Ellen. *Literary Women*. London: Women's Press, 1963.

Monk, Claire. *Heritage Film Audiences: Period Films and Contemporary Audiences in the UK*. Edinburgh: Edinburgh University Press, 2011.

Moravia, Alberto. "Un idillio nato tra i bacilli." *L'espresso*, no. 11 (March 14, 1971).

Morgan, Fergus. "Ivo van Hove's Obsession Starring Jude Law—Review Roundup." *The Stage*, April 26, 2017. https://www.thestage.co.uk/review-round-ups/ivo-van-hoves-obsession-starring-jude-law--review-round-up1.

Morreale, Enrico. *Così Piangevano: Il cinema melò negli anni cinquanta*. Rome: Donzelli Editore, 2011.

Murray, Simone. *The Adaptation Industry: The Cultural Economy of Contemporary Literary Adaptation*. London: Routledge, 2012.

———. "Materializing Adaptation Theory: The Adaptation Industry." *Literature/Film Quarterly* 36, no. 1 (2008): 4–20.

Musumeci, Mario. "Una scabrosa vicenda filmata." In *Il cinema di Luchino Visconti*, edited by Veronica Pravadelli, 5–64. Venice: Marsilio, 2000.

Naglia, Sandro. *Mann, Mahler, Visconti: Morte a Venezia*. Rome: Ikona Liber, 2013.

Naremore, James. *More Than Night: Film Noir in Its Contexts*. Berkeley: University of California Press, 1998.

———. "Authorship and the Cultural Politics of Film Criticism." *Film Quarterly* 44, no. 1 (Autumn 1990): 14–23.

Neale, Steve. "Questions of Genre." *Screen* 31, no. 1 (Spring 1990): 45–66.

Nichols, Bill. "The Voice of Documentary." In *New Challenges for Documentary*, 2nd ed., edited by Alan Rosenthal and John Corner, 17–33. Manchester: Manchester University Press, 2012.

———. *Introduction to Documentary*. Bloomington: University of Indiana Press, 2001.

Nothomb, Amélie. "Noir Strangulation (2): Amélie Nothomb and Intertextuality." In *French and American Noir: Dark Crossings*, edited by Allistair Rolls and Deborah Walker, 94–114. Basingstoke: Palgrave, 2009.

Noto, Paolo. *Dal bozzetto ai generi: Il cinema italiano dei primi anni Cinquanta*. Turin: Kaplan, 2011.

Nowell-Smith, Geoffrey. *Luchino Visconti*, 3rd ed. London: BFI, 2003.

———. *Luchino Visconti*. London: BFI and Secker and Walburg, 1967.

O'Leary, Alan. "Seminar 3 (2013): Heritage Cinema." *Tumblr*, n.d. https://italiancinema-mumbai.tumblr.com/post/59310319891/seminar-3-2013-heritage-cinema (accessed March 10, 2021).

O'Leary, Alan, and Catherine O'Rawe. "Against Realism: On a Certain Tendency in Italian Film Criticism." *Journal of Modern Italian Studies* 16, no. 1 (2011): 107–28.

O'Leary, Alan, and Neelam Srivastava. "Violence and the Wretched: The Cinema of Gillo Pontecorvo." *The Italianist* 29, no. 2 (2009): 249–64.

O'Rawe, Catherine. "Anna Magnani: Voice, Body, Accent." In *Locating the Voice in Film: Critical Approaches and Global Practices*, edited by Tom Whittaker and Sarah Wright, 157–72. Oxford: Oxford University Press, 2017.

———. *Stars and Masculinities in Contemporary Italian Cinema*. Basingstoke: Palgrave Macmillan, 2016.

———. "Gender, Genre, and Stardom: Fatality in Neorealist Cinema." In *The Femme Fatale: Images, Histories, Contexts*, edited by Helen Hanson and Catherine O'Rawe, 127–42. London: Palgrave, 2010.

OED. "adaptation, n." OED Online, December 2020. Oxford University Press. https://www-oed-com.proxy.binghamton.edu/view/Entry/2115?redirectedFrom=adaptation.

Orlando, Francesco. *L'intimità e la storia: Lettura del 'Gattopardo.'* Turin: Einaudi, 1998.

Ovid. *The Metamorphosis*. Translated by Stanley Lombardo, edited by W. R. Johnson. Indianapolis, IN: Hackett, 2011.

Pacifici, Sergio J. "Existentialism and Italian Literature." *Yale French Studies*, no. 16 (1955): 79–88.

Paliaga, Simone. "Quel sospetto sulla Valli: 'È una spia fascista.' " *Libero* (Milan), January 6, 2012.

Pamerleau, William C. *Existentialist Cinema*. Basingstoke: Palgrave Macmillan, 2009.

Pandolfi, Vito. "*Rocco e i suoi fratelli*." In *Film 1961: Avventure e prospettive del nuovo cinema*, edited by Vittorio Spinazzola, 23–25. Milan: Feltrinelli Editore, 1961.

Parigi, Stefania. "Vaghe stelle dell'Orsa: Il deposito della memoria." In *Il cinema di Luchino Visconti*, edited by Veronica Pravadelli, 221–34. Venice: Marsilio, 2000.

———. "Il dualismo linguistico." In *La terra trema: Analasi di un capolavoro*, edited by Lino Micciché, 141–64. Turin: Lindau, 1996.

Pasolini, Pier Paolo. "The Cinema of Poetry." Translated by Marianne de Vettimo and Jacques Bontemps. *Movies and Methods vol. 1*, edited by Bill Nichols, 542–58. Berkeley: University of California Press, 1976.

———. "Lettera aperta di Pier Paolo Pasolini a Luchino Visconti: Quel faro di motocicletta." *Tempo* 31, no. 47 (November 22, 1969).

Past, Elena. "The Dying Diva: Violent Ends for Clara Calamai in *Ossessione* and *Profondo Rosso*." *Forum Italicum* 42, no. 2 (2008): 296–312.

Pavese, Cesare. *La letteratura americana e altri saggi*. Turin: Einaudi, 1953.

Pellizzari, Lorenzo, and Claudio M. Valentinetti. *Il romanzo di Alida Valli*. Milan: Garzanti, 1995.

Pergolari, Andrea. *Pasquale Festa Campanile, ovvero, La sindrome di Matusalemme*. Rome: Aracne, 2008.

Pescetti, Luigi. *D'Annunzio e Volterra*. Verona: Mondadori, 1943.

Pietrangeli, Antonio. "Harlem." *Bianco e nero* 7, no. 6 (June 1943): 34–35.

Pietrangeli, Antonio, and Luchino Visconti. "Proposta di un soggetto per un film sulla borghesia milanese per la Lux." In *Controversia Visconti*, edited by Fernaldo di Giammatteo, 73–78. Rome: Edizioni dell'Ataneo e Bizzari, 1976.

Pirandello, Luigi. *Shoot! The Notebooks of Serafino Gubbio, Cinematograph Operator*. Translated by C. K. Scott Moncrieff. Chicago: University of Chicago Press, 2005.

Pistoia, Marco. 2008. "*Rocco e i suoi fratelli*: questioni di drammaturgia." In *La macchina e le muse*, edited by Federica Mazzocchi, 35–46. Bari: Edizioni di Pagina, 2008.

Porfirio, Robert. "No Way Out: Existential Motifs in the Film Noir." In *Film Noir Reader*, edited by Alain Silver and James Ursini, 77–94. New York: Limelight Editions, 1996.

Pravadelli, Veronica. "Italian 1960s Auteur Cinema (and Beyond): Classic, Modern, Postmodern." In *A Companion to Italian Cinema*, edited by Frank Burke, 228–48. Oxford: Wiley Blackwell, 2017.

Puppa, Paolo. *Teatro e spettacolo nel secondo Novecento*. Rome-Bari: Laterza, 2007.

Quaglietti, Lorenzo. *Storia economico-politica del cinema italiano, 1945–1980*. Rome: Riuniti, 1980.

Re, Lucia. *Calvino and The Age of Neorealism: Fables of Estrangement*. Stanford, CA: Stanford University Press, 1991.

Redmon, Allen H. "Rewatching *Shutter Island* as a Knowing Audience." *Adaptation* 8, no. 2 (2015): 254–67.

Reed, Philip. "Aschenbach Become Mahler: Thomas Mann as Film." In *Benjamin Britten: Death in Venice*, edited by Donald Mitchell, 178–83. Cambridge: Cambridge University Press, 1987.

Reed, T. J. "Mann and His Novella: 'Death in Venice.' " In *Benjamin Britten: Death in Venice*, edited by Donald Mitchell, 163–67. Cambridge: Cambridge University Press, 1987.

Reich, Jacqueline. *Beyond the Latin Lover: Marcello Mastroianni, Masculinity, and Italian Cinema*. Bloomington: Indiana University Press, 2004.

Rhodie, Sam. *Rocco e i suoi Fratelli*. London: BFI, 1992.

Ricci, Steve. *Cinema and Fascism: Italian Film and Society, 1922–1943*. Berkeley: University of California Press, 2008.

Rigoletto, Sergio. *Masculinity in Italian Cinema: Sexual Politics, Social Conflict and Male Crisis in the 1970s*. Edinburgh: Edinburgh University Press, 2014.

Ripari, Edoardo. *Storia cinematografica della letteratura italiana*. Rome: Carocci, 2015.

Rondi, Gian Luigi. "Il primo Visconti: Intervista di Gianluigi Rondi." In *La terra trema un film di Luchino Visconti dal romanzo I Malavoglia di Giovanni Verga*, edited by Sebastiano Gesù, 281–84. Lipari: Salarci Immagini, 2006.

———. *Il cinema dei maestri: 58 grandi registi e un'attrice si raccontano*. Milan: Rusconi, 1980.

Rondolino, Gianni. *Luchino Visconti*. Turin: UTET, 2003.

———. "La formazione, fra letteratura e cinema." In *Studi viscontiani*, edited by David Bruni and Veronica Pravadelli, 31–48. Venice: Marsilio, 1997.

Rosen, Lisa. "Sound and Temporality: Voice-over in Visconti's *La terra trema*." *Luchino Visconti*, n.d. http://www.luchinovisconti.net/visconti_al/visconti_sound.htm#_ (accessed March 10, 2021).

Rosenstone, Robert A. "The History Film as a Mode of Historical Thought." In *A Companion to the Historical Film*, edited by Robert A. Rosenstone and Constantine Parvulescu, 71–87. Oxford: Wiley Blackwell, 2016.

Rosi, Francesco. "Dieci mesi tra i pescatori." In *L'avventurosa storia del cinema italiano raccontata dai suoi protagonisti, 1939–1959*, edited by Franca Faldini and Goffredo Fofi, 137–41. Milan: Feltrinelli, 1979.

Ruberto, Laura E., and Kristi M. Wilson, eds. *Italian Neorealism and Global Cinema*. Detroit: Wayne State University Press, 2007.

Rubin, Gayle S. "Thinking Sex: Notes for a Radical Theory of the Politics of Sexuality." In *Pleasure and Danger: Exploring Female Sexuality*, edited by Carole S. Vance, 267–319. Boston: Routledge and Kegan Paul, 1984.

Rusconi, Marisa. "Il Leone d'oro al magnetofono." *Sipario* 20, no. 34 (1965): 11–13.

Said, Edward. *On Late Style: Music and Literature against the Grain*. London: Bloomsbury, 2006.

Sainati, Augusto. "Lo zoom e la bellezza." In *Il cinema di Luchino Visconti*, edited by Veronica Pravadelli, 271–80. Venice: Marsilio, 2000.

Sartre, Jean-Paul. *Existentialism Is a Humanism = (L'Existentialisme est un humanisme)*. Translated by Carol Macomber, edited by John Kulka. New Haven, CT: Yale University Press, 2007.

Schifano, Laurance. *Luchino Visconti: The Flames of Passion*. Translated by William Byron. London: Collins, 1990.

Sciascia, Leonardo. *Pirandello e la Sicilia*. Milan: Adelphi, 1996.

Scütte, Wolfram. "Morte a venezia." In *Visconti: scritti, film, star e immagini*, edited by Marianne Schneider and Lothar Schirmer, 206–23. Milan: Electa, 2008a.

———. "L'innocente." In *Visconti: scritti, film, star e immagini*, edited by Marianne Schneider and Lothar Schirmer, 256–72. Milan: Electa, 2008b.

Seaton, Matt. "I Feel Used." *The Guardian*, October 16, 2003.

Semprebene, Roberto. *La terra trema: Rapporti tra cinema e politica nel secondo dopoguerra*. Turin: Effatà Editrice, 2009.

Serandrei, Mario."Editor as Screenwriter." In *Titanus: Family Diary of Italian Cinema*, edited by Sergio M. Germani, Simone Starace, and Roberto Turigliatto, 348–51. Rome: Edizioni Sabinae, 2014.

———. "La contessa Serpieri." In *L'avventurosa storia del cinema italiano raccontata dai suoi protagonisti, 1939–1959*, edited by Franca Faldini and Goffredo Fofi, 325–29. Milan: Feltrinelli, 1979.

Serra, Ilaria. "From Literature to Film through Figurative Arts: Italian 'Imagistic Substitutions.' " *Adaptation* 4, no. 2 (September 2011): 137–66.

Servadio, Gaia. *Luchino Visconti: A Biography*. New York: Watts, 1983.

Shiel, Mark. *Italian Neorealism: Rebuilding the Cinematic City*. London: Wallflower Press, 2006.

Shirer, William. *The Rise and Fall of the Third Reich*. New York: Simon and Schuster, 1960.

Shookman, Ellis. *Thomas Mann's Death in Venice: A Novella and Its Critics*. Columbia, SC: Camden House, 2003.

Singer, Irving. *Reality Transformed: Film as Meaning and Technique*. Cambridge, MA: MIT Press, 2000.

Sitney, P. Adams. *Vital Crises in Italian Cinema: Iconography, Stylistics, Politics*. Austin: University of Texas Press, 1995.

Small, Pauline. "Producer *and* Director? Or, 'Authorship' in 1950s Italian Cinema." In *Beyond the Bottom Line: The Producer in Film and Television Studies*, edited by Andrew Spicer, A. T. McKenna, and Christopher Meir, 109–24. London: Bloomsbury, 2016.

———. "The Maggiorata or Sweater Girl of the 1950s." In *The Italian Cinema Book*, edited by Peter Bondanella, 116–17. London: BFI, 2014.

Sontag, Susan. *Under the Sign of Saturn*. New York: St. Martin's Press, 1980.

Sorlin, Pierre. *Italian National Cinema, 1896–1996*. London: Routledge, 1996.

———. *La storia nei film: Interpretazioni del passato*. Florence: La Nuova Italia, 1980.

———. *Sociologia del cinema*. Translated by Luca S. Budini. Milan: Garzanti, 1979.

Spackman, Barbara. *Decadent Geneologies: The Rhetoric of Sickness from Baudelaire to D'Annunzio*. Ithaca, NY: Cornell University Press, 1989.

Sperry, Eileen. "'Milk for Gall': Elizabethan Power Strategies in Macbeth." In *Breastfeeding and Culture: Discourses and Representation*, edited by Ann Marie A. Short, Abigail L. Palko, and Dionne Irving, 34–49. Bradford, ON: Demeter Press, 2018.

Spinazzola, Vittorio. "Rocco e i suoi fratelli." In *L'opera di Visconti, atti del convegno di studi Fiesole 27–29 giugno, 1966*, edited by Mario Sperenzi, 304–11. Florence: Tip. A Lipari, 1969.

Spitzer, Leo. "L'originalità della narrazione nei 'Malavoglia' (1955)." In *Verga: Guida storico-critica*, edited by Enrico Ghidetti, 294–99. Rome: Editore Riuniti, 1979.

Stam, Robert. "Beyond Fidelity: The Dialogics of Adaptation." In *Film Adaptation*, edited by James Naremore, 54–76. London: Athalone Press, 2000.

Stam, Robert, and Alessandra Raengo, eds. *Literature and Film: A Guide to the Theory and Practice of Film Adaptation*. Malden, MA: Blackwell, 2005.

———, eds. *A Companion to Literature and Film*. Malden MA: Blackwell, 2004.

Steimatsky, Noa. *Italian Locations: Reinhabiting the Past in Postwar Cinema*. Minneapolis: University of Minnesota Press, 2008.

Stirling, Monica. *A Screen of Time*. New York: Harcourt Brace Jovanovich, 1979.

Strindberg, August. *Strindberg: Five Plays*. Translated by Harry G. Carlson. Berkeley: University of California Press, 1983.

Subini, Tomaso. "Il difficile equilibrio tra Storia e melodrama in *Senso*." In *Il cinema di Luchino Visconti tra società e altre arti*, edited by Raffaele De Berti, 47–78. Milan: Cuem, 2005.

Tarratt, Margaret. "The Damned: Visconti, Wagner, and the 'Reinvention of Reality.'" *Screen* 11, no. 3 (Summer 1970): 44–56.

Testa, Carlo. "Literature and Cinema from 'Adaptation' to Re-creation: Coping with the Complexity of Human Recollection." *Between* 2, no. 4 (2012): 1–36.

———. "Vadetecum: A Manifesto of Inter-Media Re-Creation." In *Watching Pages, Reading Pictures: Cinema and Modern Literature in Italy*, edited by Giorgina Torello and Daniela de Pau, 75–95. Newcastle: Cambridge Scholars, 2008.

———. *Masters of Two Arts: Re-creation of European Literatures in Italian Cinema*. Toronto: University of Toronto Press, 2002a.

———. *Italian Cinema and Modern European Literatures*. Westport, CT: Praeger, 2002b.

Testori, Giovanni. *Il ponte della Ghisolfa*. Milan: Garzanti, 1985.

Tinazzi, Giorgio. *La scrittura e lo sguardo*. Venice: Marsilio, 2007.

Tomasino, Renato. "Lo straniero." *Filmcritica* 18, no. 181 (September 1967): 428–29.

Trueman, Matt. "Obsession: An Interview with Ivo van Hove." *National Theatre Blog*, n.d. https://www.nationaltheatre.org.uk/blog/obsession-interview-ivo-van-hove (accessed February 12, 2019).

Truffaut, Francois. "A Certain Tendency of the French Cinema (1954)." In *Auteurs and Authorship: A Film Reader*, edited by Barry Keith Grant, 9–18. Oxford: Blackwell, 2008.

Tudor, Andrew. *Image and Influence: Studies in the Sociology of Film*. London: George Allen & Unwin, 1974.

Urbano, Michaela. "Un film per la tv fa rivivere *Rocco*." *Il Messaggero*, December 19, 2010.

Valli, Alida. "Scuole: Quelli del 'Centro.' " In *L'avventurosa storia del cinema italiano raccontata dai suoi protagonisti, 1939–1959*, edited by Franca Faldini and Goffredo Fofi, 40–43. Milan: Feltrinelli, 1979a.

———. "Amanti, eroi, reduci, tenori." In *L'avventurosa storia del cinema italiano raccontata dai suoi protagonisti, 1939–1959*, edited by Franca Faldini and Goffredo Fofi, 96–107. Milan: Feltrinelli, 1979b.

Van Watson, William. "Luchino Visconti's (Homosexual) *Ossessione*." In *Re-Viewing Fascism: Italian Cinema, 1922–1943*, edited by Jacqueline Reich and Piero Garofalo, 172–93. Bloomington: Indiana University Press, 2002.

Venturini, Piero. "La poesia dello slancio: L'*Adagietto* della Quinta sinfonia di Mahler." In *Venezia nel cinema di Luchino Visconti*, edited by Stefano Toffolo, 70–81. San Donà di Piave: Edizioni Nattan, 2006.

Verga, Giovanni. "Verga a Dina 20.II 1912." In *Verga e il cinema*, edited by Gino Raya, 30. Rome: Herder, 1984a.

———. "Verga a Dina 24.IV 1912." In *Verga e il cinema*, edited by Gino Raya, 33. Rome: Herder, 1984b.

———. "Dedicatoria della novella 'L'amante di Gramigna' (1880)." In *Verga: Guida storico-critica*, edited by Enrico Ghidetti, 59–60. Rome: Editore Riuniti, 1979.

———. *The House by the Medlar Tree*. Translated by Raymond Rosenthal. Berkeley: University of California Press, 1964.

Villa, Federica. "Giorgio Bassani e le occasioni letterarie per Luchino Visconti." In *La macchina e le muse*, edited by Federica Mazzocchi, 239–58. Bari: Edizioni di Pagina, 2008.

Vincendeau, Ginette. "French Film Noir." In *European Film Noir*, edited by Andrew Spicer, 23–54. Manchester: Manchester University Press, 2007.

———. "Introduction." In *Film/Literature/Heritage*, edited by Ginette Vincendeau, xi–xxiv. London: BFI, 2001.

Visconti, Luchino. "Pensieri sull'opera e su Maria Callas." In *Visconti: scritti, film, star e immagini*, edited by Marianne Schneider and Lothar Schirmer, 37–46. Milan: Electa, 2008.

———. Interview with Michel Ciment and Jean-Paul Török. In *Luchino Visconti, cineaste*, ed. Alain Sanzio and Paul-Louis Thirard, 145–52. Paris: Persona, 1986.

———. "La contessa Serpieri." In *L'avventurosa storia del cinema italiano raccontata dai suoi protagonisti, 1939–1959*, edited by Franca Faldini and Goffredo Fofi, 325–29. Milan: Feltrinelli, 1979.

———. *La terra trema*. Bologna: Cappelli, 1977.

———. *Leggere Visconti*. Edited by Giuliana Callegari and Nuccio Lodato. Pavia: Amministrazione Provinciale, 1976. (*LV*)

———. *Morte a Venezia*. Bologna: Cappelli, 1971.

———. *Two Screenplays: La terra trema, Senso*. Translated by Judith Green. New York: Orion Press, 1970a.

———. *Three Screenplays: White Nights, Rocco and His Brothers, The Job*. Translated by Judith Green. New York: Orion Press, 1970b.

———. *La caduta degli dei (Götterdämmerung) di Luchino Visconti*. Bologna: Cappelli, 1969.

———. *Il Film 'Il Gattopardo' e la regia di Luchino Visconti*. Bologna: Cappelli Editore, 1963.

Von Der Lippe, George B. "Death in Venice in Literature and Film." *Mosaic: An Interdisciplinary Critical Journal* 32, no. 1 (March 1999): 35–54.

Wagstaff, Christopher. *Italian Neorealist Cinema: An Aesthetic Approach*. Toronto: University of Toronto Press, 2007.

Warfield, Nancy D. "After *The Damned*." *Little Film Gazette of N.D.W.* 9, no. 1 (January 1981): 8.

Webber, Andrew. "Mann's Man's World: Gender and Sexuality." In *The Cambridge Companion to Thomas Mann*, edited by Richard Robertson, 64–83. Cambridge: Cambridge University Press, 2002.

Willinger, David, ed. *Ivo van Hove Onstage*. New York: Routledge, 2018.

Wilper, James P. "Rewritings, Adaptations, and Gay Literary Criticism: Thomas Mann's *Death in Venice*." *Adaptation* 8, no. 1 (2014): 1–15.

Wilson, Michael. "Art Is Ambiguous: The Zoom in Death in Venice." *Literature/Film Quarterly* 26, no. 2 (1998): 153–56.

Wood, Mary P. "Italian Film Noir." In *European Film Noir*, edited by Andrew Spicer, 236–72. Manchester: Manchester University Press, 2007.

———. *Italian Cinema*. Oxford: Berg, 2005.

Wood, Robin. "Ideology, Genre, Auteur." *Film Comment* 13, no. 1 (January–February 1977): 46–51.

Woodward, Kath. *The "I" of the Tiger: Boxing, Masculinity and Identity*. New York: Routledge, 2007.

Woolf, Virginia. "The Cinema." *Nation and Anthenaeum*, July 3, 1926, 381–83.

Youdelman, Jeffrey. "Narration, Invention, and History." In *New Challenges for Documentary*, edited by Alan Rosenthal, 397–408. Berkeley: University of California Press, 1988.

Zagarrio, Vito. "Le 'quinte' della storia: riflessioni sulla regia." In *La terra trema: Analasi di un capolavoro*, edited by Lino Micciché, 117–39. Turin: Lindau, 1996a.

———. "Lo sguardo dell'eccellenza. Note sulla regia." In *Il Gattopardo*, edited by Lino Micciché, 62–73. Napoli: Electa, 1996b.

Zangara, Mario. "I malavoglia e la terra trema." *Rivista del cinema italiano* (March 1953): 35–42.

Zavattini, Cesare. "Una grossa botta in testa al neorealismo." In *Antologia del Cinema Nuovo 1952–1958: Dalla critica cinematografica alla dialettica culturale*, edited by Guido Aristarco, 888–91. Rimini-Florence: Guaraldi, 1975.

———. "Some Ideas on Cinema." In *Film: A Montage of Theories*, edited by Richard Dyer MacCann, translated by Pier Luigi Lanza, 216–28. New York: Dutton, 1974.

Zeffirelli, Franco. "Come un toscano insegnò il siciliano per conto di un Lombardo." In *La terra trema: Analasi di un capolavoro*, edited by Lino Micciché, 27–41. Turin: Lindau, 1996.

Filmography

Aldrich, Robert, dir. *Whatever Happened to Baby Jane*. The Associates and Aldrich Company, 1962.

———. *Sodom and Gomorrah*. Titanus, Pathé Consortium Cinéma, Sociéte Générale de Cinématographie, 1962.

Alessandrini, Goffredo, and Francesco Rosi, dirs. *Camicie rosse*. Produzione Grandi Film, Grand Films Francais, 1952.

Anderson, Lindsay, dir. *This Sporting Life*. Independent Artists, Julian Wintle/ Leslie Parkyn Productions, 1963.

Antonioni, Michelangelo, dir. *Le amiche*. Trionfalcine, 1955.

———. *Blow-Up*. Carlo Ponti Production, Bridge Films, MGM, Premier Productions, 1966.

———. *Professione: Reporter*. MGM, Compagnia Cinematografica Champion, Les Films Concordia, CIPI Cinematografica S.A., 1975.

Astruc, Alexandre, dir. *Un vie*. Agnes Delahaie Productions, Cino del Duca, 1958.

Ballerini, Piero, dir. *L'ultimo combattimento*. Novissima Film, 1940.

Batzella, Luigi, dir. *La bestia in calore*. Eterna Film, Sonora Films, 1977.

Bava, Mario, dir. *La ragazza che sapeva troppo*. Galatea Film, Coronet s.r.l., AIP, 1963.

———. *Sei donne per l'assassino*. Emmepi Cinematografica, Les Productions Georges de Beauregard, Monachi Film, Top Film, 1964.

Bertolucci, Bernardo, dir. *La commare secca*. Cinematografica Cervi, Cineriz, 1962.

———. *Il conformista*. Mars Films, Marianne Productions, Maran Film, 1970.

———. *La strategia del ragno*. Rai Radiotelevisione Italiana, Red Film, 1970.

Borghesio, Carlo, dir. *Il campione*. ICI, Leo Film, 1943.

Brass, Tinto, dir. *Salon Kitty*. Coralta Cinematografica, Cinema Seven Film, Les Productions Fox Europa, 1976.

———. *Caligula*. Penthouse Films International, Felix Cinematografica, 1979.

Brook, Peter, dir. *Lord of the Flies*. Two Arts, 1963.

Brooks, Richard, dir. *The Brothers Karamazov*. Avon Productions, 1958.

Callegari, Gian Paolo, dir. *Eran trecento*. Pandora Filmproduktion, 1952.

Canevari, Cesare, dir. *L'ultima orgia del III Reich*. Cinc Lu.Ce., 1977.

Capra, Frank, dir. *It's a Wonderful Life*. Liberty Films, 1946.

Carné, Marcel, dir. *Le Quai des brumes*. Ciné-Alliance, 1938.

———. *Hotel du Nord*. SEDIF, Impérial Film, 1938.

———. *Le Jour se léve*. Productions Sigman, 1939.

Cavani, Liliana, dir. *Il portiere di notte*. Italnoleggio Cinematografico, Lotar Film Productions, 1974.

Chenal, Pierre, dir. *Crime et châtiment*. Général Productions, 1935.

———. *Le dernier tournant*. Gladiator Productions, 1939.

Clément, René, dir. *Gervaise*. Agnes Delahaie Productions, Silver Films, CICC, 1956.

Curtiz, Michael, dir. *Kid Galahad*. Warner Bros., 1937.

D'Amico de Carvalho, Caterina, and Vieri Razzini, dirs. *Per Luchino Visconti*, episodes 1–8. Rai Tre, 1987.

de Limur, Jean, dir. *Apparizione*. SAFIC, Società Italiana Cinema, 1943.

De Santis, Giuseppe, Mario Serandrei, Marcello Pagliero, and Luchino Visconti, dirs. *Giorni di Gloria*. Titanus and ANPI, 1945.

De Sica, Vittorio, dir. *Sciuscià*. Società Cooperativa Alfa Cinematografica, 1946.

———. *I sequestrati di Altona*. SGC, Titanus, 1962.

De Sica, Vittorio, Federico Fellini, Mario Monicelli, and Luchino Visconti, dirs. *Boccaccio '70*. Cineriz, Concordia Compagnia Cinematografica, Francinex, Gray-Film, 1961.

Duse, Vittorio, dir. *Il nostro campione*. Mundini, 1955.

Duvivier, Julien, dir. *Pépé le Moko*. Paris Film, 1937.

Edmonds, Don, dir. *Ilsa: She Wolf of the SS*. Aeteas Filmproduktions, 1975.

Fellini, Federico, dir. *La dolce vita*. Federico Riama Film, Cinecittà, Pathé Consortium Cinéma, 1960.

Ferrero, Mario, dir. *Gli innamorati*. RAI Radiotelevisione Italiana, 1955.

Fiermonte, Enzo, dir. *L'atleta di cristallo*. Monte Film, 1946.

Flaherty, Robert J., dir. *Man of Aran*. Gainsborough Pictures, 1934.

Ford, John, dir. *How the West Was Won*. MGM, Cinerama Productions, 1962.

Franciolini, Gianni, Alfredo Guarini, Roberto Rossellini, Luchino Visconti, and Luigi Zampa, dirs. *Siamo donne*. Titanus, Film Costellazione Produzione, 1953.

Fuqua, Antoine, dir. *Southpaw*. Escape Artists, Fuqua Films, Riche Productions, Wanda Productions, 2015.

Gagliardi, Giuseppe, dir. *Tatanka*. Margherita Film, Gruppo Minerva International, MiBAC, 2011.

Gallone, Carmine, dir. *Scipione l'africano*. Consorzione "Scipio L'Africano," ENIC, 1937.

———. *Oltre l'amore*. Grandi Film Storici, 1940.

———. *Harlem*. Società Italiana Cines, 1943.

Garnett, Tay, dir. *The Postman Always Rings Twice*. MGM, 1946.

Genina, Augusto, dir. *Il cielo sulla palude*. Arx, Film Bassoli, 1949.

Germi, Pietro, dir. *Il brigante di Tacca del Lupo*. Lux Film, Rovere, Società Italiana Cines, 1952.

Giannini, Ettore, dir. *Carosello napoletano*. Lux Film, 1954.

Girolami, Marino, dir. *Walter e i suoi cugini*. Marino Girolami, 1961.

Girolami, Marino, and Giorgio Simonelli, dirs. *Era lei che lo voleva!* Excelsa Film, 1952.

Grierson, John, dir. *Granton Trawler*. New Era Films, 1934.

Griffith, D. W., dir. *Way Down East*. D. W. Griffith Production, 1920.

Heusch, Paolo, dir. *Un uomo facile*. Serena, 1958.

Hitchcock, Alfred, dir. *Rebecca*. Selznick International Pictures, 1940.

———. *Shadow of a Doubt*. Universal Pictures, 1943.

Ivory, James, dir. *Howard's End*. Merchant Ivory Productions, 1992.

———. *Maurice*. Merchant Ivory Productions, Cinecom Pictures, Film Four International, 1987.

———. *A Room with a View*. Merchant Ivory Productions, Goldcrest Films International, NFFC, Curzon Film Distributors, Film Four International, 1985.

Käutner, Helmut, dir. *Die letzte Brucke*. Cosmopol-Film, UFUS, 1954.

Kazan, Elia, dir. *On the Waterfront*. Horizon Pictures, 1954.

Koch, Carl, dir. *Tosca*. Scalera Films, 1941.

Kubrick, Stanley, dir. *Lolita*. A.A. Productions, Anya, Harris-Kubrick Productions, Transworld Pictures, 1962.

Kurosawa, Akira, dir. *Rashomon*. Daiei Motion Picture, 1950.

Lean, David, dir. *Lawrence of Arabia*. Horizon Pictures, 1962.

Longoni, Angelo, dir. *Tiberio Mitri: il campione e la miss*. Cristaldi Pictures, 2011.

Magni, Luigi, dir. *Nell'anno del signore*. Francos Film, Les Films Corona, San Marco, 1969.

Mamoulian, Rouben, dir. *Golden Boy*. Columbia Pictures, 1939.

Mankiewicz, Joseph L., dir. *Cleopatra*. 20th Century Fox, MCL Films, Walwa Films, 1963.

Milestone, Lewis, dir. *Of Mice and Men*. Hal Roach Studios, 1940.

Milestone, Lewis, and Carol Reed, dirs. *Mutiny on the Bounty*. Arcola Pictures, 1962.

Monicelli, Mario, dir. *I soliti ignoti*. Cinecittà, Lux Film, Vides Cinematografica, 1958.

Morassi, Mauro, dir. *Il cocco di mamma*. Cineproduzione Emo Bistolfi, Pallavicini, 1958.

Mulligan, Robert, dir. *To Kill a Mockingbird*. UI, Pekula-Mulligan, Brentwood Productions, 1962.

Pasolini, Pier Paolo, dir. *Salò e le 120 giornate di Sodoma*. Produzioni Europee Associate, Les Productions Artistes Associés, 1975.

Pontecorvo, Gillo, dir. *La battaglia di Algeri*. Casbah Film, Igor Film, 1966.

Questi, Giulio, dir. *La morte ha fatto l'uovo*. Summa Cinematografica, Cine Azimut, Les Films Corona, 1968.

Radford, Michael, dir. *Il Postino*. Cecchi Gori Group Tiger Cinematografica, Penta Film, Esterno Mediterraneo Film, Blue Dahlia Productions, K2 Two, Canal+, 1994.

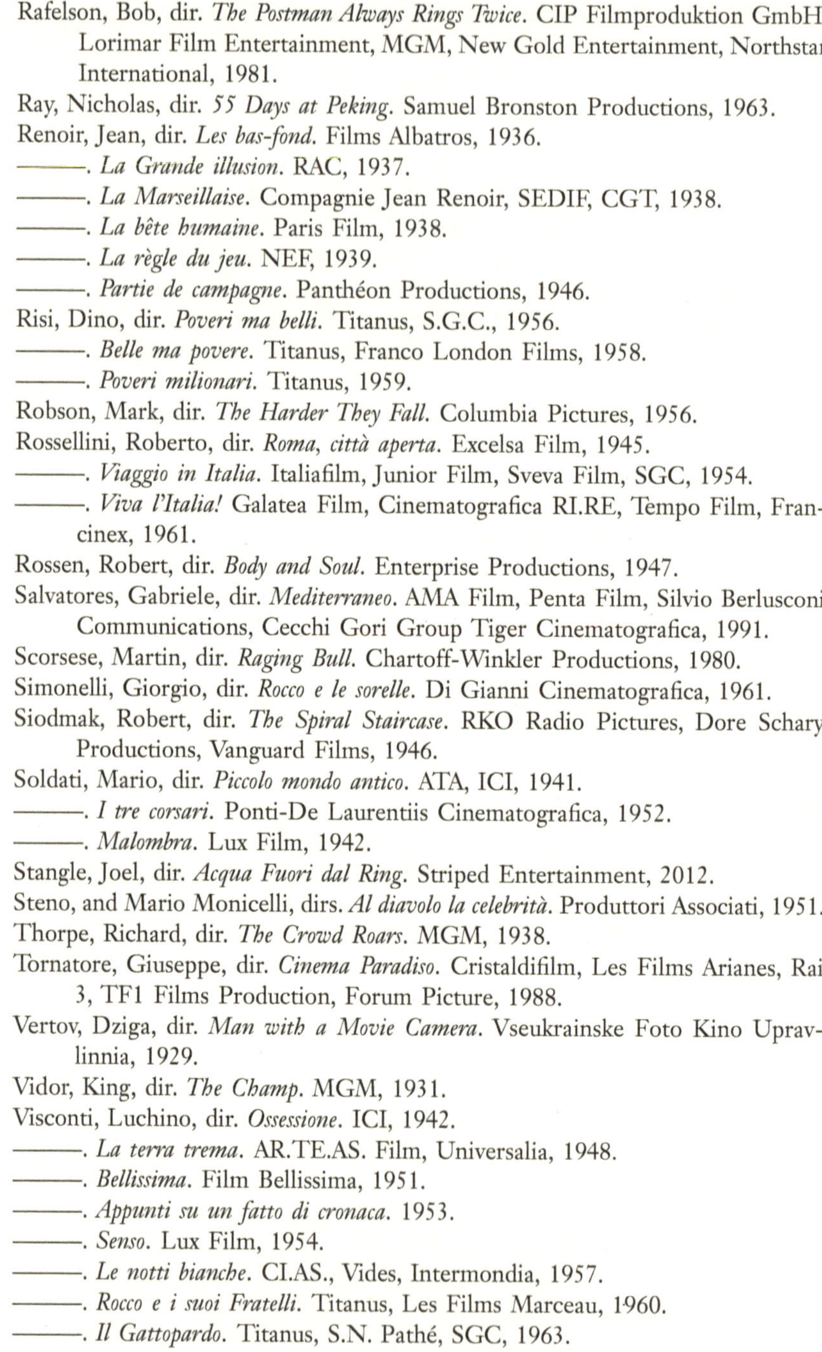

Rafelson, Bob, dir. *The Postman Always Rings Twice*. CIP Filmproduktion GmbH, Lorimar Film Entertainment, MGM, New Gold Entertainment, Northstar International, 1981.

Ray, Nicholas, dir. *55 Days at Peking*. Samuel Bronston Productions, 1963.

Renoir, Jean, dir. *Les bas-fond*. Films Albatros, 1936.

———. *La Grande illusion*. RAC, 1937.

———. *La Marseillaise*. Compagnie Jean Renoir, SEDIF, CGT, 1938.

———. *La bête humaine*. Paris Film, 1938.

———. *La règle du jeu*. NEF, 1939.

———. *Partie de campagne*. Panthéon Productions, 1946.

Risi, Dino, dir. *Poveri ma belli*. Titanus, S.G.C., 1956.

———. *Belle ma povere*. Titanus, Franco London Films, 1958.

———. *Poveri milionari*. Titanus, 1959.

Robson, Mark, dir. *The Harder They Fall*. Columbia Pictures, 1956.

Rossellini, Roberto, dir. *Roma, città aperta*. Excelsa Film, 1945.

———. *Viaggio in Italia*. Italiafilm, Junior Film, Sveva Film, SGC, 1954.

———. *Viva l'Italia!* Galatea Film, Cinematografica RI.RE, Tempo Film, Francinex, 1961.

Rossen, Robert, dir. *Body and Soul*. Enterprise Productions, 1947.

Salvatores, Gabriele, dir. *Mediterraneo*. AMA Film, Penta Film, Silvio Berlusconi Communications, Cecchi Gori Group Tiger Cinematografica, 1991.

Scorsese, Martin, dir. *Raging Bull*. Chartoff-Winkler Productions, 1980.

Simonelli, Giorgio, dir. *Rocco e le sorelle*. Di Gianni Cinematografica, 1961.

Siodmak, Robert, dir. *The Spiral Staircase*. RKO Radio Pictures, Dore Schary Productions, Vanguard Films, 1946.

Soldati, Mario, dir. *Piccolo mondo antico*. ATA, ICI, 1941.

———. *I tre corsari*. Ponti-De Laurentiis Cinematografica, 1952.

———. *Malombra*. Lux Film, 1942.

Stangle, Joel, dir. *Acqua Fuori dal Ring*. Striped Entertainment, 2012.

Steno, and Mario Monicelli, dirs. *Al diavolo la celebrità*. Produttori Associati, 1951.

Thorpe, Richard, dir. *The Crowd Roars*. MGM, 1938.

Tornatore, Giuseppe, dir. *Cinema Paradiso*. Cristaldifilm, Les Films Arianes, Rai 3, TF1 Films Production, Forum Picture, 1988.

Vertov, Dziga, dir. *Man with a Movie Camera*. Vseukrainske Foto Kino Upravlinnia, 1929.

Vidor, King, dir. *The Champ*. MGM, 1931.

Visconti, Luchino, dir. *Ossessione*. ICI, 1942.

———. *La terra trema*. AR.TE.AS. Film, Universalia, 1948.

———. *Bellissima*. Film Bellissima, 1951.

———. *Appunti su un fatto di cronaca*. 1953.

———. *Senso*. Lux Film, 1954.

———. *Le notti bianche*. CI.AS., Vides, Intermondia, 1957.

———. *Rocco e i suoi Fratelli*. Titanus, Les Films Marceau, 1960.

———. *Il Gattopardo*. Titanus, S.N. Pathé, SGC, 1963.

———. *Vaghe stelle dell'Orsa*. Vides Cinematografica, 1965.
———. *Lo straniero*. Dino de Laurentiis Cinematografica, Master Film, Marianne Productions, Casbah Film, 1967.
———. *La caduta degli dei*. Italnoleggio, Praesidens, Pegaso, Eichberg Film, 1969.
———. *Alla ricerca di Tadzio*. Rai Radiotelevisione Italiana, 1970.
———. *Morte a Venezia*. Alfa Cinematografica, Warner Bros., PECF, 1971.
———. *Ludwig*. Mega Film, Cinétel, Dieter Geissler Film Produktion, 1972.
———. *Gruppo di famiglia in un interno*. Rusconi Film, Gaumont International, 1974.
———. *L'Innocente*. Rizzoli Film, Les Films Jacques Leitienne, Imp.Ex.Ci., Fracoriz Production, 1976.
von Sternberg, Josef, dir. *Der blaue Engel*. UFA, UFA Tonfilm, 1930.
Wise, Robert, dir. *The Set-Up*. RKO Radio Pictures, 1949.
———. *Someone Up There Likes Me*. MGM, 1956.
Wyler, William, dir. *Roman Holiday*. Paramount Pictures, 1953.
———. *The Big Country*. Anthony Productions, Worldwide Productions, 1958.

Index

Also in the series

William Rothman, editor, *Cavell on Film*

J. David Slocum, editor, *Rebel Without a Cause*

Joe McElhaney, *The Death of Classical Cinema*

Kirsten Moana Thompson, *Apocalyptic Dread*

Frances Gateward, editor, *Seoul Searching*

Michael Atkinson, editor, *Exile Cinema*

Paul S. Moore, *Now Playing*

Robin L. Murray and Joseph K. Heumann, *Ecology and Popular Film*

William Rothman, editor, *Three Documentary Filmmakers*

Sean Griffin, editor, *Hetero*

Jean-Michel Frodon, editor, *Cinema and the Shoah*

Carolyn Jess-Cooke and Constantine Verevis, editors, *Second Takes*

Matthew Solomon, editor, *Fantastic Voyages of the Cinematic Imagination*

R. Barton Palmer and David Boyd, editors, *Hitchcock at the Source*

William Rothman, *Hitchcock: The Murderous Gaze, Second Edition*

Joanna Hearne, *Native Recognition*

Marc Raymond, *Hollywood's New Yorker*

Steven Rybin and Will Scheibel, editors, *Lonely Places, Dangerous Ground*

Claire Perkins and Constantine Verevis, editors, *B Is for Bad Cinema*

Dominic Lennard, *Bad Seeds and Holy Terrors*

Rosie Thomas, *Bombay before Bollywood*

Scott M. MacDonald, *Binghamton Babylon*

Sudhir Mahadevan, *A Very Old Machine*

David Greven, *Ghost Faces*

James S. Williams, *Encounters with Godard*

William H. Epstein and R. Barton Palmer, editors, *Invented Lives, Imagined Communities*

Lee Carruthers, *Doing Time*

Rebecca Meyers, William Rothman, and Charles Warren, editors, *Looking with Robert Gardner*

Belinda Smaill, *Regarding Life*

Douglas McFarland and Wesley King, editors, *John Huston as Adaptor*

R. Barton Palmer, Homer B. Pettey, and Steven M. Sanders, editors, *Hitchcock's Moral Gaze*

Nenad Jovanovic, *Brechtian Cinemas*

Will Scheibel, *American Stranger*

Amy Rust, *Passionate Detachments*

Steven Rybin, *Gestures of Love*

Seth Friedman, *Are You Watching Closely?*

Roger Rawlings, *Ripping England!*

Michael DeAngelis, *Rx Hollywood*

Ricardo E. Zulueta, *Queer Art Camp Superstar*

John Caruana and Mark Cauchi, editors, *Immanent Frames*

Nathan Holmes, *Welcome to Fear City*

Homer B. Pettey and R. Barton Palmer, editors, *Rule, Britannia!*

Milo Sweedler, *Rumble and Crash*

Ken Windrum, *From El Dorado to Lost Horizons*

Matthew Lau, *Sounds Like Helicopters*

Dominic Lennard, *Brute Force*

William Rothman, *Tuitions and Intuitions*

Michael Hammond, *The Great War in Hollywood Memory, 1918–1939*

Burke Hilsabeck, *The Slapstick Camera*

Niels Niessen, *Miraculous Realism*

Alex Clayton, *Funny How?*

Bill Krohn, *Letters from Hollywood*

Alexia Kannas, *Giallo!*

Homer B. Pettey, editor, *Mind Reeling*

Matthew Leggatt, editor, *Was It Yesterday?*

Merrill Schleier, editor, *Race and the Suburbs in American Film*

Neil Badmington, *Perpetual Movement*

George Toles, *Curtains of Light*

Erica Stein, *Seeing Symphonically*

Alexander Sergeant, *Encountering the Impossible*

www.ingramcontent.com/pod-product-compliance
Lightning Source LLC
LaVergne TN
LVHW050150080826
844660LV00002B/147

9781438484976